Ben Pobjie is the author of *100 Tales from Australia's Most Haunted Places*, *Error Australis*, *Mad Dogs and Thunderbolts* and *Second Best*, as well as countless articles about TV, sport, politics and the meaning of life scattered throughout the Australian media landscape. He lives in Sydney, where he spends his days panicking about deadlines.

100 *Weirdest* TALES FROM ACROSS AUSTRALIA

BEN POBJIE

affirm
press

First published by Affirm Press in 2023
Boon Wurrung Country
28 Thistlethwaite Street,
South Melbourne, VIC 3205
affirmpress.com.au

10 9 8 7 6 5 4 3 2 1

 A catalogue record for this
book is available from the
National Library of Australia

ISBN: 9781922930071 (paperback)
Cover design by Josh Durham/Design by Committee © Affirm Press
Typeset in Garamond Premier Pro by J&M Typesetting
Proudly printed in Australia by McPherson's Printing Group

To Freda, who is helping me write the weirdest tale of all

Contents

Introduction

Australia, there can be no doubt, is a weird country. Not that it's alone in this: most countries have a bit of weirdness to call their own – just check out the United States' electoral system or the time the Dutch ate their own prime minister, for a start.

But Australia's weirdness isn't only pervasive and compelling, it is also quintessentially Australian, as well as being greatly underrated. Too many people don't realise just how weird Australia is, and that's a shame, because daily life in this country is far richer and more vivid when you have a true understanding of how bizarre is the country, the culture and the history that surround us.

It's hard to say why Australia turned out so strange. Maybe it's because, although home to the oldest continuing culture on Earth, it was colonised quite recently by an unstable mixture of petty criminals and drunken policemen, none of whom actually wanted to be here and all of whom were horribly inappropriately dressed. Maybe it's because Australians have always had a peculiar set of priorities, which caused them to form a national cricket team before they actually had a nation and to express their much-vaunted sense of anti-authoritarianism through unwavering loyalty to the British Royal Family. Maybe it's because it gets quite hot here and our brains have gone a bit funny.

But whatever the reason, weirdness is an essential part of Australia, and we should embrace that. Within these pages, all varieties of Aussie oddness are revealed, explored and celebrated. From micronations to cryptozoology, from disappearing ships to unhinged prime ministers,

1

from fake medieval castles to giant fruit, and from scary things in the sky to baffling murders: this book has them all, and a poo jogger too!

So it is my privilege to invite you here and now to cast off the shackles of normalcy, abandon your childish belief that you are living in a sane and comprehensible country, and dive with patriotic glee into the wild, woolly, whirlwind world of Weird Australia.

You'll never be the same again.

The One-Sided Decider

The grand final is a treasured part of Australian life in a variety of sports. Australian rules football and rugby league, in particular, venerate the final day of the season, when all is on the line and a champion will be crowned. Many of the greatest moments in Australian footballing history have come on grand final day, as have many of the most disappointing anticlimaxes, which just shows how high expectations are.

Grand final day carries many cherished traditions, but perhaps the most cherished of all is that the grand final itself be played between two teams. This tradition is today closely adhered to, and most pundits agree that having two teams contest the biggest game of the year – as opposed to, for example, three or eight or ten point six– ensures the highest possible quality.

But as is often the case with traditions, this was not always so religiously observed. At the beginning of the New South Wales Rugby Football League – the competition that would evolve into today's NRL – a certain amount of experimentation was undertaken, which is why in 1909, in only the NSWRFL's second year, a grand final was played, and won, with only *one* team taking part.

There's a story behind it, of course (which is fortunate, given I'm writing a book here).

The 1909 grand final – or, as they termed it at the time, the 'final'* –

---

* The distinction between a final and a grand final is a subtle and devilishly complex one, and cannot be gone into in depth here. Suffice it to say that, whatever it was called, this was the game which would determine the champion team of 1909.

3

was to be between the Balmain Tigers, named after the huge jungle cats that roamed Sydney's inner west in the early 20th century, and the South Sydney Rabbitohs, named after the men who roamed Sydney's inner south carrying dead rabbits.

The 1909 NSWRFL season took place against a backdrop of financial hardship for the professional league, which had only come into existence the previous year, having broken away from the amateur code of rugby union. It was due to this hardship that the league had arranged a series of matches between the Kangaroos (Australia's best rugby league players who had defected from rugby union last year) and the Wallabies (Australia's best rugby league players who had defected from rugby union just now, in order to play in this series of matches).

This clash was a sure-fire money-spinner, but the hoo-ha began when the NSWRFL decided to schedule the fourth game of the series on the day of the Balmain–Souths final – and, further, to put the final on *before* the Kangaroos–Wallabies game, as a curtain-raiser.

The Balmain club was incensed at the disrespect shown to the teams and the competition, and declared that this insult would not be ignored. They would, in fact, boycott the match.

And here is where things get murky. Because if you listen to Balmain folk, the agreement was that both teams would refuse to play the final in protest at the degradation of their league, and their opponents were guilty of an act of infamous bastardry. If you listen to the Souths side, however, the Tigers were nothing but sore losers, who had gone off on their own in this mad windmill-tilting exercise, while the Rabbitohs were always going to do their duty and play the game.

On the appointed day, 18 September, the Balmain team showed up at the Sydney Showground in driving rain and picketed the entrance. Unfortunately, they didn't do a great job of it, as not only did a large crowd manage to get in, so did the South Sydney team.

Having arrived, the Rabbitohs duly took the field, while the Tigers duly did not. When the referee blew the whistle, Souths kicked off, chased the ball downfield, picked it up and ran it over the line for a try.

The referee then blew the whistle again, declared the match over and South Sydney the winners. Thus the Rabbitohs earned both the 1909 premiership and the everlasting enmity of all 'Balmainiacs'*.

It emerged later that the boycott by the Tigers had been part of a backroom intrigue concocted between the Balmain and North Sydney clubs to bankrupt the league by ruining the gate receipts of the Wallabies–Kangaroos match. The players had been mere pawns in this ultimately unsuccessful powerplay.

It didn't really matter, anyway: the political manoeuvrings were quickly lost in the mists of memory. Today, all that remains is a powerful grudge and a historical curiosity: the day they held a grand final and only one team showed up.

---

* A nickname bestowed on the Balmain club by others, in recognition of the fact that they were from Balmain and also mentally ill.

The Tragedy of the Beaten Favourite

As a rule, Australians don't much care about the death of horses – or, to put it more accurately, Australians care about the death of horses for one day a year, the same day on which Australians also care about the relative speed of horses, the people who sit on horses and the importance of wearing ugly hats while vomiting in the vicinity of horses.

Nobody really knows why Australians decide horses are important for that one day a year – possibly it has something to do with brain parasites – but it is certainly an essential part of our national psyche. Very occasionally, however, a horse comes along that penetrates more deeply into Australian culture, such that even when it's not the first Tuesday in November people are vaguely interested in it. Such a horse was Phar Lap, a horse that combined the two qualities that most fascinate humans: extreme speed and being involved in a murder mystery.

Like most great Australians, Phar Lap was born in New Zealand before realising how awful it was and leaving – just like Russell Crowe, if Russell Crowe had four legs and no testicles. Once arrived in a proper country, he demonstrated an amazing talent for running very fast as long as a tiny man sat on his back and hit him repeatedly – an activity that, we presume, Phar Lap enjoyed enormously. He was named after the Thai word for 'lightning', due to his amazing speed and the fact that his owner planned to eventually sell him to a restaurant. Others called him 'Big Red', due to his close resemblance to Rhonda Burchmore.

The whole nation fell in love with Phar Lap, which was an extremely weird thing for a nation to do – in fact, possibly that alone would be enough to include him in this book. However, the truly bizarre part of the Phar Lap story is his death.

Some might say his cards had been marked since the day before the 1930 Melbourne Cup, when gangsters took a shot at him, knowing the only way to avoid the colossal losses that would result from Big Red's victory was to plug him good. This was yet more evidence of how great a horse he was: there is no higher compliment for a thoroughbred than to get shot at. It's just a shame Phar Lap never really knew how generously he had been complimented. Then again, it's a shame Phar Lap never knew he was a racehorse in the first place, so in a way his whole life was a story of depressing ignorance.*

It was in the United States that Phar Lap met his demise, and in circumstances that can only be described as 'a bit off, eh'. It happened after he won the Agua Caliente Handicap** in Mexico in 1932, shocking the world with the revelation that horseracing happens in Mexico. In retrospect, his fate was sealed as soon as he won that race: there were powerful men who knew that if Phar Lap could win in Mexico, he may very well also win in America, and that simply would not do.

Remember, this was during the Great Depression, and the psyche of the American people had already taken a battering. If, on top of the economic despair, Americans had been forced to accept that not even their horses were the best in the world anymore, the entire country might've crumpled and gone to bed to cry.

And so the fact that – on 5 April 1932, as he prepared for his US debut at a ranch near Menlo Park, California – Phar Lap woke up with a high temperature and in terrible pain,*** and subsequently died of a massive haemorrhage later that day, is exceedingly suspicious.

The public was devastated by the death of their favourite five-year-old

---

* This is, perhaps, the most Australian thing of all.

** In English the 'Hot Water Handicap' – a special race in which the better the horse's record, the more boiling water was poured onto its face prior to the race.

*** I wonder how horses let people know that they're in terrible pain. There must be some kind of signal they give to indicate that something hurts for reasons unrelated to a jockey hitting them to make them run faster.

and demanded answers. Wild theories quickly sprang up and persisted for decades: had Phar Lap been deliberately poisoned? Had he been accidentally poisoned? Had he just had a bit of a tummy bug? Had he killed himself over an unhappy love affair? Impossible to tell, although the last one is unlikely, given he was a gelding.*

Many years after Phar Lap's death, veterinary science had made great advances: in the 1930s it was still normal to assume that any ailment from which a horse was suffering was most likely due to a witch's curse. In the 21st century, though, proper analysis could be done on a dead horse – and, fortunately, Phar Lap had been safely preserved, with his skin in Melbourne, his skeleton in Wellington and his heart in Canberra.** Testing on his remains proved that, before death, the mighty horse had ingested a massive amount of arsenic.

The question is: why? Perhaps the arsenic had been slipped into his feed by evildoers intent on cutting short Phar Lap's reign. Perhaps it had been given to him innocently by his own trainer, as back in those days, for some reason, people thought arsenic was good for horses. I'm not even joking about that: people genuinely gave arsenic to horses to give them a pep-up. Never forget, reader: people in the past were idiots.

Perhaps we'll never know the truth about just why Phar Lap died. And perhaps it's better that way, for when it comes to intriguing national legends, the Story of the Mysterious Horse Death is a lot more appealing than the Story of the Horse Who Died and We All Know Exactly What Happened. So for marketing's sake, if nothing else: God bless whoever gave Phar Lap his arsenic breakfast.

---

* Then again, maybe that's why the love affair was so unhappy ...
** For the same reason the royal family always take separate planes.

The Spectral Sailor of Armit Island

The Whitsunday Islands can go toe to toe with any other spot in the world when it comes to natural beauty, and Armit Island, in the Whitsundays' Northern group, is as gorgeous as any of them. Small, tranquil and little touched by humans, it is a stunning oceanic idyll, no good for anyone seeking tourist traps but paradise for those who would prefer to swim in clear, warm waters, catch sight of spectacular birdlife, or recline on a beach and imagine themselves beyond the reach of civilisation.

Okay, the tourism brochure is over – now let's talk ghosts.

It was no doubt the beauty and tranquillity of Armit that led an eccentric fellow by the name of Heron* to lease Armit Island from the Queensland government in the 1890s, back when that was apparently a thing you could do. Heron built a hut on Armit's beach and settled into a happily solitary life, spending his days collecting exotic plants. Occasionally, passing boats would anchor at Armit and their crews would come ashore and chat to Heron. Inevitably they would ask the hermit whether life did not get terribly lonely on his deserted island.

'Oh, no,' Heron would casually reply. 'A sailor keeps me company.'

This was confusing, as there were definitely no people on the island apart from Heron. And when a certain Captain Gorringe came to Armit and camped there for a week, the plot thickened.

Gorringe, like his predecessors, got to chatting with Heron, and like his

---

* There is some disagreement among historians as to whether he was a man or an actual heron.

predecessors was informed of the sailor whom he had befriended. However, after a few days on the island, during which time no sailor popped up to say hi, Gorringe decided to make further enquiries. Where the dickens, he asked, is this sailor pal of yours? Heron obliged with an explanation.

Shortly after arriving on Armit Island, Heron told Gorringe, he was woken in his hut by some night-time noise. Walking out onto the beach, he heard a dreadful scream of pain from the scrub at the beach's edge. A moment later a man, in the old-fashioned garb of a sailor from some bygone age, emerged from the scrub and strolled calmly down to the water. Heron called out to the man, but he ignored the call and continued straight into the sea, eventually disappearing.

Heron was alarmed by what he had seen, but over the years he became far more sanguine, for the strange sailor was not lost beneath the waves: to the contrary, it became quite a regular occurrence for Heron to wake at night, hear the agonised cry and watch the sailor walk determinedly into the water.

Despite Captain Gorringe's view that Heron was a sensible and intelligent sort,* it would be easy to dismiss this story as the hallucination of a crazed hermit – were it not for the fact that Heron was not the only witness to the phantom sailor's night walk. In 1908 Mr Charles Anderson anchored his cutter off Armit and saw Heron's nautical companion making his way to the water, where, as per earlier assertions, he vanished. Anderson described the sailor as not walking but floating 'a few inches above the sand', and said that he appeared to be dressed in the style of the 17th century. The writer Alexander Vennard – better known to his fans as Bill Bowyang – claimed the ghost was dressed after the fashion of 'a sailor of Nelson's days', i.e. the early 19th century. Vennard, who saw the apparition when he camped on Armit Island in the late 1930s, also attested to the fact that the man floated above the sand rather than walking on it.

---

* On the one hand, he was clearly crazy because he chose to live in a hut on an island remote from the rest of humanity. On the other hand, he was obviously smart enough to choose to live in a hut on an island remote from the rest of humanity.

Various other witnesses to the Armit spectre described his pigtail, a kerchief around his head, a short jacket with large buttons and three-quarter-length sailor's trousers. It is believed he is the shade of a sailor who met a grisly end in the island scrub. There is no record of any sailor being lost on Armit Island, but this should not deter the dedicated ghost-believer: the Whitsundays were once riddled with pirate ships and escaped convicts who kept no records. And even before the British arrived on the east coast, Portuguese and Spanish sailors may have come across the islands.

In light of all the evidence, is it really possible that all the witnesses were mistaken and the Armit Island ghost does not exist? Of course it is, but don't spoil the fun.

The Peculiarities of Piscine Precipitation

If there is one principle on which there is near-universal consensus in the scientific world, it is this: fish belong in the water rather than the sky. Yet, supreme irony of ironies, fish themselves insist on violating this very principle over and over again.

Australia has a rich and proud history of ... well, of everything, really. That's what makes us such a great country: you name it, we have a rich and proud history of it. And fish falling from the sky is no exception: in fact, the only reason that our national sporting teams do not wear badges depicting falling fish is because of the corporate stranglehold of Big Roo.*

The fish rain capital of Australia is the town of Lajamanu, in the Northern Territory. This tiny berg of just over 600 people is 890 kilometres from Darwin and 560 kilometres from Katherine.** Most of its inhabitants are members of the Warlpiri people, and it has a hot, dry climate alleviated only occasionally by fish storms.

Lajamanu locals have reported numerous occurrences of piscine precipitation. In 2010 hundreds of spangled perch*** plummeted down upon the populace. 'These fish fell in their hundreds and hundreds,' said local Christine Balmer. 'The locals were running around everywhere picking them up.'

Why were the locals so desperate to pick up the perch? Was it an

---

* Not to be confused with Little Roo, played by Justine Clarke.
** Even further when Katherine is on holiday.
*** These can be easily recognised by the fact they are exactly like ordinary perch, but with spangles.

indictment of the sparse seafood options on offer in the town? Perhaps. But it was also the latest proof of the hamlet's status as a climatic fish magnet. A similar fall struck in 2004, and in the early 1980s Lajamanu was also bombarded by piscatorial aviators – at least according to Les Dillon, who was very clear that he was not drunk at the time. In fact, this is a common theme in stories of fish-falls: the witnesses, in almost every case, were not drunk, swear to God.

And although Les Dillon might've had a few drinks before stepping out of the pub and reporting a bunch of fish on the ground, Christine Balmer was quite clear: she *saw* the fish fall from the sky. And tell me: has Christine Balmer ever lied to you?

If more evidence were needed, in February 2023 it happened again. For the fourth time in fifty years, the perch precipitated. 'When the rain started, we've seen fish falling down as well,' said Central Desert councillor Andrew Johnson. 'We saw some freefalling down to the ground, and some falling onto the roof.' He added, 'I think it's a blessing from the Lord,' and if a man believes having fish fall on you is a blessing, I say good for him.

In a way, the latest Lajamanu fish rain is a blessing for all of us, for the fact that it further confirms the reality of the phenomenon. We all want to believe that it can rain fish, for the simple reason that life is boring and we long for something to break the monotony. So if you can spice up your life simply by believing that every time you go outside there is a non-zero chance that fish will start falling on you ... keep watching the skies.

That Sinking Feeling

As the saying goes, when life gives you lemons, make lemonade. But could it not just as easily say, when life gives you a big ugly hole in the ground, make a garden? No, it could not. But that's still a thing you can do, and not only can you do it, in 1886 James Umpherston did.

Umpherston was a remarkable man. Most people react with horror to the idea of doing gardening, but James Umpherston really seemed to enjoy it. What's more, he had that spark of genius within him that allowed him to see beyond the obvious, to glimpse the possibilities in the most apparently possibility-free situation.

James Umpherston's story began, like most stories do, 40 million years ago. South Australia was underwater at this time, which is how the period got its nickname, 'The Golden Age of SA'. Layers of limestone forming on the seabed were then eroded by water over the years, resulting in caves below the surface. Later, when the Mount Gambier region became dry land, the ceilings of the caves collapsed, thus creating sinkholes. The south-east corner of South Australia is home to over fifty sinkholes, which today serve as a warning to travellers from the east to stay away from Adelaide.

A sinkhole, of course, is one of those fascinating natural geographical features that serve to remind us that Hell is real and we are forever on the brink of eternal damnation. When God in His wisdom created the Earth, he decided that making it so that gigantic holes would occasionally just open up in the ground would be a good way to keep us on our toes, and it's worked pretty well.

But when James Umpherston came along, he saw more than just a manifestation of his own deepest fears written in the landscape: he saw the potential for great beauty. And so he bought up seventy-two hectares of sinkhole-infested land and set to work transforming one particular crater into something fragrantly gorgeous.

So it was that James Umpherston hopped down into the abyss and started planting, and building, and shaping the hole into a modern-day inverted Hanging Gardens of Babylon. He planted beds of gorgeous flowers, constructed lovely fountains and laid out impeccably manicured lawns, until he had himself a wonderfully lush sanctuary twenty metres below the ground. From a grim and foreboding threat to life and limb, the visionary Umpherston had created a glorious patch of lush serenity – a testament to both the beauty of nature and the ingenuity of humanity.

Fortunately for us all, Umpherston's tending of the sunken garden was maintained after his death, and you can still go to the Umpherston Sinkhole on the outskirts of Mount Gambier. There, you can marvel at how one man's refusal to accept that a horrible pit was a horrible pit led to the perfect place for a summer day's stroll.

The Hermetic Hermit of Deliverance Island

Deliverance Island – now officially known as Warul Kawa Indigenous Protected Area so as to avoid any associations with Burt Reynolds – is a tiny coral speck in the Torres Strait, 200 kilometres north of Thursday Island and thirty-four kilometres south of Papua New Guinea. It is not a place of great appeal as a residence, unless you are a bird, a turtle or an extremely strange Danish sailor.

As it happens, a man who fitted at least one of the above descriptions was Harry Envoldt, who was variously dubbed the 'modern Crusoe' and the 'Deliverance Island Hermit'. Envoldt spent the better part of four decades on Deliverance Island, in open defiance of the fact that this was an extremely silly thing to do. Nobody really knows why he pursued such a lifestyle: he kept his own counsel, and whatever dark secret or personality disorder drove him to the island life, he took it to his grave – or at least to the beach he died on.

Of course, living on islands comes naturally to Danes, who come from a country containing 443 of them. But this doesn't explain why Harry eschewed the joys of Danish islands, which are much colder and damper and full of reindeer and Lego, for the blinding sun and oppressive heat of Deliverance Island. Among those who knew of him, rumours abounded about what had brought him there: some said he was a Danish prince forced by scandal to flee his country; then as now, it was almost impossible for Australians to conceive of a Danish person who was not a member of the royal family.

The truth of how Envoldt had fetched up on Deliverance – or at least

16

a more plausible version of the truth than the disgraced prince theory – came from an unexpected source: acclaimed English author Somerset Maugham, who ran into the hermit during his travels in the South Seas in the 1920s. Maugham wrote a story about Envoldt titled 'German Harry', which was apparently what North Queenslanders had dubbed him, even though it was well known he was from Denmark – a classic case of racism if ever I've heard one.* Maugham found Harry a terse and surly character, a wild and hairy fellow who displayed precious little appreciation for guests who pop round.

The story Maugham heard about German Harry the Dane was that he'd been born in Denmark in 1849 and became a sailor as a teenager. After many years sailing the seven seas, Envoldt was working on the Austrian ship *Gibraud*, bound for Batavia, when that vessel was wrecked in the Torres Strait. Deciding that the shipwreck gods clearly wanted him there, Harry stayed and began selling beche-de-mer** around Thursday Island and the New Guinea coast.

For a while the beche-de-mer trade flourished, and German Harry and his partner Louis the Greek*** enjoyed the fruits of their labours, as well as the fruits of the sea, as well as, occasionally, actual fruit. But the devious doings of an interloper known as French Joe**** saw the collapse of the business and the break-up of the partnership, and Harry Envoldt was left all alone on Deliverance Island.

This occurred in the late 1890s, and Envoldt would spend the remaining thirty years of his life in isolation on the island. He built himself a little hut and lived on turtle meat and fish, rarely coming into contact with other humans apart from the occasional visiting pearler.

What sort of life did Harry lead on Deliverance Island? When, with long beard and leathery skin, he sat on the beach and gazed out to sea, did he long for his old life, or did he revel in the freedom and simplicity

---

* And believe me, I have.
** French for 'bech of the mer'.
*** I really just can't with these people's naming conventions.
**** Eyeroll ...

of his new one? Did he ever yearn for human company? Was it contempt for worldly society that had led him to detach himself from it, or was it simply a lack of ideas? How does a man spend decades in his own company, on a bare strip of sand in the middle of the ocean, without books or music or entertainments of any kind? Even Robinson Crusoe had Friday to hang out with. Surely it must've driven Harry mad. Surely he must've been mad in the first place.

Eventually, Harry Envoldt met the kind of end so commonly met by island hermits: an end both predictable and gross. He used to cure his fish and turtle meat by placing it in a wire cage which he anchored offshore, letting the saltwater do its job. It was while attending to his cage on 27 January 1928 that Harry was attacked by sharks. He managed to get free of the beasts and make it back to the beach, but several bits of him were missing. Collapsing on the sand, he bled out. His body was found by a pearler.

Harry Envoldt was seventy-eight years old and had lived on Deliverance Island for nearly forty years, the last thirty of them alone. He led a life of adventure and romance that captured the imagination of many, not least the esteemed Maugham. But the secrets of that life, and what made Harry choose it, remained as elusive at his death as they were the day he decided that the sarcastically named Deliverance Island would be his home forevermore.

The Pride of Prince Leonard

Australia is a great place. Wonderful climate, stunning natural beauty, single-handedly won two world wars, probably would've won several football World Cups if other countries weren't cheaters ... the reasons to be proud of this nation go on and on.

And yet there are some people whose feelings about the country are more complex. There are those who find themselves so conflicted about the greatness or otherwise of Australia that although they cannot bring themselves to leave, they nevertheless cannot in good conscience stay.

The solution? Make your own country, right where you are. You'll become a citizen of a foreign land without having to go anywhere.

This was exactly the course taken by Prince Leonard of Hutt River, when faced with the West Australian government's draconian wheat production quotas.

You might say that's a pretty extreme reaction. You might say, 'Hey, we've all had to deal with draconian wheat production quotas, but we don't go about creating our own countries.' To which Prince Leonard might say, 'Your loss.'

Prince Leonard was born Leonard Casley, to commoner parents, and was forty-five years old when, in 1970, the West Australian government got all up in his face about the wheat. The quotas were preventing him from selling as much wheat as he wanted – which was a lot. Having had no luck appealing to the state's governor, Leonard became desperate, only to stumble upon the answer to his problems. As he pored over the Constitution and laws of the Commonwealth of Australia, in search of something that would grant him relief from his travails, he discovered one fascinating and highly significant fact: there is literally no law in this country against being a weird crazy guy on a farm.

Armed with this legal principle, Leonard promptly declared himself the head of state of the newly founded Principality of Hutt River, a tiny yet proud nation, seventy-five square kilometres in area and 517 kilometres north of Perth, capital city of the hated oppressors.

Leonard cited several justifications for his decision to secede from Australia. First of all, he claimed, international law supplied just such a right to all. This was interesting but, even if true, it didn't mean much: according to historical precedent, everyone in the world is allowed to ignore international law.

He also claimed that the governor-general's office had written to him once and referred to him as 'the Administrator of the Hutt River province'. Leonard, demonstrating an innate legal perspicacity verging on the hallucinogenic, pointed out that this constituted officially binding recognition of the principality.

His next move was to formally dub himself 'His Majesty Prince Leonard I of Hutt', which was only fair given that a principality must of necessity have a prince. He also kept on selling all his wheat – illegally, according to the law of Western Australia, but perfectly legally according to the law of Hutt, which stated that selling wheat was great and should be done as much as possible.

But there were dark days ahead. In February 1977, Australia prosecuted Prince Leonard for failing to supply the Australian Taxation Office with required documents, raising the question, 'What part of "sovereign nation" do you not understand, guys?' Following his fine for the offence, Leonard retaliated in December of that year by declaring war on Australia. He then displayed superb strategic talent, keeping his enemies off-balance by ending the war a few days later. The Australian leaders, their heads spinning, didn't know what was going on. Hutt had them right where they wanted them.

Over the next forty years, the Principality of Hutt River thrived and prospered, a peaceful utopia in the western wilderness. It spent its time selling wheat, issuing the occasional stamp or coin, and defending further legal cases brought against Prince Leonard for – among other things – tax evasion, conducting a shop without a permit, and unpaid debts to the publisher of his memoir *The Man* – a seminal work about Prince Leonard and why he is The Man. The prince and the ATO became an almost inseparable couple: always bickering, yet you sensed there was real love there.

But nothing lasts forever, not even micronations with no legal status. In 2017, after a forty-five-year reign, Prince Leonard I announced he would be abdicating in favour of his son Graeme. This signalled the beginning of the end for the Principality of Hutt River: no nation has ever survived having a prince called Graeme.

In January 2020, Hutt closed its borders, devastating millions of tourists worldwide. In August 2020, the nation was formally dissolved, and its lands sold to pay tax debts, in a final note of surrender to the tyrannical superpower that had for five decades been attempting to stuff Hutt River into its gaping maw. And so Prince Leonard's dream died, teaching all the lesson: you cannot fight City Hall, particularly when City Hall is the Australian federal government and you are an extremely strange and angry wheat farmer.

The Suspicious Saga of the Frantic Flyer

Sir Charles Kingsford Smith, known as 'Smithy' because 'Kingsfordy' is awkward to say, was a bona fide Australian hero. Having demonstrated his ability to not just fly a plane but also land it, he thrilled the public in the 1920s and 1930s by constantly whizzing about over their heads, waving cheerfully and wishing his plane had a toilet in it.

Smithy was the first man to fly across the Pacific Ocean, and made the first nonstop flights across Australia and between Australia and New Zealand. He broke numerous records and won many races during his short life, which ended in 1935 when he disappeared over the Andaman Sea: a demise which, frankly, anyone could have warned him was likely to happen if he insisted on going about flying all the time.

Before he disappeared, however, Charles Kingsford Smith was involved in one of the more peculiar incidents in early aviation history, an incident which did great damage to his reputation as a loveable knockabout Aussie larrikin.*

It all began so innocently: Smithy, determined to reach out to the underprivileged of the world, decided to fly to England. This was a bold decision, as in the first half of the 20th century, England was still quite a long way away from Australia.** But having flown just about everywhere else, he was sure he could manage it. So he set off in his plane, the *Southern*

---

* Not that he *was* a loveable knockabout Aussie larrikin, but it's generally assumed that any Australian man who becomes famous must be a loveable knockabout Aussie larrikin.

** It's much closer now due to global warming.

Cross, which he had named after his favourite direction and his favourite emotion. He took with him several companions who were not famous and therefore are of little importance.

The trip to England began well, with the plane both staying up in the air and moving forward. However, as they flew over the Kimberley region of Western Australia, the *Southern Cross* suffered a serious fault known in technical aviation terms as 'no longer being above the ground'. Having been caught in a storm, they lost their bearings and were forced to land on a mudflat.

Knowing that search parties would be sent out, Smithy and his less interesting pals settled down to wait for rescue. For thirteen days they sat on the mudflat and drank coffee, having forgotten to bring anything good to drink. It might seem that thirteen days is a long time to find some guys and a plane, but it's important to remember that Western Australia is a very big place, and also that this was history, when people were generally bad at their jobs.

Eventually, Smithy and friends were discovered by a search plane, but, tragically, one of the other planes had been lost during the search, and its crew – Kingsford Smith's friend Keith Anderson and mechanic HS Hitchcock – had been killed.

It was a terrible tragedy, but just one of those unavoidable accidents that sometimes happen when people insist on following their insane desire to hurtle through the air in little metal canoes. Or was it?

Rumours began to circulate that there was more to this affair than at first assumed, and the public began to turn some dark looks towards the once-loved Smithy. Was it not a strange coincidence, people asked, that this famous pilot, who had been struggling to make a go of his new business venture, Australian National Airways, and could really do with a bit of publicity, suddenly was caught up in a grand and romantic tale of adventure and survival just when it came in handy?

The suggestion was that the downing of the *Southern Cross* was a deliberate publicity stunt on the pilot's part, and that he had therefore caused the deaths of the brave searchers simply for his own personal gain.

One can imagine the potential headlines: 'PILOTS DIE IN SMITHY SCAM'; 'CHARLIE GUZZLES COFFEE WHILE HEROES PERISH'. Making it even worse was the fact that the beverages the stranded flyers had been partaking of were of the brand 'Coffee Royal'. 'Oh, good working man's coffee isn't good enough for these toffs,' the 1920s equivalent of talkback radio hosts might have ranted. 'They drink Coffee *Royal*, while the poor bastards looking for them crash and die with no coffee at all!'

The saga became known as the Coffee Royal Affair, making it sound much sexier than it really was, and an official enquiry was held to investigate the question of whether Anderson and Hitchcock had died because of Kingsford Smith's deviousness or just because of his incompetence. The enquiry found that no blame attached to the national treasure – which was a great relief to him, if somewhat generous. I mean, there had to be a *little* bit of blame attached to him. He was the one who had decided to fly to England, after all.

Although Kingsford Smith was cleared, a small cloud hovered over his reputation for the rest of his life – which, admittedly, wasn't very long, because, in a shocking twist nobody could have predicted, he disappeared while flying a plane. These days, people don't remember Smithy for the Coffee Royal Affair, any more than they remember him for belonging to a paramilitary fascist organisation.* He is a national hero, which is only fair given how long he spent in the sky and how comparatively infrequently he fell out of it.

Nevertheless, in the Smithy story there will always be that one odd blip: the time he spent a couple of weeks sitting in mud and drinking coffee, while his friends died looking for him.

---

* The famous US pilot Charles Lindbergh was a fascist too. Something about flying long distances really pushes people to the right.

The Wacky World of White Australia

When we look back at our history, we are always in danger of fixating on certain aspects at the expense of others. People concentrate so much on Queen Victoria's humourlessness, for example, that they forget about her extreme sexual perversity. In the same vein, Australians can tend to focus heavily on how racist the White Australia policy was, and thereby miss the pertinent point that it was also batshit insane. The latter point is best highlighted by the tale of Egon Kisch.

Kisch was an Austrian-Czechoslovakian communist writer who was known for his crusading journalism and his fierce opposition to Nazism, even before people knew that Nazism was bad. He was living and working in Germany when Hitler came to power, and was promptly arrested and expelled from the country because he was a) Czechoslovakian; and b) mean to Hitler.

The next year, 1934, Kisch came to Australia to attend the All-Australian Congress Against War and Fascism, which sounds like a reasonable thing to do – but as we've mentioned, people didn't yet know fascism was wrong, and most of them reckoned war was positively awesome, so being *against* them both made everyone deeply suspicious. 'What sort of person,' they asked, 'is against both war AND fascism? Some kind of radical or homosexualist?'

And so it was that the Australian government, led by Prime Minister Joseph Lyons, refused Kisch entry to the country on the grounds that he was the kind of anarchistic ruffian who, if left to his own devices, might jeopardise Australia's friendly relations with the Third Reich.

Here the first genuine weirdness occurred.* When the RMS *Strathaird* arrived in Melbourne, with Kisch in the custody of the captain, having already been informed by government officials that he would not be allowed entry, the maverick commie took matters into his own hands and made a running jump from the ship's deck. He flew five metres onto Station Pier, impressing everyone watching – but he broke his leg in the process, making further flight rather more challenging.

The police quickly bundled the injured Kisch back onto the ship, which continued on its course to Sydney, where Kisch again attempted to enter Australia – this time with the backing of High Court justice Dr HV Evatt, who had in the meantime ruled that the exclusion of Kisch was unlawful and that he must be allowed in.

At this point, the Australian government, spearheaded by bovver-boy Attorney-General Robert 'Pig Ignorant' Menzies, brought out the big gun: the *Immigration Restriction Act*. This was a clever law passed by the government a few decades earlier that found a way to keep non-white people out without actually saying 'Whites Only' – which, even in the early 1900s, would've been considered a gauche way of framing legislation.

The act achieved its aim by specifying that 'any person who ... when an officer dictates to him not less than fifty words in any prescribed language, fails to write them out in that language in the presence of the officer' could be denied entry to Australia. It was an ingenious law: in theory it was simply an attempt to ensure that anyone trying to get in would be able to communicate with the locals, but in practice it meant that if anyone with the wrong skin colour tried to sneak in, the immigration officials could kick them out on the grounds that they weren't fluent in Basque.

The sheer madness of a government so desperate to keep Asians away that they would invent this hilariously stupid entrance test was laid bare by the arrival of Egon Kisch. Kisch, of course, was white, but to the Lyons regime he was just as undesirable as any black, brown or yellow chap, and so Australian history came to perhaps its most absurdist moment yet: the

* I'm not counting the Australian government liking Nazis as weird – and if you look over history, neither will you.

day that a Czechoslovakian communist was ordered to write the Lord's Prayer in Scottish Gaelic to prove that he was of suitable character to visit Australia. And if you've ever read a sentence more divinely deranged than that, I want to see it.

Kisch, displaying an admirable intolerance to bullshit, but also a disappointing lack of enthusiasm for Dadaist performance art, refused to take the test on the grounds that it was clearly freaking nuts. He was arrested and released on bail, whereupon his lawyers went back to the High Court and successfully demonstrated that the policeman designated to administer the test didn't actually know Scottish Gaelic himself. This would've made the fairness of the process somewhat dubious, but the court ruled that it didn't matter anyway, because the *Immigration Restriction Act* specified that the language of the test had to be a 'European language', and Scottish Gaelic didn't count because it was only spoken by, like, twelve people and a few sheep.

Thus was Egon Kisch released and allowed to tour Australia, albeit after one final attempt by Lyons to have him kicked out: an attempt which Justice Evatt screwed up into a ball and threw at his head. Kisch subsequently travelled the country, addressing thousands at rallies and letting everyone know that Hitler was a bad dude. This point of view caught on, to the extent that, in 1939, Pig-Face Menzies, once so sorrowful over the idea of people being mean to Hitler, actually declared war on him. And the rest is history, and lots and lots of movies.

Egon Kisch was a Nazi-fighting hero and deserves great recognition for his activism. But at least some of the acclaim given to him should be reserved for the part he played in exposing the Australian government as not only extremely racist, but completely and undeniably weird.*

---

* How much has changed? You decide.

Arthur's Hair-Raising Tale

Arthur Marrin was a simple, humble man, a loving husband to Catherine and father to May and Irene. He was not a man who craved fame or sought out the spotlight. All he desired was the safety and happiness of his family, and to go quietly about his business, travelling the Southern Highlands of New South Wales selling cordial.

Many had scoffed at Arthur as a young man when he declared his intention to dedicate his life to cordial-making. They also scoffed at him as a middle-aged man when he actually made cordial. People scoffed at Arthur a lot. But they couldn't deny that he was a decent and honest man whose love of cordial in no way detracted from his positive qualities.

So it is that we cannot dismiss Arthur Marrin's tale of the day he came across the terrifying 'hairy man' on the road from Braidwood to Captain's Flat. On that bright, sunny day in 1893, Arthur was wide awake and completely sober – of course he was, for all he had with him was a wagon full of cordial. As he rattled serenely down the track, his dog came scampering out of the roadside undergrowth, eyes wide and whimpering in terror.

Arthur Marrin was not a man to let anyone scare his dog without facing the consequences. Grasping his whip firmly in one hand, he alighted from the wagon and stepped off the road and into the bush to investigate.

As he looked about for the source of the dog's alarm, a fearsome sight leapt from the brush: a terrifying beast, looking upon the frightened cordial-man with chilling mien. Although often later dubbed 'the hairy man', it was nothing human: covered with fur, it had reared up on its hind legs, according to the *Goulburn Evening Penny Post*,* 'with its two fore feet stretched out like the two arms of a man'.

In that pose, it was clear the thing was either going to attack him or give him a hug, and Arthur didn't fancy either. Frantic with horror, he picked up a rock and hurled it at the beast. The rock struck the creature's head, and it fell to the ground. Seizing his chance, Arthur ran up to it and, showing remarkable if unnerving initiative, beat it to death with the handle of his whip.

This may have demonstrated that the creature was surprisingly easy to kill, or that Arthur Marrin was a frighteningly violent psychopath. Perhaps a bit of both. But the upshot was that Arthur went home with a big, hairy corpse to show all his friends.

He put the body on display out the front of his cordial factory, thinking, not unreasonably, that if anything was going to get people in the mood for a cool, refreshing glass of cordial, it was seeing the bloodied cadaver of a nightmarish monster.

Whether it was successful in provoking a profitable thirst in the people of Braidwood is not recorded, but what is recorded is the observations of a reporter from the *Braidwood Dispatch*, who got a good look at the creature and wrote down all the ways in which it did not at all resemble a man:

> It was four feet long, 11 inches across the forehead and had a face very much like a polar bear. It weighed over seven stone [forty-four kilograms]. Its forearms were very strong with great paws that would be capable of giving a terrible grip. It was a tan colour like a possum with strong hair on its skin.

Learning that it weighed just forty-four kilograms and stood only four feet tall puts Arthur's killing of the creature into perspective: more

---

* Ranked in the top five most reliable posts of the Goulburn evening eighteen years running.

and more, the cordial-maker is coming across as a bully.

Sadly, further investigation into exactly what the hairy man of Braidwood might've been was stymied by Arthur Marrin's wife, who decided that having a rotting animal corpse outside the cordial factory was less than genteel, and demanded her husband bury the thing without delay. This Arthur did, being a dutiful husband and valuing domestic harmony more than dead monsters.

He interred the body behind the cordial factory, but unfortunately nobody knows the exact spot, which means we are unable to dig it up and look at its remains for ourselves, which would be a fun way to spend an afternoon.

So all we have to go on are the contemporary descriptions of the beast. That Arthur Marrin met and murdered something weird is undeniable: there were eyewitnesses. But just what was it?

His grandson, Lawrie St Hill, believes it was 'something similar to a tree kangaroo', which sounds reasonable, although we should note that a) 'something similar' would need to encompass 'not all that similar' for this to be true, as tree kangaroos are closer to two feet and seven kilograms, and unlikely to terrify either a cordial-maker or his dog to any great extent; and b) Lawrie St Hill has no more idea than anyone else, since seeing legendary beasts is not hereditary.

Others have speculated that the thing might have been a giant wombat, or an 'Australian gorilla', which is an intriguing hypothesis but also unlikely given there's no such thing.

But whether wombat, kangaroo, gorilla, bear or just a small child in a costume unlucky enough to run into Arthur on a bad day, the hairy man lives on today in our imaginations, even if it fails to live on in a shallow grave out the back of the old cordial factory.

The Coital Corpses

The passengers on the first train from Sunnybank were looking forward to a jolly Christmas Eve as they chugged towards Brisbane. A busy day of last-minute Christmas shopping, or attempting to remain polite to last-minute Christmas shoppers, awaited them. If any of them had any creeping sensations of ghastly foreboding running down their spines, they would've put it down to the fact that they still had no idea what to get for Aunt Hilda this year.

But today would be no ordinary city jaunt for the Sunnybank train. As it pulled into Park Road Station, the driver and the fireman* noticed something disturbing: two figures lying in the paddock near the railway line, which was 'a well-known rendezvous for canoodling couples'. The figures were a man and a woman, and a glimpse of their faces told the railway workers that their utter stillness was not by choice.

Both the man and the woman had a huge hole right where the back of the head is more traditionally found, having been shot where they lay. Even more grimly,** it was clear, from their position and the dishevelled state of their clothes, that the couple had been engaged in what might delicately be called intimate relations – but what might indelicately be called DOING IT – in the paddock when they were surprised by someone with a grudge and a gun.

The pair were identified as Mrs Eileen Gladys Walsh and Acting Police Sergeant Marquis Cumming, and it's an indication of the gravity

---

*   Not that kind of fireman, the train kind of fireman. Whatever that is.

**   Or, if you're the author of a book about weird occurrences, luckily.

of the tragedy that people hardly laughed at all at his name. Mrs Walsh was a recently separated mother of two, and Cumming was a married father of five, so it might be said that getting up to paddock shenanigans wasn't the nicest way to behave, but we can all agree that, even for grassy adultery, a bullet in the head is a huge overreaction.

Well, most of us can agree. Clearly, there was at least one person who thought it was an entirely proportionate response. The question was, and remains: who was that person?

Mrs Walsh's wedding ring had been removed, as had Cumming's belt, handcuffs and keys – but his watch and wallet were still on him, so the killer seemed not to have been motivated by robbery. Which was good news for true-crime buffs, because nothing takes the spice out of the murder of two people banging in a field like finding out it was just a boring robbery.

Suspicion alighted on Cumming's wife, Theresa, who in the past had been aware of her husband's nominatively determined indiscretions and was known to be fed up to the back teeth with them. There was also the possibility the crime was committed by the sergeant's son Stanley, who had had heated arguments with his father and, like his mother, was generally sick of the randy old sod. The fact that Cumming's locker at the station was filled with lurid love letters, and that he had apparently fathered an illegitimate child with a woman from Mount Morgan, gave heft to the possible motive of his wife and child.

These facts also suggested that scattered all around Brisbane were men whose wives and girlfriends had grabbed themselves a slice of Cumming, and who no doubt would've liked to have seen the copper with a ventilated skull.

But then there was also Eileen's husband, James, a brutish drunk from whom she had recently fled, and a man who was unlikely to take such a development with gentle good humour. James Walsh had an alibi for the night in question – but as anyone who's ever watched *Midsomer Murders* can tell you, they always do.

However, there are further murky waters to be waded through in this most sordid, yet also kind of exciting, case.* For one thing, a witness claimed that on the night of the murder he saw two shadowy male figures following Walsh and Cumming as they headed towards Boggo Road Gaol – near where they were killed. For another, a woman known as 'Miss X' told the *Truth* newspaper** that a policeman she'd been dating had left her at 9pm on the night of the murder, but asked her to swear he'd been with her till midnight. The next night, so Miss X said, the man blurted out that he was a murderer and that she had to leave Queensland or he would 'scatter your brains like I did Cumming's'.

The identity of Miss X was never revealed, and neither was the name of the policeman in question, who had supposedly been dating another of Cumming's paramours. After investigating the evidence, the police decided it wasn't worth reopening the case – which is pretty bloody convenient, if you ask me.

It may be that the truth will never be known about who gunned down the unhappy lovers as they got frisky in the meadow just before Christmas. We will forever be free to speculate, theorise and make podcasts about it. And in a way, that's the most satisfying conclusion for us all.***

---

* Murder is always exciting when it happened long ago enough not to care about the victims.

** Irony etc.

*** Though not, obviously, for Eileen and Marquis.

The Horror of Hook Island

The oceans of our world are filled with strange and mysterious creatures, almost all of them absolutely disgusting. If you're looking to find the ugliest thing you've ever seen in your life, just dive to the bottom of the sea, where the Lord God has deposited all of His most repulsive creations so He doesn't have to look at them.

But though we have discovered many of the sea's revolting monsters, it's a fact that vast swathes of the world's oceans remain unexplored, and there could be even stranger, even uglier freaks swimming around out there. It's a chilling thought, but one we must face bravely, especially in light of stories like that of the Hook Island monster.

Hook Island is a near-uninhabited island in the Whitsundays, off the central coast of Queensland, named after its discoverer, who came across the island while fleeing a crocodile. It is not a place of any great note, and were it not for the monster it would be best known as an excellent snorkelling spot for anyone who wants to be killed by a jellyfish.

It was in December 1964 that Breton* photographer Robert Le Serrec, his family, and friend Henk De Jong were crossing Stonehaven Bay, Hook Island, in a motorboat and came across a quite extraordinary creature in the shallow waters of the lagoon. It was like nothing they had ever seen before, and Le Serrec, being a man of science, possessed of insatiable curiosity and quite alert to moneymaking opportunities, decided to have a closer look.

---

* Some kind of biscuit, apparently.

Le Serrec and De Jong moved gradually towards the beast, taking photos, and eventually slipped into the water in an attempt to film it. As soon as they began to film, however, it bolted. The stills Le Serrec captured, however, have become legendary among cryptozoology enthusiasts, and to this day provide some of history's most compelling evidence of the existence of ambiguous photographs.

The creature was, Le Serrec estimated, about seventy-five to eighty feet long, and shaped either like a tadpole or a sperm, depending on how your mind tends to work, with a broad head and a long, whiplike tail. It was mostly black, with brown stripes and smooth skin. Its eyes were on top of its head in order to allow it to spot passing Bretons.

As is always the case when a new horror is discovered to be lurking in wait to devour our children, the news of Le Serrec's find caused enormous excitement around the world and gave Hook Island a profile that, frankly, it did not deserve.

Today, nearly sixty years after Robert Le Serrec first cried 'Mon Dieu!', myriad questions about the Hook Island monster remain unanswered. Was the photographer's story true? Is the creature dangerous? Is it still alive? Can we safely go swimming off Hook Island without fear of being swallowed by a giant sperm? Could the seemingly irrelevant fact that Robert Le Serrec was in debt and had several years earlier told people that he had a great idea for making money that involved a sea serpent be a factor? When you get down to brass tacks, what the hell was it?

Many theories have been advanced. Some believe it may have been a giant synbranchid, or swamp eel. Some believe it could be an as-yet-unknown species of shark. Still others think it might've been simply a tightly bunched shoal of fish, though to be fair those others are not very bright. Sadly, however, the most widely accepted theory today is that it was a hoax, just like the Loch Ness Monster and the moon landing. The hoax hypothesis is a depressingly sensible one for those of us who truly want to believe that the world is a more magical and wondrous place than it seems, and that there are huge tadpoles splashing about somewhere.

Until someone with a better camera comes along, we'll have to remain ignorant as to the true identity of the monster. Was it a rare new ocean predator? Was it a prehistoric monster that has survived to the present day? Was it actually a tadpole, meaning that somewhere out there is a 200-foot frog? Was it a big sheet of plastic cut into the shape of a sea monster by a complete jerk of a Frenchman? We'll never know. So let's just assume, until we're forced to change our minds, that it was whichever thing you find the most interesting.

The Mystifying Myth of the Marree Man

It is of course well known that art is a waste of time. But if it's a waste of time to make a drawing, how much more futile a use of one's limited time on Earth is it to make a drawing that is nearly three kilometres long and covers over 600 acres? And what sort of person would do such a deranged thing?

These are the questions that were raised in 1998 by the discovery of the Marree Man, also known as Stuart's Giant, a huge geoglyph* sixty kilometres west of Marree, in South Australia. The picture depicts – or seems to depict, to the casual observer – an Aboriginal man wielding a boomerang or woomera. The man is 2.7 kilometres tall, and his outline is twenty-eight kilometres long. The lines of the drawing are twenty to thirty centimetres deep in the ground.

The Marree Man wouldn't be such a deep mystery if it were very, very old. As all students of history know, people in the olden days were weird as hell, and if they'd scratched a picture of a giant in the ground, it could be written off as one of the symptoms of the well-recognised brain parasites that pretty much everyone before about 1950 suffered from.

But the truly weird thing about the Marree Man is that it's not old at all. It was only discovered in 1998, because it was only MADE in 1998. Satellite images of the site show that on 27 May 1998 there was no Marree Man, and on 12 June 1998 there was one. So at some point in that sixteen-day window, a person or persons unknown headed out to the countryside

---

* Greek for 'big weird picture drawn by making lines in the ground'.

and drew a giant, and for the last few decades that person or persons has steadfastly refused to let us in on why the hell they did it.

The more one looks into the mystery, the more it deepens. For example, the proprietor of the William Creek Hotel, north-west of Marree, claimed that a fax was sent to the hotel informing them of the location of the drawing. This is positively baffling: who on Earth would actually own a fax machine? Yet the story of Marree Man is like that: bizarre and inexplicable and full of obsolete technology.

After the discovery of the Marree Man, the flames of intrigue were fanned by a series of anonymous press releases about the work. These caused some to speculate that the picture was created by Americans, due to oddly jarring phrases in the statements such as 'Your state of SA', 'Queensland Barrier Reef' and 'Boy, howdy, what a roundup!'.*

The American connection was strengthened by the discovery of a small glass jar near the Marree Man, containing a satellite photo of the artwork and a note which featured the US flag and references to the Branch Davidians, the cult that had recently engaged in a robust debate with the FBI on biblical interpretation.

In January 1999, another fax** was sent to anyone who could receive it, informing them that there was a plaque buried just under the Marree Man's nose. The plaque also had an American flag on it, as well as the Olympic rings and the words, 'In honour of the land they once knew. His attainments in these pursuits are extraordinary; a constant source of wonderment and admiration.' This is a quotation from the book *The Red Centre*, describing wallaby hunts by Pitjantjatjara men.

Another notable feature of the Marree Man is that it is a close match for a reverse image of the Artemision bronze figure of Zeus raised from the Adriatic Sea in 1928, a fact that many believe to be evidence of something or other.

What does it all mean? When you put together a picture of a hunting man, an ancient Greek bronze, the Olympic rings, the US flag and the

---

* One of these I made up.

** Seriously!

persistent use of fax machines, what do you get? The answer, of course, is 'someone who likes to annoy people and does not have a real job'. But that's not necessarily a totally satisfying solution to the whole mystery.

Some have suggested that the Marree Man was created by Bardius Goldberg, an artist who had expressed interest in making an artwork visible from space. Goldberg refused to say whether he was the artist. Others think the Australian or US Army might have done it, as part of the merry hijinks so typical of the military. However, the armies also refuse to say whether they were responsible, so we are left to ponder.

The only thing we can know for sure is this: in the history of enormous effort being expended on extremely difficult yet entirely pointless things, the Marree Man is as shining an example as you'll ever see.

The Part-Time Lake

Anyone who has driven down the Federal Highway from Sydney to Canberra has enjoyed the sight of the shining tranquil waters of Lake George. Unless, of course, they have instead enjoyed the sight of sheep grazing on the lush grass of the big field where Lake George used to be. If they travel regularly on the highway, they'll see both, and most likely think to themselves, 'Bit weird.'

For Lake George is only a part-time lake. Technically known as an endorheic lake, meaning it has no outflow to rivers or oceans, it is a depression* that fills up with water when there is enough rain. But if the rain stays away, it's just a big bunch of grass and trees and things.

The lake is believed to be a million years old, although there are few reliable eyewitnesses who are willing to confirm this. It used to be connected to the Yass River, but at some point the Lake George Escarpment rose – which is so typical of that particular escarpment, known in the escarpment community for its capricious and selfish behaviour. This resulted in the drainage being blocked and Lake George going all endorheic and having no friends.

The original inhabitants of the region around Lake George called it *Werriwa*, meaning 'bad water', because the lake is one of the saltiest bodies of water in inland New South Wales. In fact, other lakes hardly ever talk to it because of how easily it takes offence; one word in the wrong place and it goes dry and sulks for months.

___
* Due to being so close to Canberra.

40

The first European to stumble across or into the lake was Joseph Wild in 1820. Wild blamed the lake's saltiness on mental illness, and thus it was named after George III. George III had been dead for nearly a year by this stage, but the governor was adamant that the lake was definitely *not* named after George IV.

The history of Lake George has been rich and varied, quite apart from its indecisive approach to moisture. In the 1800s there was a billabong at one end of the lake,* which the landowner filled with Murray cod. When the rains caused the billabong to overflow, the cod gleefully swam into the lake, only to find that in the 1890s the Federation Drought happened and all the water was gone, making the cods look like complete idiots, though not as stupid as the humans who had decided that a good way to celebrate Federation was to have a drought.

At one point it was mooted to place Australia's capital next to Lake George, its filling-and-emptying routine to provide a powerful metaphor for market economics. In the end, Canberra was built reasonably close to the lake, although not close enough that MPs can go swimming – or, in dry times, crawling – there.

Some have theorised that the reason Lake George fills and empties as it does is that it's connected deep beneath the surface of the Earth to lakes in Africa and South America – although this theory is considered less fun than most because it's too blatantly stupid even for crazy people to get on board with.

A visit to Lake George is always worthwhile, as a reminder to us all that nature is, indeed, weird as hell.

---

* And at the other end, a Paddle Pop.

Jurassic Ark

A museum is a great place in which to learn more about the world. But where can you go if you want to know *less* about the world? No problem: just head out to Bells Bridge, Queensland, and visit Jurassic Ark, an open-air museum that stands out from the crowd by dedicating itself to teaching visitors 100 per cent untrue facts.

Jurassic Ark was created by John Mackay, founding director of Creation Science, who became frustrated with the pro-evolution bias exhibited by many museums and wanted to present the alternative view that the Bible is true and science is a conspiracy to stop children feeling ashamed of their bodies.

At Jurassic Ark, you will find copious evidence that the Biblical account of the creation of the Earth and Noah's Ark is entirely true, like signs saying that it is. There's also a big mural of pictures depicting the story, and when has a mural ever lied to you?

Then there are the fossils. Real ones, of plants, that demonstrate beyond any possible doubt that the owners of Jurassic Ark have put some fossils in it. As the museum explains, none of these fossils show any evidence of evolution whatsoever: every single one of them is a fossil of a thing rather than a fossil of two things turning into each other. Take THAT, Charles Darwin, says the museum, in its quiet understated way.

The museum also features special experiments that demonstrate that fossils don't actually take a long time to form: you can make them pretty quickly if you've got the right machinery. Which presumably God does have, because He's God, isn't He.

Naturally any museum called 'Jurassic Ark' needs dinosaurs, and they've got them. Huge and lovingly crafted models of prehistoric beasts, shown alongside modern-day animals, proving that actually dinosaurs lived quite a short time ago. Otherwise, how would the people who made the models know what they looked like standing next to a duck? As the Jurassic Ark website says, 'the Chinese still call dinosaurs dragons just like the English and many other cultures did until it became politically incorrect due to evolution'.

And that's Jurassic Ark in a nutshell: an enormous and vivid rebuke to the forces of political correctness and their attempts to infect modern life with the lie that the world is old.

It's a refreshing change from all the non-Biblical museums, like, for example, the Gympie Bone Museum, just down the road from Jurassic Ark. The Gympie museum has a fascinating collection of bones but shamefully neglects to tell visitors that the bones were made by Jesus.

So, if you're looking for paganistic indoctrination by amoral perverts, go to a 'mainstream' museum. But if you want to learn the wonderful story of the Bible in mural form, find out more about how fossils are formed extremely quickly, rejoice in the knowledge of God's plan for humanity and how He drowned all the dinosaurs because they were too slow to get on the boat, there is only one place to go: Jurassic Ark, where facts go to repent.

The Parable of the Prime Minister's Trousers

O ne of the greatest things about being Australian is that only on the very rarest of occasions are we forced to contemplate the places into which our political leaders' private parts get stuck.* Say what you like about the calibre of human selected by the Australian people for the highest office, at least they generally have the grace and tact to avoid inviting the public consciousness into their underpants.**

But even the most serendipitous of national traits have exceptions, and Australia got a particularly unsavoury one in 1986 when former prime minister Malcolm Fraser was found stumbling about the lobby of Memphis's Admiral Benbow Inn wearing a shirt, a tie and a disturbingly skimpy towel wrapped about his nether portions.

Before relating the facts of the matter, it's important to provide a little bit of background about the sort of character Malcolm Fraser was, for it is only by understanding Malcolm Fraser the man that we can truly appreciate how funny this episode was.

Malcolm Fraser was prime minister of Australia from 1975 to 1983, during which time he nurtured a reputation as the kind of calm, sober hand on the tiller that a country needed when it was in danger of not being clinically depressed. His best-known catchphrase was 'Life wasn't

---

* Something that cannot, sadly, be said about our American cousins, who since the 1990s have been unable to avoid thinking about presidential penises for more than a few hours at a time.
** I know you're thinking about Tony Abbott, but technically Speedos are not underpants, and reducing the wonderful work done by our lifesaving community to cheap jokes about genitalia is disgusting. Shame on you.

meant to be easy', but he wasn't quite as much fun as that might suggest. Overall, he was the prime minister brought in after the wild party of the Whitlam years to clean up the place and ground the whole country until it had done its chores.

It was only after Fraser left office – defeated by Bob Hawke, a man who quite enjoyed whipping off the trousers himself, but with the innate political nous to avoid doing so in hotel lobbies – that Australia was forced to confront the fact that for eight years it had been under the control of a genuine pants man.

The seeds of this confrontation were sown when Fraser, having ascended in his post-politics career to the position of chairman of the Commonwealth Eminent Persons Group, went to Memphis as guest speaker at the Memphis Country Club. Later he would say, 'I wish I'd never been to bloody Memphis', and he was by no means the first or last to say so.

After his speaking engagement, Fraser went to Beale Street to listen to the blues, just like Elvis once had, but unlike Elvis he did not end up revolutionising western popular music, not even a little bit. He went drinking at the Peabody Hotel, a luxury establishment quite at the opposite end of the spectrum from the Admiral Benbow Inn, where he later checked in under the name 'John Jones'. The next morning, 'John Jones' stumbled into the Benbow lobby sans trousers, complaining that his watch, passport, wallet and $600 had gone the way of the pants.

Fraser was robbed of his possessions and his dignity, as the Australian people had to come to terms with learning that their staid ex-PM was the sort of man who checked into cheap hotels under fake names and then exposed their thighs to the general public. They then had to try to figure out exactly what sort of man that was. They knew it wasn't exactly the sort of thing you put on your résumé.

Fraser himself denied that he was to any extent a dirty dog, claiming that it was a straightforward case of drink spiking, and that he had no idea how he'd ended up at the Admiral Benbow. His wife, Tamie, opined that the ex-PM must have been set up, saying, 'He might have gone off with someone here or there at some time but he wouldn't go to a bar to meet someone on the off chance – they were setting him up. Poor old boy. It's really horrible. He was so embarrassed.' So, if nothing else, we can at least be sure of one fact: Tamie Fraser was a really cool wife.

Elsewhere, speculation ran rampant as to what had really happened in Memphis. Some believed that the Israeli intelligence agency Mossad had targeted Fraser because of his interference in an arms deal Israel was conducting with South Africa. This is a most attractive theory, but most of the available evidence from history suggests that when Mossad targets someone, their goal is to achieve a bit more than getting them pantsless in public.

The likely explanation is that the granite-faced statesman Malcolm Fraser was stung by a tall Texan blonde, who in subsequent months enacted similar humiliations on various Memphis plutocrats. Reportedly, the lady had a tattoo above her breast and a winning way with the wealthy, and Fraser could rest easy knowing he was far from the only nitwit who fell into the trap.

In the end, the Texan blonde may have done Fraser a favour. It can be of great benefit to a public figure who is seen as stern and aloof to be humanised in the mass consciousness, and few things humanise a man like wandering around a dodgy motel with only a towel to hide his shame. In many ways, the Admiral Benbow Inn was the location for Malcolm Fraser's transformation from autocratic party-pooper to absolute dude. Next time you're in Memphis, you should drop in and savour that pantsless atmosphere.

The Lady of the Swamp

In the middle of a Gippsland swamp, its grand facade crumbling piece by piece into the bog, stood Tullaree, the former stately home of the once-wealthy Clement family. Before World War I, the Clement sisters had held court there, entertaining the rich and powerful and revelling in their place at the pinnacle of Victorian society. However, by 1950 the family's wealth had been frittered away by extravagant spending, poor investment decisions and an approach to land cultivation that could best be described as 'Oh god I just can't be arsed'. With the money all gone and the high-society shindigs a thing of the past, the mansion had become a ruin from a horror movie: a ghastly wreck swathed in scrub and tangles of blackberries, overrun by rats and snakes, where Margaret and Jeanie Clement hid away from the world, penniless and relying on charity to feed and clothe themselves.

That year, Jeanie died, and police had to wade through miles of waist-deep swamp to retrieve her body. With the public alerted to the Gothic grotesquerie of the Clements' decline, the press made its way through the swamp to interview Margaret, who became known as 'The Lady of the Swamp'.

Margaret, now alone in the house apart from her dog and legions of vermin, would walk eleven kilometres through the murky water to get supplies from the nearest town. She spent her time at home reading detective stories by the light of kerosene lamps, writing to her relatives begging for money, and reliving the days of blazing lights, sumptuous banquets and ballrooms full of dancing people, which still swirled and sparkled in her head.

For two years Margaret lived alone at Tullaree, the destitute object of widespread public fascination, until in May 1952 she simply disappeared.

For a week the police searched with the assistance of 200 volunteers, scouring the ruins and staggering through the swamp, but no trace of Margaret was found. The first theory was that the poor old dear had slipped into the swamp waters and drowned, but more sinister ideas arose when Margaret's walking stick was found intact and mud-free in the house. Foul play was very much on the menu.

Suspicion alighted on Stan Livingstone, who was not only Margaret's neighbour but also a retired footballer, so it was hard to believe he wasn't guilty of something. Livingstone and his wife, Esme,* had bought Tullaree in 1951, promising Margaret a lifetime tenancy in a cottage on the property. The Livingstones eventually did very well out of Tullaree, fixing it up and selling it twelve years later. But they denied having any hand in Margaret's death, for what that was worth.**

The Livingstones pointed the finger at Margaret's nephew, Clement Carnaghan. Clement Carnaghan pointed the finger straight back at the Livingstones. It was a classic game of fingerpoint ping-pong, with no resolution in sight.

Margaret Clement was declared legally dead in 1954 – and it is to be hoped that, by that time, she really was dead, as if she was still alive, the shock of being declared dead could've killed her. In 1980 a coronial inquiry was held into her death, under the auspices of the Victorian Department of Taking Ridiculous Amounts of Time to Get Around to Things. The coroner returned an open finding – the official legal version of the shrug. The inquiry had been convened after human remains were found at Tullaree in 1978, but nobody could agree whether they were Margaret's bones or those of some other woman nobody cared about.

The fence-sitting of the coroner did nothing to quiet the interest in Margaret Clement's disappearance. In 1982 Clement Carnaghan died. In 1986 the Livingstones, seeing an opportunity to kick a man while he

---

* Probably the same one from *A Country Practice*.
** Not very much, because murderers usually do.

was down – typical of a Footscray player – issued a press release claiming that Clement had kidnapped his aunt, a frankly rude move. In 1997 the coroner, whose obsession with Margaret Clement was starting to get a bit weird, said that it was 'one of the great unsolved mysteries, but not one beyond resolution'.

As of 2023, the coroner still looks a twit, because so far the Clement case has very much been beyond resolution. Perhaps the truth about Margaret really was lost forever in the Tullaree swamp in 1952. Where and how the lonely woman met her lonely end remains as mysterious as ever. We can but hope that when her eyes closed for the last time, the crowds in the Tullaree ballroom were still waltzing behind them.

The Kingdom of the Kelly Skull

There is a powerful irony in the fact that of all the pieces of Ned Kelly's body, it's his head – the part he was most proud of – that ended up going missing.

Kelly paid for his crimes on 11 November 1880, the date chosen to commemorate the dismissal of Gough Whitlam. Sentenced to death for killing three policemen and impersonating a bin, Kelly was hanged at Old Melbourne Gaol after delivering his famous last words: 'Sucks, this life.'

Following his execution, Kelly was buried, but this was perfectly normal and mainly done for reasons of hygiene. The problems began not when he was buried, but when he was dug up again in 1929, to make room for a new development for living people.

It was assumed that Kelly's bones would have disintegrated, as it was the practice at the time to cover bodies in quicklime when they were buried. And given that quicklime was the quickest variety of lime yet discovered, it was expected that his grave would be empty (and resistant to scurvy).

This was not, however, the case. Either the quicklime had been forgotten or the Melbourne Gaol lags' bones were made of particularly stern stuff, because when they began digging the old coffins up a bunch of bones spilled out everywhere.

The crowd that had for some reason gathered to watch some guys dig up some graves went mad, diving in like children around a smashed gumball machine to grab a bone for themselves. This being an era of few entertainment options, having a bone at home could keep a family amused for months.

Contractor Harry Lee grabbed Kelly's skull for himself and bolted, but later, like many of his fellow grave-robbers, he repented and returned it. All the bones that could be found were put into new coffins and reburied at Pentridge Prison.*

The skull, however, was just beginning its grand adventure. It was not buried, but kept around on a detective's desk like a kind of primitive Funko Pop, until it was donated in 1931 to the Australian Institute of Anatomy. For forty years the denizens of the institute kept the skull, occasionally getting it out to look at.

Then, in a clever call-back, the skull was given back to the Old Melbourne Gaol, which was no longer a gaol but a museum, where tourists and schoolchildren could come to learn more about traditional glass cases. In one of those cases was Kelly's skull, right next to Kelly's death mask, so people could see the difference between Kelly with skin on and Kelly with skin off, and decide for themselves which suited him better.

For most of the 1970s, Kelly's skull thrilled Kelly lovers and skull fans alike, until in 1978 it disappeared from its case, an action which most biologists say a skull is unlikely to perform on its own.

As the saga of the skull began to resemble the journey of Bobo the Bear in the *Simpsons* episode 'Rosebud', a farmer called Tom Baxter popped up in 2009 to say he had the skull in a Tupperware container, having come into possession of it by means of shut up, it's none of your business.** He handed the skull over to forensics experts to have it confirmed that it was indeed the legendary bushranger's bonce.

A long process of people in white coats poking at the skull and looking in microscopes ensued until, through DNA analysis,*** two things were determined: 1. The skull was definitely the one taken by Harry Lee

---

* I suspect putting men who have died in prison into another prison after they died is some kind of double-jeopardy violation, but I am not a lawyer and I never even saw that movie, so I could be wrong.

** Specifically, he said he 'did not consider it theft' and 'I haven't admitted to being the person who took it', so you can see why nobody considered him suspicious at all.

*** Don't ask; it's complicated.

in 1929; and 2. The skull was definitely *not* Ned Kelly's.

In other words, the skull that had been on the detective's desk, in the Australian Institute of Anatomy, on display at the Old Melbourne Gaol and in Tom Baxter's Tupperware had never been a famous bushranger's skull at all – just some random dead convict's.

Later on, Kelly's skeleton was discovered at Pentridge and identified. But his skull was still missing. Where is it? Nobody knows. Does it matter? Well, it's a matter of respect. To remove a man's head is generally considered an ill-mannered act, and that rule isn't necessarily waived just because the man is dead. If Ned Kelly had known his head was going to be stolen, he may well have never agreed to be hanged in the first place. Dirty trick to play on a fella.

All we can hope is that one day the skull will be found and reunited with the rest of his bones, and we can finally pay proper respect to this country's most beloved multiple murderer.

The Legend of the Glowing Cross

I t was in 1978 that the *Northern Star* newspaper ran a story about a woman who had reported visiting the North Lismore Pioneer Cemetery, where she had seen a cross on one of the graves glowing like a lightbulb.

The *Northern Star* was not a publication with a massive circulation, but of the select group who read this particular issue, someone passed it on, and someone passed it on again, and again, and suddenly the story of the glowing cross was crackling through the national press and captivating people around the country.

Lismore became the centre of a good old-fashioned public palaver, as media descended on the town to wring every drop from the story, while stonemasons, geologists and various other sciencey types also arrived to figure out just what the deal was.

As was quickly uncovered, the deal was that this glowing cross was no new fad. In fact, this cross had been glowing for more than half a century, and its story began with a tragedy in 1907.

Railway worker William Steenson was killed in horrible circumstances, by a runaway train carriage at Mullumbimby. He died a hero, trying to stop the train and save the passengers. Buried in the Pioneer Cemetery, his grave was adorned by a fine large cross of Balmoral red granite.

It was eleven years after his death, in 1918, that the cross took up its new hobby of lighting up. The glowing cross was well known to Lismore locals, being dubbed 'the ghost on the hill'; local children would dare each other to approach it.

Albert Dann recalled that as a child he had been offered a penny if he would read the epitaph on William Steenson's tombstone.

Forcing myself towards the main gate, suddenly, as I edged closer, a dazzling beam of white light flashed from the centre of the cemetery and struck me in the eyes. I was rooted to the spot with a horrible fear ... Somehow I remember forcing my unwilling body about and with every ghost and devil after me I sprinted back along the metalled road to the comfort of a gas lamp, beneath which the boys were howling and laughing, you couldn't do it, you couldn't do it.

Heartwarming episodes of juvenile psychological torture aside, Lismore grew used to the glowing cross and it became a humdrum part of small-town life; news of the phenomenon did not break through to the wider world until the *Northern Star* sent it viral in '78.

After interest in the cross exploded, numerous explanations for the unearthly glow were suggested and rejected. It was not a reflection of moonlight: the cross glowed on moonless nights. It was not a fluorescent or radioactive variety of rock. It was not the remains of glow-worms – these cannot be found in granite.*

Nobody could satisfactorily explain the glow, which multitudes had witnessed. The cross kept on glowing and keeping its mysteries to itself until 1986, when Lismore woke up one morning to find it had vanished. Taken up to its celestial home? Well, no, probably just stolen. Frankly, a dick move on someone's part.

William Steenson's family erected an identical cross, also made of Balmoral red granite, but it has never glowed. The original remains lost, hidden away in someone's shed or sitting at the bottom of a river, bearing the words that can't help but seem eerily apt:

---

* I mean, it's hard to believe that particular suggestion was ever taken very seriously.

Though sorrow and darkness encompass the tomb
Thy saviour has pass'd through its darkness before thee
And the lamp of his Love
Is thy guide through the gloom.

The Land of Submarines

The town of Germanton had a problem. It had borne that name proudly since 1858, in honour of local publican John Christopher Pabst, who had been, through no fault of his own, German. This had been fine and dandy for all concerned for many years, but in 1914 World War I came along and being called Germanton was suddenly not such a marker of status.

During World War I, changing your name to sound less German was all the rage. Even the British Royal Family changed its name from 'The House of Saxe-Coburg and Gotha' to 'The House of Windsor', in order to emphasise to their subjects that they were definitely not German and that nobody should drop bombs on them.

But Germanton, a little hamlet on the road between Sydney and Melbourne, was ahead of the curve: the royal name change was still two years away in 1915 when the people of Germanton decided that it was in terribly bad taste to have 'German' in your name when those were the very people we were sending our young men to kill. Accordingly, a new name for the town was sought.

The settlement was originally known as Ten Mile Creek, but returning to the old name was viewed as both retrograde and boring. Besides, with the war raging and every Australian seeking to do his or her bit, what they really wanted was a *patriotic* name: a name that didn't just say 'We aren't German' but emphasised 'We are absolutely balls to the wall for this lovely war'.

As in innumerable history exams, the answer came from the

Dardanelles. On 13 December 1914, the submarine HMS *B11*, a clapped-out pile of junk under the command of 26-year-old Lieutenant Norman Douglas Holbrook, pulled off a classic little-engine-that-could manoeuvre when it passed under five rows of mines to torpedo and sink the Turkish ship *Mesudiye*. Under heavy fire from torpedoes and gunboats, Holbrook then guided the *B11* back to safety in the Mediterranean. For his actions, Holbrook became the first submariner to be awarded the Victoria Cross.

Holbrook's heroism greatly impressed the Germanton folk. 'Now there's a fella,' they told each other, 'who represents all that is good about Australia: courage, grace under fire, being English, etc.' Moreover, in killing thirty-seven Turks, Holbrook had proven himself truly dedicated to the war effort and was therefore about as far from a German as it was possible to get.

And so it was that Germanton renamed itself Holbrook in honour of the gutsy submariner, and it has been Holbrook ever since.

But the people of Holbrook never were ones for half-measures. When they had an idea, they carried it all the way to the end of the line. It took eighty years for them to do so, but in 1995 the true potential of Holbrook was realised. It was in that year that, having reasoned that if a town was to be named after a submarine commander it only made sense that that town should have a submarine in it, the town finally got its patriotic hands on one.

The Navy decommissioned the HMS *Otway* in 1995 and, not wanting to pay to take it to the tip, they gave it to Holbrook instead. Or, rather, they sold it to Holbrook. Or, rather, they sold some of it to Holbrook: specifically, the part of the hull above the waterline. In a way, this was even better than getting the whole thing, as it meant that when the sub was placed in a public park, it gave the appearance of serenely sailing about on top of the grass. Funnily enough, the park in which the *Otway* is situated is called Germanton Park, which seems to kind of defeat the purpose, doesn't it?

Holbrook's submarine stands as a beautiful reminder of what a local community can do when driven by violent xenophobia. World War I had many impacts that could broadly be called negative, but if there was one positive to come out of the Great War, it is that to this day there stands, just off the Hume Highway, more than 100 kilometres from the sea, a magnificent submarine, commemorating the bravery of Norman Holbrook – commander of a completely different submarine – and the determination of the people of Germanton that nobody would call them traitors. The mills of history do indeed grind slow, but they also grind exceedingly weirdly.

The Burrawang Bunyip

This story is about the bunyip that lives in the swamp in the valley below Burrawang, in the Southern Highlands of New South Wales.* But it could be about any bunyip, anywhere. The important thing is not any specific bunyip, but to embrace and appreciate *all* the bunyips that bless us with their presence and bring such vitality and colour to our great country.

But anyway. On to the story of the horrible monster.

What a bunyip looks like is a matter of wide disagreement, like Renée Zellweger. It either looks like a large dog or seal with a shaggy coat, a long-necked creature with tusks and the head and tail of a horse, or possibly an emu, or it might look like a really big starfish, or an owl.

Leaving aside the challenge of synthesising these descriptions, the main point of bunyips is not what they look like but what they do – and what they do is lurk in the water waiting for unwary folk to wander by, whereupon they jump out and eat them. Somewhat antisocial of them, but everyone's got to eat.

Most bunyips come to us in stories from Aboriginal mythology, but the Burrawang bunyip is a more recent phenomenon, being attested to in the 20th century, which was supposed to be the century when people stopped believing in crazy monsters. Railway workers in the 1930s heard the bunyip bellowing and growling in the swamp and ran away in terror, wisely following the old aphorism, 'Nothing that bellows in a swamp is good for you.'

---

* Incidentally, a lot of weird stuff seems to go on in the Southern Highlands. Someone should look into that.

In the 1960s, possibly in protest at the increasingly lax morals of Western society, the bunyip was frequently heard roaring by Burrawang residents, who consequently denied themselves the pleasure of a swim in the swamp. It was said to have a long neck, be covered with feathers, have a long horn in the middle of its head and stand on two legs. Some people said it could fly, but let's not entertain wild rumours.

Ed Woolfrey, a former publican at the Burrawang pub, recalled that the bunyip's roar was loud enough to shake the bottles off the top shelf of the bar, while dairy farmer Ken Sharpe testified that it was a remarkably fast mover, as it could be heard at one end of the swamp and then at the other end just minutes later.

There are stories of the Burrawang bunyip taking cattle, but it seems to have generally left the human population unharmed, except for some broken bottles.

Why does the bunyip roar? One presumes it is angry about something, or suffering from persistent toothache. Or perhaps it just wants to keep people away from its territory – just like humans, animals often resent strangers barging into their homes, and just like humans, they will often bellow aggressively at them if they try.

It is unfortunate that most eyewitness accounts of the Burrawang bunyip are actually earwitness accounts: everyone claims to have heard it, but it's tough to find anyone who's seen it. Although clearly someone has – otherwise how would we know it has feathers and a horn? But even if sightings are thin on the ground, it's a scientific fact that if noises are happening, something is making those noises, and you can look that up.

And while it is, theoretically, possible that roaring from the Burrawang swamp is not a bunyip, it is also possible that it is. So fifty-fifty, really.

The Peculiar Puzzle of the Pyjama Girl

One of the saddest days in anyone's life is when they discover that in real life, when murders happen, there are no eccentric genius detectives to come along and make the police look like fools by noticing the clue nobody else did and solving the case. In real life, it's really hard to solve murders, and the only people who make the police look like fools are the police.

A perfect example of this is the 'Pyjama Girl' case, in which the police were unable to solve a murder even after the murderer confessed.

In early September 1934, Tom Griffith was, for some reason, leading a bull along Howlong Road* near Albury when he noticed two things: one, a strong smell of kerosene, and two, a body in a culvert alongside the road. Investigating further, he discovered a third thing: the body was a dead one. This, to Tom's mind, was quite serious, and so as a courtesy he let the police know.

The body was dressed in yellow silk pyjamas adorned with Chinese dragons, which in rural Australia in the 1930s could've been enough to get you killed by itself. The victim was badly beaten and had a bullet in her neck. Her head was wrapped in a towel, suggesting she had been murdered just after washing her hair.

The pyjama girl was determined to be a woman in her twenties, meaning it was incorrect and sexist to call her a 'girl' and we're all being very sexist when we do so. Having made this determination, the police

---

* Dunno why they don't just measure it.

threw their hands up and said, 'Buggered if we know.' With no idea who the body was, they did the only thing they could: sent her to the Sydney University Medical School and put her on public display.

From the perspective of our modern society, it is only natural to respond to this by asking, 'They did *what*?' But it's important to remember the context of the period: people back then were weird and stupid.

The pyjama girl's body was preserved in formaldehyde, which was probably a smart move, as without it identification would've become difficult in quite a short space of time. As it was, the body stayed at the uni for eight years before being moved to police headquarters. This proved a masterstroke, as in the twinkle of an eye – or, rather, two years – there was a breakthrough in the case.

Earlier in the investigation, the police had considered the possibility that the pyjama girl was missing woman Linda Agostini. Upon reviewing the evidence, they decided it couldn't be her. In 1944, ten years after the body was found, they looked at the evidence again and discovered that actually it was Linda Agostini. On a roll, the cops went round to Linda's husband's place and asked him if he'd killed his wife. Tony Agostini, probably amazed that nobody had thought to ask him before, said yes.

Agostini admitted to accidentally shooting his wife in one of those wacky mishaps that happen in every marriage. Afraid of being accused of murder, he had driven the body to Albury, dumped it in the culvert and set it on fire. To many people, this made him look *more* like a murderer. He was not convicted of murder, however, but of manslaughter, and after serving three years was deported to Italy, where he led a peaceful, carb-heavy life until he died in 1969.

Case closed! Except not. Because although Agostini had confessed to killing his wife, and in all likelihood had killed his wife, the conclusion that Linda Agostini was the pyjama girl is by no means a foregone one. In his book *The Pyjama Girl Mystery: A True Story of Murder, Obsession and Lies*,* Richard Evans notes that the pyjama girl had a different-shaped

---

* Sounds pretty sexy when you put it that way.

nose to Linda Agostini, and a different bust size – seems a bit sleazy to be looking at dead women's boobs, but still. Also, the pyjama girl had brown eyes and Linda Agostini had blue eyes, which raises the question: seriously, what the hell were the police thinking? Or at least it would raise that question, if it hadn't already been raised back in the 1930s and continuously since.

Essentially, we still don't know who the pyjama girl was, and maybe we never will, unless we can find something that has hitherto existed only in fiction: a clever detective.

The Weeping Woman Caper

Of all the reasons why a woman might want to have a cry, the fact that she knows Pablo Picasso is going to make her look like a creepy green alien in one of the world's most famous paintings is not a common one, but it is undoubtedly one of the most publicly notable. Certainly it caught the attention of the National Gallery of Victoria,* which in 1985 bought Picasso's *The Weeping Woman*.

This was not *the* *The Weeping Woman* but one of a series of *Weeping Womans* that Picasso painted in the 1930s. The main one is in the Tate Modern in the United Kingdom, and is bright and colourful. The one bought by the NGV, conversely, is sickly green and purple and looks like the woman is weeping because she doesn't like the make-up job done on her as an extra for *The Walking Dead*.

Still, nightmarish colour scheme and weird pointy face aside, the painting cost the gallery $1.6 million.** This was the most ever paid for a painting by an Australian gallery, even more than the National Gallery of Australia*** had paid for Jackson Pollock's *Blue Poles* – though, to be fair, *The Weeping Woman* did actually look like something, so was definitely worth more than *Blue Poles*. 'This face is going to haunt Melbourne for the next 100 years,' said NGV director Patrick McCaughey, possibly not realising how that sounded.

---

* By the way, that gallery calling itself the *National* Gallery? That's a whole other irritating story.

** In today's money, fifteen billion Euros.

*** An *actual* National Gallery.

Soon after its acquisition, the face began to haunt Melbourne in a very different way from how McCaughey intended. On 2 August 1986, thieves – ironically, the very type of people that the gallery didn't want to break into it – broke into the gallery. Unscrewing the painting from the wall, they took it out of the gallery and ran away. That's right! Stealing a valuable masterpiece is just that easy! Why not try it yourself this weekend?

It took two days for anyone to notice that *The Weeping Woman* was missing, not because it was really small, but because the thieves had cleverly left a card stating that it had been removed for routine maintenance. The card carried the term 'ACT', which stood for 'Australian Cultural Terrorists', but which NGV staff assumed meant the painting had been taken to the National Gallery in Canberra. This provided police with a strong clue: the thieves had clearly had enough inside information to know that staff at the NGV were incredibly slow-witted.

The ACT – the terrorists, not the territory – wrote to the Victorian arts minister, Race Mathews, with their demands: an increase in arts funding of 10 per cent over three years, and the establishment of a $25,000 art prize called the Picasso Ransom Prize, for artists under 30.

These demands were actually pretty good ideas, but the government refused to agree to them because the thieves had called the minister a 'pompous fathead' and a 'tiresome old bag of swamp gas', which were true but hurtful. The ACT promised that if their demands were not met within seven days, *The Weeping Woman* would be destroyed.

The deadline passed, with demands unmet and the painting unfound. On 19 August, more than two weeks after the theft, police received an anonymous phone call that led them to locker 227 at Spencer Street Station. Inside they found *The Weeping Woman*, wrapped in brown paper, tied with string, undamaged and as creepy and gross as ever. There was also a letter from the thieves, which stated: 'Of course we never looked to have our demands met ... Our intention was always to bring to public attention the plight of a group which lacks any of the legitimate means of blackmailing governments.'

They certainly achieved their aim: the theft of *The Weeping Woman* shone an undeniable spotlight on the plight of art thieves. That's a legacy that will hopefully last forever.

Rain Harder

We have already learned of the strange and entertaining phenomenon of fish rain, as seen in the Top End town of Lajamanu, where fish fell from the heavens much like manna to the Israelites in the Bible, except with higher levels of omega-3.

However, Lajamanu isn't the only place to have reported such surprising downpours. In 2016 residents of Winton in Queensland also found themselves blessed with an unexpected bounty of spangled perch. In 2020 another Queensland town, Yowah, experienced the same thing.

The Winton fish-fall was recorded by Tahnee Oakhill, who captured footage of the tenacious little buggers flapping about on her family's farm, while her children ran around scooping them up from the mud because it was Queensland and what else is there for children to do?

In Yowah the fish were discovered by caravan park owner Rick Shiells, who was on his way to check the rain gauge – which unfortunately was not fitted with a fish setting – when he saw a fish swimming in a puddle.

'I thought, "Geez, that's unusual"', said Mr Shiells, and scientists later confirmed that yes, it was.

It is interesting that in all these cases, the fish in question were spangled perch. There is something about this species, also known as *Leiopotherapon unicolor*, or the spangled grunter, due to its loud snoring, that makes it peculiarly well suited to long air journeys. Perhaps it is simply the fact that, having the widest distribution of any freshwater

grunter in Australia,* it's more likely than most fish to be on the spot
when the tornados strike. Perhaps it is the fish's small size, making it easily
portable for weather systems. Perhaps it is the species' natural love of
pranks and practical jokes. Or is it just that this is God's favourite fish, so
He always chooses it when he needs to throw something at us?

As was the case in Lajamanu, the Winton and Yowah fish-falls were
met with scepticism by ichthyologists.** Many have pooh-poohed the idea
of fish rain, an incredibly unsanitary practice. Although some scientists
believe that it's quite a simple matter for a tornado to scoop up a bunch of
little fishies, take them on a road trip and dump them hundreds of miles
distant, others say that the far more likely explanation is that in flood
times the fish swim through shallow floodwaters and end up flopping
about in desperation when the waters dry up.

But when faced with a choice of two explanations, which is the
preferable one: the one that is 'more likely', or the one that is 'there are
fish falling from the sky'? Exactly. Besides, the fact that both the Northern
Territory and Queensland have enjoyed the blessings of sky-fish surely
adds weight to the hypothesis, according to the well-known principle
that an unlikely thing happening once is unlikely, but an unlikely thing
happening three times is more likely than a likely thing.***

We may never know the complete truth, which is so often the case
when it comes to small ray-finned vertebrates dropping on your head. But
whether you write it off to a freak of nature or devise a more complicated
theory whereby the fish rains are a side effect of a powerful weather-
control beam being wielded by the R&D team at Google as part of
their plan to make the population of the Earth entirely dependent on
genetically modified crabmeat by 2035, you can't deny that fish falling
out of the sky is, as Rick Shiells averred, unusual.

---

*   And that's saying something. You know how grunters get around.
**   From the Greek 'ichthys' meaning 'fish' and 'ologist' meaning 'guy who ruins people's
     fun'.
*** Science!

The Perplexity of the Poo Jogger

Who among us does not know the temptation of breaking taboos? The idea of violating the mores and conventions of civilised society has fascinated humans since time immemorial, and great historical figures from Caligula to Lord Byron to Dannii Minogue have dared to flout the arbitrary restraints of so-called polite society.

Add to those legendary names Andrew Douglas MacIntosh of Greenslopes, Brisbane, who will forever go down in history as the man who made Greenslopes a little less green.

Andrew MacIntosh was a silver fox of sixty-four years, with a good job at a major retirement village company and a place on the infrastructure board of the Brisbane City Council. Many in such a comfortable position live out their lives quietly playing by the rules, refusing to make a splash or rock the boat for fear of threatening their cushy, bourgeois existence.

Andrew MacIntosh was not such a man. Even as he assisted in the planning of Brisbane's infrastructure, even as he facilitated quality retirement living for thousands of Australians, he felt himself chafing at the bonds in which middle-class Western civilisation had ensnared him. He felt there must be something more to life, that living a truly authentic life required not just material success and comfort, but some conscious act of rebellion against the chains with which humanity enslaved itself.

And so it came to pass that Andrew MacIntosh, one grey dawn, decided to break free.

Andrew, like so many ageing men with a terror of mortality and an atrophied imagination, was an enthusiastic jogger. And it was while he was jogging that morning along the quiet streets of Greenslopes that his great idea struck him.

It began as a rumbling in his digestive tract. His stomach whispered to him. His bowels cried out with some urgency. And as he jogged along, his lower portions transmitting their message of equal parts distress and temptation, he looked at the pristine suburban apartment complex that he was running past, and opportunity winked its seductive eye at him.

After all, he thought, his face creasing like Bilbo Baggins contemplating ownership of the One Ring, *why shouldn't I?*

And suddenly, for Andrew MacIntosh, all the rules, all the regulations, all the pettifogging demands of middle-class respectability melted away like ice in the sun.

He stopped.

He walked over to the pathway leading into the apartment complex.

He lowered his shorts.

He sighed with the blessed relief of simultaneous bowel movement and social defiance.

And from that moment Andrew MacIntosh ascended to a higher plane.

After one has drunk of the nectar of the gods, one does not easily set the goblet down. Andrew MacIntosh had defecated in public on someone else's property, and he had a taste for it. Soon he was stopping by the same complex every day on his morning jog to unburden himself. He took to carrying a roll of toilet paper with him on his runs, for although he had a revolutionary's heart, he still had regard for personal hygiene.

For some weeks, MacIntosh lived the carefree life of the unfettered spirit, pounding the pavement and leaving his calling cards like a faecal bushranger. The papers called him 'the poo jogger', in the great media tradition of imposing romantic nicknames on famous outlaws. He became a hero to millions, although none knew his true identity.

Yet ever do the forces of conformity conspire against inspiration. Tall poppy syndrome was alive and well in Brisbane in 2018, and the residents of the Greenslopes apartment block, jealous of MacIntosh's capacity to live everyone's dream, decided that he must be destroyed. They lay in wait, and when the happy jogger made his regular stop outside their home, they sprung their trap. A photograph of a startled MacIntosh, pants down and eyes wide, was duly taken, handed to the Queensland Police and distributed widely to the media.

The dream was over. MacIntosh was taken into custody and given a hefty fine. He subsequently lost his job, and never poo-jogged again. And all those who had found hope and courage in the exploits of this Poopy Pimpernel sagged, their world once again seeming bland and hopeless.

Some might say the lesson from the poo jogger affair is that society always wins: that free thinking and creative flair, no matter how inspired, will always be crushed by the forces of authority and censoriousness. But I prefer to think it teaches us something more positive: that an artistic flame might burn briefly, yet still it might burn bright. Although happy endings are never guaranteed, in this world there is still room for the man or woman willing to throw off the shackles of neoliberal capitalism, drop their trousers and leave on the asphalt a tribute to the human spirit.

The Fairlie Odd Woman

There's a saying in Australia: 'If you want to experience the very stupidest of life, go to the Gold Coast.' This has been true ever since the late 1800s, when the Gold Coast was founded as a tax write-off by a novelty underwear company. But in all the strange and idiotic history of that sun-kissed strip known as 'Australia's perineum', few stories are as compellingly odd as that of Fairlie Arrow.

Fairlie Arrow, named after her parents' favourite adverb, was a singer at Jupiters Casino, one of Australia's most successful poverty generators. Although she had not reached any great heights of international fame, she was at least popular enough to have garnered her own personal stalker. In the six months leading up to Christmas 1991, Arrow had made multiple complaints to police about a deranged fan who had followed her, phoned her dozens of times and even broken into her home, where he had done the washing-up, fed the dogs and rearranged the furniture, but on the negative side had left creepy messages on her bathroom mirror.

The stalker's menacing behaviour reached a crescendo when, on 15 December, Arrow was abducted from her Isle of Capri* home. The disappearance created a public uproar, as the police sprang into what could loosely be called 'action'.

Fairlie Arrow's husband, George Harvey – who was a member of the vocal group the Four Kinsmen, and therefore had already suffered his share of disappointment in life – made a tearful plea for his wife's safe return.

---

*   Not the good one, the one in Queensland.

'If this man cares for her then he'll let her go,' Harvey said. 'I can understand why he's done it – she's beautiful,' he added, which was a bit weird.

Fairlie's father also made a public plea. 'I'm so scared,' he said. 'Years ago abductions were not so bad, but today people don't seem to have any scruples.' After this statement the public began to wonder whether there was anyone normal involved in this story at all.

For two days it seemed as though Arrow's husband's empathy for men who like to abduct beautiful women, and her father's longing for the days of kinder, gentler kidnappings had fallen on deaf ears. Until a miracle happened: Fairlie showed up on a remote country road, face-down, her hands tied behind her back. She was unharmed, her tormentor having apparently had a crisis of conscience.

Relief at Arrow's safe return was widespread, and yet, in their nasty cynical way, people almost immediately began to ask questions. Questions like 'Was she *really* kidnapped?' and 'Is there something a bit funny about all this?' and 'What the fuck?'.

Arrow shot back* at the sceptics, saying, 'Trust me. This is not a bad publicity stunt.'

She was telling the truth: it was in fact an extremely *good* publicity stunt. It just wasn't a very good fake kidnapping.

It wasn't long before Arrow's story began to fall apart: although she claimed to have spent forty-eight hours bound and blindfolded in an unknown location, the testimony of a cleaner at the Town and Country Motel said otherwise. According to her, a woman and a man, the former bearing a striking resemblance to Fairlie Arrow, had booked into the Town and Country and spent a pleasant couple of days there, corresponding exactly with the time Arrow was missing.

On 1 January 1992, Fairlie Arrow, in accordance with her New Year's resolution to be more straightforward about her hoaxes, admitted that she'd made the whole thing up, her story having crumbled in the face of

---

* See what I did?

the Town and Country's Do Not Disturb sign.

The nation was outraged. The people of Australia, who had opened their hearts to this quiet, unassuming blonde, could not believe that they had allowed themselves to be titillated by a tale about a brutal abduction when all along they had actually been titillated by a tale about a lying torch singer. Nothing makes an Australian angrier than to find they've been manipulated by media exploitation of the wrong thing.

The police were furious too. 'This case has been a great waste of men* and resources,' Detective Senior Constable Ron St George said. 'We have unsolved murders to work on.' Indeed, experts estimate that well over 300 unsolved murders in Queensland would have been solved were it not for Fairlie Arrow.

As for George Harvey, who apparently had known nothing of his wife's scheme, he was humiliated by the whole affair and left Arrow, returning to his career with the Four Kinsmen, which he found slightly less humiliating.

Fairlie Arrow herself claimed she'd only carried out the fake kidnapping to draw attention to the actual stalker who had been terrorising her, and emphasised her point by posing nude for *Penthouse*, causing a chastened nation to apologetically look at her bits.

Today she lives in semi-obscurity on the flashback pages of various News Limited publications, concentrating on her new passion of animal welfare and reflecting only occasionally on that brief, shining moment when she was, for a few days, Australia's favourite and sexiest victim of fake violent crime.

---

* Sexist much?

The Curse of the Headless Angel

According to Joseph Conrad, author of such famous sailing tales as *Lord Jim* and *Heart of Darkness*, the clipper *Torrens* was: 'a ship of brilliant qualities – the way the ship had of letting big seas slip under her did one's heart good to watch. It resembled so much an exhibition of intelligent grace and unerring skill that it could fascinate even the least seamanlike of our passengers.'

As the generally accepted spiritual heir of Conrad's literary tradition, I can truly appreciate the admirable style with which he described the vessel. But there was more to the *Torrens*' story than engaging prose, for, despite the qualities which moved Conrad to wax lyrical, it was a ship beset by strange and often unfortunate fates.

Built in England in 1875, the *Torrens* at first enjoyed good fortune as a carrier of many prominent passengers, and became renowned for its speed, covering the trip from Plymouth to Port Adelaide in an average of seventy-four days, which is rubbish now but was pretty nippy at the time.

In 1890, however, its original captain, the presciently named Henry Robert Angel, retired, and the *Torrens* never again attained either its past glory or its past speed. On her first trip without Captain Henry, the ship lost its foremast and main topmast, a surprising fit of absent-mindedness that was rare among clippers of the time. While being refitted in Brazil, the *Torrens* caught fire, a compound of catastrophes that nevertheless failed to convince its owners to take the hint.

In 1896, the *Torrens* was taken over by Henry Angel's son, whose name, quite implausibly, was Falkland Angel. Under young Falkland, the

Torrens met its crowning calamity, striking an iceberg in January 1899, south-west of the Crozet Islands, in the southern Indian Ocean.* In fact, it managed to hit the same iceberg three times** before the iceberg got bored and floated away, and the *Torrens* just barely managed to bob saggily into Adelaide harbour a month later. Upon surveying the damage to the ship, Adelaide locals pronounced it 'a marvellous escape', which was all to Falkland Angel's credit, but was probably little consolation for him.

The ship had lost its foretopmast, jib boom and bowsprit, all of which are, as far as we know, important on a boat, but particularly distressing was the loss of the *Torrens*' figurehead: an elegant wooden lady that had been modelled on the figure of Henry Angel's daughter Flores, Falkland's sister.

It was believed among the superstitious seafaring community that a female figurehead was good luck: the feminine spirit would calm stormy seas and keep a ship's inhabitants safe. The loss of the figurehead therefore seemed a terrible omen for the ship, although given it had both caught on fire and repeatedly hit an iceberg with the figurehead in place, you'd have thought the crew might've reconsidered its efficacy by now.

The superstition seemed well founded, however, when, after the wooden Flores Angel was detached from the ship and lost in icy sub-Antarctic waters, the *Torrens*' fortunes went from bad to worse. In 1903 a storm almost caused it to founder on Kangaroo Island, the crew narrowly escaping a brutal marsupial death. Violent winds assailed the ship all the way through that particular voyage, and at the end of it, as she was towed along the Thames, another boat tried to sail between her and the tugboat and was consequently sunk. Fed up with these shenanigans, the owners of the *Torrens* sold her to some Italians, whereupon she ran aground, was condemned to be broken up, won a reprieve due to the shipbreakers' admiration of her 'splendid lines', then once again ran onto rocks. She was

---

* Thirteen years later the *Titanic* also hit an iceberg; most historians agree that this is where it got the idea.

** The Crozet Islands are French territory, so it is probable that the iceberg did it on purpose.

76

finally put out of her misery in 1910.

One might think that was the end of the tale of the rise and fall of the *Torrens*, but one would be, as usual, wrong. For in 1973, long after everyone had forgotten about the ship and its frustrating inability to stop crashing into things, members of ANARE (the Australian National Antarctic Research Expedition) stumbled on something quite remarkable: the wooden figure of Flores Angel, in a mudhole on Macquarie Island. But Flores could no longer exactly be termed a figure*head*, as when the researchers found her a head was the one thing she lacked.

The truly remarkable thing was not just that the headless angel had survived for seventy-four years after the *Torrens* hit the iceberg, but that in order for it to fetch up on Macquarie Island, it would have had to drift more than 7300 kilometres. And that's if it took the short route: it was calculated that poor Flores could have floated around the world up to seven times before coming to her resting place on Macquarie.

There is something heartwarming about the fact that, after the fortunes of one of the world's finest clippers went into terminal decline, one part of it – the part sculpted in honour of its first captain's beloved daughter – ended up being among history's greatest sea voyagers.

The Somerton Man

'*Tamám shud*,' read the scrap of paper. That means 'is finished' in Persian, and the extreme deadness of the man in whose pocket the paper had been found suggested it was onto something.

The man had been found on Somerton Park beach, in the suburbs of Adelaide, leaning against the seawall, at 6.30am on 1 December 1948. He seemed to have died in his sleep: numerous witnesses said they'd seen him, in the same position, the previous evening.

The mystery of the man's identity and cause of death captured the public's imagination – interesting deaths were as rare in Adelaide as interesting lives. There was no clue to his identity on him: all the labels on his clothes had been removed, and he had no wallet. His dental records could not be matched to any known person. In his pockets were found an unused rail ticket, a bus ticket, a metal comb, some cigarettes and chewing gum – but this didn't help, as people of all kinds liked to smoke and chew and take public transport and comb their hair. He also had no hat, which was extremely unusual for 1948, the middle of hat-wearing's golden age, and led some to speculate that he might have been murdered by a passing hat poacher.

An autopsy was unable to determine the cause of death, but did reveal that the man had a spleen about three times the normal size. There was no law against large spleens, and the theory that he had been killed for his spleen was quickly dismissed. The autopsy revealed that his last meal was a pastie, a piece of information that was no help whatsoever.

A suitcase was found at the Adelaide Railway Station that was believed to belong to the dead man. It contained a red checked dressing gown, a pair of light brown trousers, a red felt pair of slippers, an electrician's screwdriver, a small knife, a pair of scissors and a stencilling brush, as well as four pairs of underpants. The contents of the suitcase were extremely suggestive to investigators, who concluded that the deceased almost certainly liked packing suitcases.

The real breakthrough in the case came when the scrap of paper was found in a fob pocket* sewn into the body's trousers. The 'Tamám shud' scrap had been torn out of a copy of the *Rubaiyat of Omar Khayyam*.

So the piece of paper did not provide any helpful clue as to the identity of the dead man, but it did make the case a lot more interesting, which everyone agreed was a good thing. The phrase's meaning seemed disturbingly apt, and the theme of the poetry book – living life without regrets – quite suggestive. When you consider the fact that the *Rubaiyat* tells the ancient Persian story of a man who takes a train to Adelaide and dies on a beach, it only becomes more chilling.

The copy of the book was located and found to contain indentations of lines of written text in the back that was either a fiendishly complex code or a bunch of meaningless gibberish, as well as the phone number of a nurse from Glenelg called Jessica Thomson, who claimed not to know who the dead man was – but she had kind of a look on her face, you know? You know the kind of look? Yeah, that kind of look.

Many theories about the 'Somerton man' have been floated over the years – he was a lover of Jessica Thomson's, or a dead spy, or a steamship worker, or a former woodcutter. But all the theories, claims and supposed identifications led to no positive conclusion, besides the lesson that dying without any ID is a great way to make new friends.

In the end, the mystery of the Somerton man and 'Tamám shud' remains an eerie reminder of the fact that there will always be dark corners of the world that humans can never fully illuminate.

Oh, wait: in 2022, DNA analysis revealed that the dead man was Carl

---

* A pocket used by men in previous generations to fob people off with.

Webb, an electrical instrument maker from Melbourne who was known to be suicidal. So that's that.

Bit of a letdown really, isn't it? Let's just pretend we still don't know, eh?

The Walking Zoo

At 5.30 on a Sunday morning in 1916, Jessie got up and began a bracing walk from Sydney's Moore Park north to Sydney Harbour. As she walked, she attracted curious looks from passers-by, and even press attention.

Why were people so interested in Jessie's Sunday stroll? Was it that it was quite early to be taking a constitutional? Was it that a single woman roaming the streets of Sydney in 1916 was bound to generate gossip? Or was it simply that Jessie was a fully grown Indian elephant? Who can tell?

Jessie was the largest of a cohort of over 800 residents of the Sydney Zoo at Moore Park who had to make the trek across the water to the new site at Taronga Park, a move made necessary by the fact that the old site was too small, too dry, too covered with cement and, for many of the residents, too fatal: 1916 was not a time of excessive awareness of the niceties of animal welfare, but even then there was a number of dead animals in tiny cages beyond which people began to kick up a fuss.

And so to the leafy surrounds of Taronga the zoo would relocate, where the animals could live in the open air, without ugly metal bars, free to roam spacious* enclosures and occasionally maul an unwary spectator to death.**

Some animals presented more of a problem than others. Small lizards and frogs, for example, are fairly easy to transport: you put them in a

---

* Not actually spacious, of course, but spacious for 1916, when giving an animal enough room to turn around was still seen by some as an act of environmental vandalism.

** Known in zoological circles as 'enrichment'.

shoebox and send them over in a taxi, or a carefully aimed catapult. Birds are easy too: you just give them the address and let them make their own way. Lions and tigers can be a little more problematic, but in the end as long as you have a crate big enough and you're insensitive to the cat's feelings, it should be fine.

Jessie, however, was definitely an issue: while today it is perfectly easy to transport an elephant wherever you want, simply by clicking the 'elephant' button on the removalist's website, back in 1916 there was no easy solution. There was no truck strong enough to bear an elephant's weight, and all the larger catapults were in use at the Somme. There was only one thing for it: Jessie would have to walk.

And so it was that the citizens of Sydney, hearts weighed down by the sorrow of the war that was taking so many of their young men's lives on the other side of the world, had something to lighten the mood, as the great migration from Moore Park to Taronga began. As the bulk of the creatures made their way to the new zoo, the city rang with strange and exotic noises such as had never been heard on those streets.

'Mournful yells from hyenas, angry roars from lions and tigers ... a veritable menagerie of wild beasts confined in cages, having late disturbed the early morning serenity of Sydney streets,' reported the *Evening News*.

Dwellers in city flats disturbed from their slumbers by such unusual sounds have drawn the window blinds and looked down on a unique sight. Never, it is safe to assert, has the city seen such processions of denizens of the Indian jungle, wild roamers of the African veldt, and South American pampas, bears from the Arctic and Canadian Rockies, stately ostriches, kangaroos, screeching parrots from Peru and the Australian bush, ungainly crocodiles lashed onto lorries by ropes, and hundreds of other animals.

But the main attraction was Jessie. At a stately pace, and accompanied by a devoted entourage, Jessie strolled down Sydney's streets and through the Domain, finally heading down Macquarie Street to meet the barge that would whisk her across the harbour.

By the time she reached the boat, Jessie's feet were killing her. Unused to the paved terrain (in an Indian elephant's natural habitat, there is very little asphalt), they had suffered terribly on the walk. Nevertheless, she stepped bravely and politely onto the boat, and so to Taronga, where there was a brief problem when the dignified grey lady initially refused to disembark. Pulling back from the edge, it took some sharp words from a handler, who reminded Jessie that the Bible states that man has dominion over all the beasts of the field, to persuade her to trip lightly across the pontoon to the shore.

And so it was that Jessie settled into her new home at Taronga, where she was free to roam and play and be forced to carry people on her back against her will in a shocking act of cruelty.

It is unlikely that Sydney will ever again see such a sight as hundreds of animals being transported through its streets, let alone an elephant lumbering up Woolloomooloo. And although in one way that's a good thing – reflecting improved standards of animal welfare and advanced methods of transportation – in another way it's a bit of a shame, because in these dark and depressing days, surely we could all do with the sort of spiritual uplift that a public display of pachydermy can provide.

Mr Brown's Big Bucks Bomb

If the 1971 Qantas bomb hoax teaches us anything, it is that crime doesn't pay, although it also teaches us that crime *could* pay, if we put a bit more thought into it.

Peter Macari was a British expatriate who had skipped bail in 1969 and sailed to Australia. Here he met Raymond Poynting and told him about a movie he'd seen: *The Doomsday Flight*. In the movie, a man puts a bomb on a plane and asks for $100,000, but in the end the guy from *Hawaii 5-0* saves the day. 'Wouldn't that be fun?' Macari asked Poynting. Poynting agreed that it did seem like a great laugh.

After months of slightly careful planning, on 26 May 1971 Macari and Poynting put their plot into action. Calling himself 'Mr Brown' in honour of his favourite comic strip, Macari called the Australian Department of Civil Aviation and claimed to have hidden a bomb on board Qantas Flight 755. To prove he wasn't lying, Macari said there was an identical bomb in locker 84 at Sydney Airport. Police found the bomb in the locker, which did not in any way prove that Macari was not lying, but still thought it was worth taking seriously. Along with the bomb was a demand for $500,000, in exchange for instructions on how to dismantle the bomb on the plane, and a warning that it would explode if the plane went below 20,000 feet. It was just like the movie *Speed* except with better acting.

The pilot of Flight 755 was informed of the situation and instructed to stay above 35,000 feet, while not, under any circumstances, running up and down the aisle between the passengers screaming, 'We're all going to die!' He followed these instructions to the letter, while the crew searched the plane for the bomb, without success.

As the plane circled over the sea off Sydney, Qantas officials checked the manual and discovered that if planes run out of fuel they fall down. As 6pm approached, there was only an hour or so's worth of fuel left, and in recognition of the fact that the 128 people on board might raise objections to the plane crashing Qantas agreed to pay the ransom. At 5.45pm, two suitcases full of cash were handed to Macari, who was in a yellow Kombi van and wearing a fake moustache, wig and glasses, knowing that if police were watching they would be unable to act with any speed if they were doubled over with laughter.

Just after 6pm, Macari called the police again. 'Yeah, so the thing is, there isn't actually a bomb on the plane,' he said.

'Oh, you cheeky monkey!' the police cried.

'LOL,' said Macari, and hung up.

Macari and Poynting were on the loose for only a few months before the police caught up with them, mainly because Poynting, who had sadly been born without a brain, decided the best way to behave immediately after pulling off a major crime was to spend the proceeds in as obvious and public a manner as possible. After purchasing a new Jaguar and Falcon GT, he attracted the attention of the fuzz, and in August 1971 both Macari and Poynting were hauled in for some questions, which turned extremely awkward after $138,000 was discovered in Macari's house.

Both men pleaded guilty to demanding money with menaces and stealing a Kombi. Poynting was sentenced to seven years, Macari to fifteen, though he was deported to the United Kingdom after nine – on a Qantas flight, which is the kind of thing you might consider a delicious irony if you've not got a lot going on in your life. He later ran a fish and chip shop, and even later committed suicide, which is a depressing note to end this chapter on so I'll do another paragraph.

In the end, Macari and Poynting's plot was doomed because, although they had energy and ambition, they had at least one brain fewer than was needed to pull off a successful scam of this kind. But they came close, and they should still serve as an inspiration to any young Australians who harbour dreams of extorting an international airline today.

Gnomesville

'Gnomesville: a place where everybody feels at Gnome' states the Gnomesville website, immediately inspiring an intense hatred towards whoever wrote it. I mean, it doesn't even make sense: what does it mean to feel 'at Gnome'? It's a feeling I've certainly never experienced. And when it comes to Gnomesville, the feelings more likely to swell in the breasts of visitors range from a warm sensation of cosy familiarity to a creeping unease and the fear that all one's nightmares are about to come true at once.

For Gnomesville is no ordinary town. In fact, it's not a town at all. What it is is around 7000 garden gnomes placed on and around a roundabout at Wellington Mill, in Western Australia's Ferguson River Valley. Gnomesville is now one of the largest outdoor groupings of garden gnomes in the world. Or at least we assume it is. It's hard to imagine anyone's ever checked.

The origins of Gnomesville are shrouded in mystery, much as the intersection is now shrouded in gnomes. Legend tells of a day, back in the mists of history in 1995, when the council built a roundabout. Locals, who had lived all their lives without having to go in a circle and didn't wish to change now, were outraged. They took to the streets to protest in the only way they knew how: by placing garden gnomes on the roundabout.

Why was this the only way they knew how to protest? The answer to this, history does not relate. Possibly they thought that the gnomes would terrify the council workers and cause them to flee à la the construction workers in *Ernest Goes to Camp*. Maybe they thought that the gnomes would create a traffic hazard, causing dozens of deaths and forcing the abandonment of human settlement in the area. Perhaps they believed that the gnomes would come to life and destroy the roundabout at night.

Of course, there are alternative explanations for the original placement of gnomes, such as that the first gnomes were put there to 'stand guard' over the roundabout, or that they were put there as a simple symptom of mental illness.

It doesn't really matter why the gnomes first appeared. What matters is that their numbers grew. As people passed by and saw the gnomes at Gnomesville, more and more of them added their own gnomes to the collection, despite the fact that garden gnomes are expensive and the economy is in a shocking state. After a number of years the Wellington Mill community realised that they had thousands of gnomes on their hands, and they could capitalise on this by appealing to that sector of the tourism market that seeks an experience that chills you to the bone and forces you to question the possibility of a loving God.

You can go to see the gnomes today, if you wish. Head out to the junction of Wellington Mill Road and Ferguson Road and drink in the sight of thousands of dead, unseeing eyes staring at you, their frozen smiles seeming to mock all the comfortable preconceptions you have about Man's place in the universe. When you're in Gnomesville, it's very easy to imagine an army of gnomes annihilating humanity and ushering in a millennium of darkness and violence.

Frankly that doesn't make me feel at Gnome at all.

The Rise and Fall of the Great Coningham

The crowd buzzed with anticipation – albeit a seemly, decorous sort of buzz in appreciation of the fact that it was 1894 and people still had manners. At one end stood Archie MacLaren, the captain of Lancashire and England's shining hope. Of all the flower of English youth, MacLaren was the floweriest. The following English summer, he would break the world record for a first-class innings with a knock of 424, but right now he stood at the crease on the Melbourne Cricket Ground, preparing for a pleasant day's Australian-hammering.

In the distance stood Arthur Coningham, taking the field in a Test match for the first time and entrusted with the new ball on debut. A nerve-racking situation for any young cricketer, but Coningham was not a man whose self-confidence was ever easily shaken. Gazing down from the top of his run at the English champion, he stroked his spectacular moustache and began loping to the wicket.

Reaching the crease, he leapt, lithe as a leopard. His left arm wheeled over. The ball snaked through the air towards MacLaren. The Englishman cautiously poked at it. But Coningham had deceived him. The ball ducked away and caught the edge of MacLaren's bat. It flew off the edge to champion Australian all-rounder Harry Trott, who closed his enormous hands around it, and the celebrations began – which, as this was 1894, meant everyone shook hands and said, 'Well done,' in friendly but measured tones.

Arthur Coningham had taken a wicket with his first ball in Test cricket. He had, without question, arrived.

Cricketers are a weird bunch to begin with, but there have been few odder birds to have played the game at the highest level than Arthur Coningham.

He was described as having 'the audacity and cunning of an ape and the modesty of a phallic symbol', and that's a recommendation anyone would love to get. He was an all-rounder in cricket and more generally, being a talented footballer, rower and shooter: just the kind of guy everyone hates. Although the MCG Test was his first, he had toured England with the Australians in 1893, distinguishing himself in more ways than one.

In London, Coningham was awarded a medal for bravery after saving a boy from drowning in the Thames, and many people believe these two things were connected. At another point in the tour, while standing in the outfield on a particularly cold day waiting for something to happen, he started a fire to keep himself warm: an action which, like French-kissing an umpire, is not technically against the Laws of Cricket but tends to make the establishment look askance. But though unconventional, it spoke volumes about Coningham's character: rebellious, resourceful, iconoclastic, disrespectful of authority and prone to chills.

Perhaps the most remarkable thing about Coningham's cricket career is that after that perfect start, he never played another Test. Australia smashed England out for 75 at the MCG but lost the game, and Coningham was dropped, never to return to the team.

It was a blow for fans of Coningham's cricketing skills, but happily he refused to give up being weird. An easily distracted man, he tried many lines of work over the years: though claiming to be a chemist, he was at various times a tobacconist, a bookmaker and an extremely unsuccessful billiards gambler.

After a stint of bankruptcy, Coningham became fed up with having no money and hit upon a new source of funds: suing Catholics. He sued his wife Alice for divorce, which in itself would not have been especially lucrative, but named Father DF O'Haran, administrator of St Mary's Cathedral and private secretary of Cardinal Moran, as co-respondent. Accusing O'Haran of an affair with Alice, he demanded £5000 in damages.

Alice admitted the affair. O'Haran denied it. The case captured the public imagination and gave a shot in the arm to the often under-resourced sector of Australian sectarian bigotry. Protestants fell in behind Coningham, while Catholics rallied in support of O'Haran. The Reverend WM Dill Mackay gave Coningham a revolver in case the judge changed the trial to one by combat.

In the end, Coningham neither shot nor won damages from Father O'Haran. On the priest's behalf, investigators discovered that Arthur and Alice Coningham were in cahoots, teaming up to scam cash from the church. The jury found against Coningham, who was so shattered that he had no option but to move to New Zealand.

In New Zealand Coningham sold books and went to gaol for fraud, before his wife, somewhat ironically, divorced him for adultery. Many years later, after returning to Australia, he was admitted to the Gladesville Mental Hospital in Sydney, where he died in 1939. His son was Air Marshal Sir Arthur Coningham, a World War I flying ace and hero of the North African theatre in World War II – continuing the family business of high achievement, if not for bankruptcy and crime.

Arthur Coningham met a sad end, and in many respects had a sad life. But the highs that came were seriously high, and it'll always be a shame that one of Australia's most memorable cricketers only played the one Test.

Gone to the Dogs

The car hurtled down the country road, ran straight over the top of an innocent pedestrian and sped off into the distance without pause. Watching from a nearby paddock, a local farmer was outraged. Admittedly, this was Campbelltown, but it was also 1939, so people still tended to behave a bit better than that.*

The farmer ran down to the roadside, hurling 1930s-style swearwords at the car as it disappeared over the horizon. Arriving at the prostrate victim's side, he was shocked by the extent of his gruesome injuries. He inquired after the mangled man's welfare. The man assured him he was fine, but the farmer, looking at the hideous wounds covering him, could not accept this. He ran off and dialled 000, or whatever people dialled back then.

Fifteen minutes later an ambulance arrived on the scene to tend to the stricken man. Shortly after that the police showed up, demanding details of the incident and a description of the egregious hit-and-runner. Upon arriving, both police and ambos were quickly informed that an unacceptable waste of emergency services resources had occurred: they had been summoned to a film set, to find the actor George Wallace in perfect health despite the convincing motor accident make-up he'd been slathered in.

Such was life in the early Australian film industry: just the kind of obstacle that the producers of seminal Aussie comedy *Gone to the Dogs*

---

* Other events in 1939, it should be noted, represent a fairly strong counterpoint to this.

had to put up with. *Gone to the Dogs* is one of the most important movies in Australian history: not only a remarkable document of the fashions and styles of popular entertainment in 1930s Australia, but a fascinating reminder that there used to be a time when not only were movies made in Australia, but people watched them.

Gone to the Dogs was the second collaboration between director Ken G Hall – who would later direct Australia's first Oscar-winning film, *Kokoda Front Line!* – and the comedian George Wallace, known as Australia's answer to Charlie Chaplin (although it was not necessarily a correct answer). Hall and Wallace's first film together was *Let George Do It*, which, as the title suggests, was about a man called Joe trying to kill himself. But in *Gone to the Dogs*, the pair expanded their creative horizons beyond such basic concepts as George and letting him do it, and came up with a truly labyrinthine plot about a zookeeper who turns his greyhound magic. They quite literally do not make them like that anymore.

The film was made by Cinesound Productions, a company founded on the belief that the Australian film industry existed. Cinesound had a reputation for excellence, and for *Gone to the Dogs* they secured writers of the calibre of *Ginger Meggs* creator Jim Bancks and co-stars that included Wallace's sidekick John Dobbie and Lois Green, an actress of such ability that, after the film, she was actually able to leave Australia. The film also starred Hughie the dog, selected from 100 auditioners, and professional wrestler Fred Atkins, who played not one but two gorillas – a feat still described by most experts as the greatest achievement in acting history. Atkins lost three stone* while filming due to the heat of the gorilla suit, but it was worth it. Anyone who has seen *Gone to the Dogs* has been stunned by the poignant and essential truth conveyed by his performance as both gorillas.

The set built for the movie was 12,000 square feet, the biggest in Australian history, only surpassed in later years by that of Ollie Martin's *Houseboat Horror*. Location shooting was done at Taronga Zoo – where

---

* Three stone = fifty-six centimetres, or half a furlong.

the real gorillas reportedly accepted Fred Atkins as one of their own – and of course at Campbelltown, scene of the infamous hit and run that wasn't.

The film had its world premiere in Launceston, which is one of the rarest sentences ever written in the English language, and became a commercial and critical hit. Ken Hall went on to win an Oscar. George Wallace went on to influence generations of Australian comedians. Fred Atkins went on to win the NWA British Empire Championship, whatever that is.

Gone to the Dogs, a remarkable film, is just one of many examples of cinematic achievement in the weirdest of all times: a time when Australian films had verve, imagination, greyhounds doing ballet, wrestlers playing multiple gorillas, and, most bizarrely of all, audiences.

Latin Australia

Australia has a proud tradition of people getting so sick of how terrible this country is that they angrily say they are going to leave: a tradition made even prouder by their willingness to stay here and keep saying it indefinitely. However, in 1893 a group of surprisingly task-oriented Australians did the near unthinkable: they said they were leaving, and then they did.

This, then, is the story of New Australia, the socialist utopia that didn't last as long as Old Australia but had more monkeys.

New Australia was the brainchild of William Lane, a British journalist who came to Australia and became involved in the labour movement, only to become disillusioned when the labour movement decided to remove the u from its name. Lane teamed up with Gilbert Casey, who was Irish and therefore predisposed to kicking up a fuss. Lane and Casey conceived of a better way to build a society, striking on the idea of taking a gaggle of like-minded folk to some faraway place where they could start Australia from scratch and this time do it right. Casey even donated his house as a prize in a fundraising raffle, something no modern unionist is willing to do, which is why industrial relations in this country are such a mess.

The New Australia movement recruited many notable figures, including the scholar James Murdoch, suffragette Rose Summerfield, pharmacy tycoon George Birks, and writer and $10 note model Mary Gilmore. They dreamed of a society based on six principles:

- A common-hold, rather than a common-wealth. This meant each member should be able to take their wealth out of the society if they chose.
- A brotherhood of English-speaking whites. This meant they were all pretty racist.
- Life marriage. This meant that anyone who got married should ideally be alive.
- Preservation of the colour line. This meant that they were, seriously, really racist.
- Teetotalism. This meant that they'd get on each other's nerves very soon.
- Communism. This meant that they'd accidentally put the big one at number six.

With these lofty ambitions, the New Australia Co-Operative Settlement Association set sail in July 1893 for Paraguay, which they had selected as the ideal location for their new civilisation because of its interesting climate and plentiful supplies of soybeans.

Despite the high ambitions of the settlers, the attempt to build a communist paradise in South America by a few hundred people whose chief qualification for founding a new nation was the ability to engage in internecine left-wing power struggles ran into early trouble. The Paraguayan government, which was very keen on white people, had given the New Australians a fertile block of land, but the colonists proved less than able to take advantage. Fights broke out over principle number five, with some declaring that abstention from alcohol was necessary to create a proper working-class utopia, while others declared that they wanted a freaking drink.

William Lane quickly made himself unpopular too, by persistently being rubbish at his job. 'I can't help feeling,' wrote colonist Tom Westwood, 'that the movement cannot result in success if that incompetent man Lane continues to mismanage so utterly as he has done up to the present.' The dissatisfaction reached the point that Lane, fed up with these ingrates and their graceless bitching, despite the fact that they wouldn't even be in Paraguay struggling to survive if it weren't for him, upped sticks and left.

With fifty-eight followers who still, unfathomably, believed in him, Lane set off south and founded a new settlement called Cosme, having rejected the name New New Australia. Cosme, too, was based on noble principles of freedom, working-class solidarity and shoving it up the ungrateful bastards up north. Sadly it was not a success, as suspicions grew that Lane was a lot better at saying, 'Hey, guys, let's go make our own country!' than he was at, like, doing things.

It had taken less than two years for New Australia to disintegrate, and shortly afterwards the Paraguayan government dissolved the cooperative, gave the New Australian settlers each their own plot of land, and told them to shut up and get on with their lives. Some stayed, some went back to Australia and some headed elsewhere, still chasing the dream of a homeland where people wouldn't be annoyed by them.

Today there are 2000 descendants of the New Australia colonists in Paraguay, carrying on the legacy of one of the strangest projects in Australian history: the attempt to reboot the whole country on the other side of the world.

Full-Contact Cricket

Dennis Lillee was a proud man. One of Australia's greatest ever cricketers, he was known as much for his fiery temper as he was for his perfectly pitched outswingers.* In Perth in 1981 he caused a massive stir by committing an act that, if committed by a Test player today, would result in public dismemberment and over sixty incredibly boring opinion pieces.

The scandal was the result of the coming together of two combustible elements: first, the proud and irritable Lillee; and second, the great Pakistani batsman Javed Miandad, whose skill with the willow was matched only by his ability to be the most annoying person on the face of the Earth.

On this occasion, Javed was more irritated than irritating, his pride suffering some deep wounds due to the hammering Pakistan was taking in the Test match. After being rolled for only 180 in their first innings, Australia had struck back with venom, Lillee and Terry Alderman destroying Pakistan for just 62. The home team then piled on 424 to set Pakistan 543 to win, or two days to bat out for a draw: both near-impossible tasks.

Making things worse for Javed was the fact that, as captain, he was following a venerable Pakistani cricket tradition of being deeply unpopular with the team. Numerous Pakistan players had not wanted him appointed skipper, some even wanting the position for themselves

---

* If you don't understand what this means, tough. Go watch some cricket and come back.

despite the fact that being Pakistan captain was clearly the worst job on Earth.

So Javed was already mightily fed up when, his side reeling early in the second innings at 27–2, he walked out to bat in what seemed a futile task. However, he showed those qualities that made him one of Pakistan cricket's immortals, fighting hard in partnership with the mortal-but-still-pretty-gutsy Mansoor Akhtar to survive a torrid barrage from the Australian quicks.

This, of course, just made Dennis Lillee angrier. There was nothing Lillee hated more than batsmen surviving his torrid barrages. The Pakistanis had been extremely obedient in doing the right thing and collapsing like a straw house in the first innings: he considered it the height of rudeness to pull this swifty and start batting properly in the second.

Forty minutes before tea on the fourth day, Javed flicked a ball from Lillee off his pads and strolled a single. What happened next was broadcast on Australian television for all to see, and yet still became a matter of ferocious dispute.

As Javed completed his run, Lillee stepped to the side into the Pakistan captain's path. Javed responded by lifting his bat and pushing the bowler out of his way. Infuriated, Lillee turned as Javed walked away and kicked the batsman in the leg. Javed immediately whirled in a rage, bat raised above his head in preparation for bashing Lillee's head in. He may have done exactly that, had umpire Tony Crafter not stepped between the two men to prevent Javed from bringing the bat down, and then to block Lillee, who after initially stepping back to avoid Javed's blow had attempted to spring forward to belt him one.

The cricket world immediately exploded. As many wise observers have said, cricket is not like football. Physical contact is not part of the game. Even accidental collisions between players are liable to bring gasps of alarm from traditionalists. Cricketers coming to deliberate blows is unthinkable.

Both players argued their innocence in the case. Lillee claimed that

Javed had abused him as he went past, and then as he turned that he had hit him from behind with his bat. Javed claimed Lillee deliberately tried to block his run so he pushed him out of the way.

Commentators – including Australian greats Keith Miller, Bob Simpson and Lillee's former captain Ian Chappell – denounced Lillee, but the Australian players stuck up for their proud hairy brother. Lillee apologised to the Pakistan team, but only for his reaction, not for instigating the incident. The Pakistanis told Lillee where he could shove his apology. Lillee said he would retire if he was suspended. The Pakistan team threatened to pack their bags and quit the tour.

In the end, nothing much came of it. The Australian Cricket Board fined Lillee $120 and suspended him for two minor matches that nobody cared about. Lillee, to nobody's surprise, did not retire. The Pakistanis did not go home.* Australia won the Test easily. Both Dennis Lillee and Javed Miandad finished their careers as legends of the game.

Was the incident a case of Javed Miandad deliberately provoking the fast bowler? Or was it Lillee letting his own frustrations boil over into violence? Or perhaps it was a case of two guys both being jerks simultaneously, just like usual? Disagreement persists, though it is certain that had it happened in today's game, both players would have copped lengthy suspensions and had to go on *Dancing with the Stars* to redeem themselves. So let us all breathe a sigh of relief that the most violent day in Test cricket history happened in the right context: the 1980s.

---

* I mean, obviously they went home *eventually*.

The Great Emu War

If there is a problem that can't be solved by sending in the army, the Australian government has not yet encountered it; indeed, the phrase 'Let the army sort it out' appears more than 600 times in the Australian Constitution. So it came as no surprise that, when faced with the problem of evil emus devouring wheat crops across the vast expanses of Western Australia, the authorities pulled their most reliable card out of the back pocket.

It happened in 1932, when Australia was struggling through the Great Depression, which had turned out to be far less fun than expected. Wheat prices were cratering, and in the Campion district of Western Australia, farmers' problems were exacerbated by over 20,000 enormous feathered nightmares showing up and cutting a swathe through their fields.

Luckily, many of these farmers had fought in World War I, and during that conflict they'd discovered a universal truth: machine guns are really good at killing stuff. They took this scientific conclusion to the defence minister, Sir George Pearce, who agreed that machine guns mowing down thousands of emus would not only be helpful to the agricultural industry, but would also look really cool.

Thus it was that in October 1932, Major Gwynydd Purves Wynne-Aubrey Meredith* of the Royal Australian Artillery, along with Sergeant S McMurray and Gunner J O'Halloran, headed into the wheatbelt to make a major dent in the avian population. They were armed with two

---

* Seriously?

Lewis guns* and had orders to cull the emu population and bring back 100 emu skins to make hats for light horsemen. This last order seemed a bit petty, but it was the Depression and hats were in short supply.

It seemed a straightforward operation: after all, the soldiers had machine guns, and the emus didn't, and everything they knew about military history told them that in an armed conflict, the side with the machine guns possessed a decisive edge over the side without any. And yet, as Major Meredith and his doughty men got to grips with the emu menace, they found affairs proceeding in an unexpected direction.

To put it bluntly, they were not killing nearly as many emus as they were supposed to be.

Oh, they were killing a few. But they found that when they showed up in emu territory, ready to spray bullets along the birds' massed ranks, the emus, rather unsportingly, split up and went galloping off in different directions. This made it difficult to fire into a large crowd of emus, because there wasn't one. In a nutshell, the emus seemed to have advance knowledge of the Australian Defence Force's movements, and frustrated them at every turn. As the army's report stated: 'each pack seems to have its own leader now – a big black-plumed bird which stands fully six feet high and keeps watch while his mates carry out their work of destruction and warns them of our approach'. On the upside, as Major Meredith wrote to his superiors, the Army had suffered no casualties – although when put into an official document, that observation seemed less like a silver lining and more like irritating sarcasm.

But what could Major Meredith do? Out-thought by his emu foes, he tried mounting one of his guns on a truck, the better to manoeuvre in the field, only to find that the emus were too fast for the truck to keep up with, and the ride was too bumpy for the gunner to get any shots away anyway.

The sad and hilarious Emu War came to an end when the federal parliament began asking pointed questions about what the hell was going

---

* Named after popular TV detective Lewis, played by Kevin Whately, who is famous for machine-gunning murder suspects.

on out in Western Australia. Minister Pearce was embarrassed by the opposition asking him whether any military medals would be struck for combatants in the war; having far less appetite for public humiliation than politicians do nowadays, he ordered the withdrawal of troops. That night the emus celebrated long into the night, toasting their victory over the hated oppressors and engaging in wild emu parties.

Major Meredith retreated from the front disappointed but filled with admiration for his adversaries. 'If we had a military division with the bullet-carrying capacity of these birds it would face any army in the world,' he wrote. 'They can face machine guns with invulnerability of tanks. They are like Zulus whom even dum-dum bullets* could not stop.'

Major Meredith's words, of course, raise the question: why *don't* we have a military division of emus? We've got tens of thousands of huge, superintelligent, strategically cunning birds that can absorb machine-gun fire and still outrun a truck. Why are we not deploying them to the world's trouble spots?

The answer, I'm afraid, is that the emus refuse to serve. We have treated them with such disrespect over the years that they will not assist us. And, frankly, who can blame them?

---

* A special kind of bullet that penetrates further into the flesh due to its extreme stupidity.

The Bloody *Batavia*

The *Batavia* was the flagship of the Dutch East India Company, a 17th-century company that was just like today's big companies except that it was allowed to invade countries and kill whomever it wanted.* In 1628, the ship sailed on her maiden voyage to Batavia – by which I do not mean she was sailing to herself, but rather to the city of Batavia, in Java, which is today known as Jakarta (possibly to avoid just this confusion).

As happens frequently in interesting stories, the ship was wrecked, foundering on Morning Reef, off the West Australian coast. Forty people drowned, but 300 or so managed to make it to nearby Beacon Island, which isn't a bad strike rate for a shipwreck. In fact, in the 1600s if a ship got away with that sort of death percentage it'd be considered a win even if it didn't sink.

Having made it to shore, the passengers of the *Batavia* were dismayed to find that they would probably have been better off going down with the ship. But this was not, as was usually the case, because Australia was hell on Earth: in this instance the group simply ran into some of the common problems associated with being marooned on a desert island with a bunch of homicidal maniacs.

One of the passengers was Jeronimus Cornelisz, a seriously dodgy character who had fled Amsterdam to avoid arrest.** On the journey,

---

* So yeah. Just like today's large companies.
** Specifically, he was wanted because he'd fallen under the influence of still life master Johannes van der Beeck and committed the Rosicrucian heresy. It was ... it was a whole other thing, man.

Cornelisz, who was always up for a caper, had plotted with the ship's skipper, Ariaen Jacobsz, to mutiny against the commander, Francisco Pelsaert, take the ship and its rich cargo to some faraway land and start a new life, à la *The Shawshank Redemption*.

The shipwreck stymied this plan, but at the same time offered a golden opportunity. Commander Pelsaert, Jacobsz and a few others took a longboat to Batavia to try to fetch help for the stricken castaways. Those who stayed behind quickly made one of history's most spectacularly incorrect decisions and elected Cornelisz their leader, a position which he relished for many horrible reasons. Still living in hope of taking the *Batavia*'s treasure and absconding to some remote paradise, and suffering from what modern scholars believe to have been a case of the batshit raving crazies, he put his plans into action immediately.

His first act was to send a group of soldiers to another island to look for fresh water, with the intention of leaving them to die there. His second act was to suggest to his friends, 'Wouldn't it be a cool idea to murder all the others?' His friends agreed that that would be pretty ace.

And so it was that Cornelisz and his pals systematically began hacking, stabbing and strangling their erstwhile shipmates at a terrific rate. This was necessary at first because Cornelisz needed to make sure the majority did not turn against him, and to make the supplies last longer. Later, it turned out they really liked killing people, so they figured they might as well keep going. There was nothing better to do on the island anyway. The whole affair was a dreadful reminder of the importance of taking a book on any long journey.

The murderers killed 110 men, women and children under the calm direction of Cornelisz. They didn't kill everyone, however, extending mercy to a few of the women so they could rape them. Many historians have suggested that this was not an entirely mitigating factor.

Cornelisz had carried out his plan to bathe Beacon Island in blood beautifully, but he'd made one fatal error: the soldiers he sent off on the pretext of seeking fresh water had actually found fresh water, and moreover were onto the little creep. Battle ensued, in which Cornelisz and his men were repeatedly thumped, and at the end of which Pelsaert returned and demanded to know, 'What the hell?'

After being informed of exactly what the hell, Pelsaert held a trial on the island and decided that Cornelisz was officially a complete psycho. He and his worst henchmen were taken to nearby Seal Island, where their hands were cut off before they were hanged – I guess so they couldn't untie the knots? The remaining murderers were taken to Batavia and either hanged, flogged or creatively tortured to death, which seems like a horrid way to treat people, but when you consider these guys had just massacred over a hundred innocent people for the hell of it, becomes quite a cheerful outcome.

The story of the *Batavia* and the madman who turned its maiden journey into a blood-soaked nightmare is one of Australian – and Dutch – history's most disturbing episodes. We can only thank the Lord that, since it happened nearly 400 years ago, enough time has passed that we can enjoy it as entertainment. Silver linings!

The Lost Colony

There is precious little of Dutch culture in Australia, despite the fact that long before the English colonised the continent Dutchmen were swarming about the place, whether it be Dirk Hartog visiting to nail a pewter plate to a post, the crew of the *Batavia* popping over to murder each other, or Abel Tasman braving treacherous seas to come down and give Tasmania the wrong name.

Yet there are some who claim that the Dutch did more than just fiddle around the edges of Australia. In 1834 an article was published in *The Leeds Mercury* – Yorkshire's most trusted source of Australian mysteries – claiming to reproduce the journal of an expedition led by one Lieutenant Nixon in northern Australia. According to this, in 1832, while exploring Palm Valley, south-west of Alice Springs, the party came across a settlement of around 300 white people, who spoke a variety of Old Dutch. They informed Nixon that their ancestors had come from 'a distant land across the great sea; and that their ship broke': their chief was said to be the descendant of an officer named Van Baerle.

If true, of course, this would be huge. It would mean that the British who settled in New South Wales in 1788 were not the first Europeans to make their home in Australia, and that the Dutch had been denied credit for the achievement. Which, to be honest, would be bad news for the Dutch, as the British could unload a bit of the white guilt on them.

Now, the trouble with people telling stories about things is that a story about things that did not happen looks pretty similar to a story about things that did happen, and it can be quite difficult to tell the difference.

It is, consequently, entirely possible that the story in *The Leeds Mercury* was a bunch of dingo's kidneys. However, it's important to remember that if we went around disbelieving things that people say just because we don't have any real evidence, we are bound to gain a reputation as mean and distrustful people with no friends. With that in mind, it's probably best to assume that everything you read, at least in this book, is true.

Certainly there are those who have worked hard to prove the story. Author Henry van Zanden wrote 'The Lost White Tribes of Australia' in an effort to support the hypothesis. He quotes Lieutenant George Grey, who in his exploration of northern Australia described encountering 'Individuals of an alien white race', which is very revealing even if calling the Dutch 'aliens' seems a bit harsh, despite their accents. Van Zanden also went to south-eastern Australia and noticed that there were stone structures built before British settlement. Noticing that there were also stone structures in the Netherlands, he put two and two together and came up with a number of some kind.

There is also the testimony of Les Hiddins, the 'Bush Tucker Man', who in straying well outside his area of expertise – i.e. bush tucker – swears blind that he has heard stories from Indigenous Australians about European settlers in Central Australia. To prove it, Hiddins has been photographed standing next to a large stack of mud, which you'll agree is fairly conclusive.

There's no way of knowing for sure whether these various speculations are true. But we do know that there was definitely a Dutch officer called Van Baerle, who disappeared along with the ship he was on, the *Concordia*, in 1708, while sailing from Batavia to the Netherlands. Most likely it went down in the Sunda Strait near Java, meaning survivors could conceivably have found their way to the north-west coast of Australia.

Another possibility is that the *Mercury* story was based on the voyage of explorer Robert Dale, who gave an account of meeting a group of white people living further west, in the Karakin Lakes region of Western Australia, also in 1832. They apparently told Dale that their ancestors had arrived 170 years earlier, which could place them on the *Vergulde Draeck*, a Dutch East India Company ship that was wrecked on a coral reef off Western Australia. Of seventy-five survivors, seven went to Batavia to fetch help, but multiple search parties failed to find any trace of the remaining sixty-eight. Was this because they settled inland, a settlement discovered 176 years later by Robert Dale?

Nobody, of course, can say. But if we've learned one thing from history, it's that it keeps on turning up ridiculous things that are actually true. So why not the lost Dutch colony? It's as likely as any other unlikely story, and more fun than most.

The Sound of the Underground

In Frank Herbert's *Dune* series, the Fremen people shelter in underground dwellings during the day, emerging only at night in order to avoid the harsh sun of their desert world. Their planet is invaded by outsiders who seek to mine the precious spice and enrich themselves, but they do not know the ways of the Fremen and so they end up hot and sweaty and in a bad mood.

It is unknown whether Herbert was inspired by the South Australian town of Coober Pedy when he dreamed up the world of *Dune*, but there are definite similarities: from the scorching desert sun and the underground homes carved out of rock to keep inhabitants safe from the heat to the presence of a precious substance that attracts greedy miners – in *Dune*'s case spice, in Coober Pedy's case opals. Whether there is a direct connection or not, it is certain that Coober Pedy is one of the few places in the world that truly does seem to have been transported directly from a science-fiction world.

The town of Coober Pedy was established just after World War I, which is surprisingly late. Not that it's surprising that it took so long for people to live there: despite the abundance of the precious gems that have made the town's fortune, it's no shock that people were slow to see the virtues of living in the middle of nowhere in unbearable heat.

No, the surprise is that it was more than a hundred years after Europeans first arrived on the Australian continent and declared that they would rather live underground than in this godforsaken dump that they decided to actually start living underground.

Coober Pedy is one of the world's strangest places: a barren and blighted desert landscape where people have dug holes, hobbit-style, to live in to avoid the hellish summer heat. It just goes to show that there is nowhere on Earth so awful that people won't find a way to live there, as long as there's something shiny to dig up.

The amazing thing, though, is that though it was the presence of opals that persuaded people it was worth the hassle to live in Coober Pedy, today the town is as reliant on tourism as it is on mining. In other words, the place that nobody would want to go to unless they could make a buck from it has turned into a place people will spend money to stay in, just to get a look at the place.

That, friends, is the power of weirdness.

For who wouldn't want to see for themselves a town set in land so unforgiving that living in a cave like a common Jedi is preferable to walking around on the surface? Where houses and mines alike are dug deep beneath the earth? Where both the Catholic and the Serbian Orthodox religions have underground churches catering to subterranean believers, and you can even stay in an underground motel? Where there is a grass-free golf course, with glowing balls so you can play at night when it's cooler?

The eerie moonscape of Coober Pedy is worth seeing for any urban dweller who doesn't know just how alien our own planet can be. But, unlike most towns, the real appeal shows when you look beneath the surface: where most civilisations keep their secrets and their dead, Coober Pedy comes alive.

The Mahogany Ship

O f all the myths and legends that swirl around our great nation, the tale of the Mahogany Ship can definitely be said to be the one that most closely resembles the plot of *The Goonies*. It's not difficult to imagine a gang of plucky youngsters uncovering the fabled wreck and saving their family's homes with the gold doubloons within.*

The Mahogany Ship is supposedly a ship that, what the hell, might as well be made of mahogany if it ever existed. The story goes that it was wrecked on the south coast of Victoria, a few kilometres west of Warrnambool. Many people have claimed to have seen a bit of the ship peeking out from the sand where it's buried, but somehow, whenever anyone went looking for it so they could get some real evidence, it was completely invisible. Unfortunately, most of the stories of the Mahogany Ship come from the 19th century, when people didn't have cameras on their phones, and their phones were in their houses anyway.

The earliest report of the ship comes from 1836, when Captain Smith of the Port Fairy Whaling Station set out with two companions to hunt seals in a whaling boat, which was obviously the wrong thing to do as whaling boats are meant for whaling. Unsurprisingly, the poorly chosen boat capsized, and while making their way back to Port Fairy they stumbled upon the wreck of an enormous ship. Excitedly assuming it to be a Spanish galleon stuffed with treasure, they reported their find, and many attempts were made to find and plunder the vessel, but it rather

---

* It is, however, hard to imagine it being entertaining.

conveniently disappeared beneath the sand and couldn't be found again.

In 1847 the *Portland Guardian* reported a 'wreck ... of a three hundred ton vessel ... thrown completely to the hummocks'. This raises the question: how does a 300-ton vessel disappear? (Also: what is a hummock?)

In 1876, in a letter to the Melbourne *Argus*, Captain John Mason asserted that he had seen the ship, which was made of a dark wood like mahogany or cedar. This letter was dated 1 April, but nobody noticed, and when Mason later tried to backpedal and say that he didn't think the ship was made of mahogany, the world told him to get stuffed: they'd started calling it the Mahogany Ship and they weren't going to stop. In 1890, another letter to *The Argus* gave instructions on where to go to get a look at the ship. A third letter* twenty years later related the story of a man who had lived near Warrnambool in the 1850s and told of 'riding into the interior' of the ship itself.

And yet, despite all these stories, to this day nobody's ever presented proof of the existence of the Mahogany Ship. There have been three Mahogany Ship symposia** held – in 1981, 1987 and 2005 – in an attempt to get to the bottom of the mystery, and in 1992 the Victorian government offered $250,000 to anyone who could find the ship. Still it remains lost, the only clues being the occasional bit of wood found on the beach – which isn't much, given science has established that not everything that is wood is an old ship.

Perhaps the Mahogany Ship was the wreck of a Spanish or Portuguese caravel that fetched up on the southern shores many years before Captain Cook? Perhaps it was a French vessel? Perhaps it was a particularly wooden-looking sperm whale? Or perhaps it was just some funny-shaped sand dunes with nothing at all under them? We may never know the

---

* Records show that over 60 per cent of the adult population of Australia in the 19th and early 20th century – the period of the so-called Stationery Rush – at some point wrote a letter to *The Argus*.

** From the Greek *symposium*, meaning 'people talking about an old boat for uncertain reasons'.

truth, unless a chest full of doubloons turns up one day.

Today, one can walk on the Mahogany Ship Walking Track, a trail set out for visitors to walk along the shoreline and look in wonder at the spot where nothing has ever been found. As thrilling as that is, though, it will never compare to the vision that rises in the imagination when you think of the Mahogany Ship, where it came from, and the treasure that may or may not have (but probably didn't, but hey, who knows it might have) packed its hold.

The History of the Hairy Folk

When the British first settled Australia, it wasn't long before they and the original inhabitants were exposing each other to the weirdest parts of their respective cultures. For example, the British introduced the First Nations to the concept of *terra nullius*, a wacky notion which everyone is still laughing about to this day. In return, Aboriginal Australia introduced white people to the hairy folk, some of the weirdest creatures ever to not exist anywhere.

It could be I'm being too sceptical here: plenty of people have told stories of having seen the hairy folk, so who am I to question them?* And although there's not a huge amount of evidence for these beings' existence, they qualify on the most important criterion of folklore: the world would be a much more interesting place if they're out there.

The hairy folk, also known as *Junjudee* or little people, are diminutive and rather cheeky tackers whose presence is attested by communities all around Australia. They are reportedly rather ugly but remarkably strong for their size, and smell terrible. How, then, is one to tell the difference between the hairy folk and an ordinary rugby prop? The answer is simple: by their mischief.

For the hairy folk are lovers of pranks and, much like other countries' magical beings, like leprechauns and Ashton Kutcher, they are said to play tricks on unwary wanderers in the bush. You may hear them when camping, making noises in the darkness to keep you awake in fear through

---

* Actually, I am the author of this book and I'll question whoever I like.

115

the night, only to find when day breaks that they've snuck in and emptied your backpack. At other times the hairy folk might pop up to throw rocks at people who've strayed into their territory, or simply amuse themselves by leaping out from trees and bushes to give travellers a scare. They have a lively sense of humour and seem quite insensitive to our feelings.

But they are also said to be well-intentioned little sprites with good hearts. Often their pranks are reserved for those who have transgressed in some way, such as by overfishing. According to this version, the hairy folk are a species akin to the Lorax, assuming the task of watching over and caring for the land, but somewhat less whimsically and without such respect for rhyme and metre. There are, it is said, areas of the outback that are under the guardianship of the *Junjudee*, and anyone who hurts the country will incur their wrath.

Sometimes the little people have been reported to kidnap humans, who upon their return have changed in deep and profound ways. This phenomenon may be the source for the several million Australian films and television shows about people returning to their home towns and struggling to reconcile who they were with who they are now, except that in those films the hairy folk, along with any other interesting or entertaining details, have been left out.

The hairy folk seem like mythical creatures from the distant mists of the past, but there have actually been some quite recent sightings. In the 1970s, teens claimed to have been attacked by little people near Charters Towers in Queensland, while others were spotted near Carnarvon Gorge in 1994. If the hairy folk ever did exist, it seems that they are most likely still active in the community, and are probably eligible for Landcare grants.

But what exactly are they? A different race of hominids, cunningly hiding themselves from the clumsy *sapiens* all these years? Or are they simply juvenile yowies, as some claim? (Though, to be fair, those 'some' are yowie hunters and the sort of people who claim pretty much everything is yowies.) Perhaps, as legend would have it, they are just crafty, clever, fun-loving magical creatures, and the occasional sighting of them offers a precious glimpse into the hidden world that exists invisibly right alongside our own?

Probably not, but it'd be nice.

Ol' Blue Eyes Hits Back

The show was sold out. Melburnians had packed in to see Frank Sinatra, in Australia for the first time in fifteen years, and were being treated to some classic crooning. But tonight they would get a bonus, as Sinatra decided to spice his inter-song banter up with some forthright views on his treatment by the Australian press.

'They keep chasing after us. We have to run all day long,' the star ranted. 'They're parasites who take everything and give nothing. And as for the broads who work for the press, they're the hookers of the press. I might offer them a buck and a half,* I'm not sure.'

Sinatra had lit the fuse and Australia duly exploded. Anyone who has ever mixed with Australian journalists knows that they are beautiful, gentle souls, who live only to give selflessly to their fellow humans, asking nothing in return and abiding by scrupulous standards of honesty and integrity at all times.** The public was accordingly outraged at this savage attack on the nation's honour by a jumped-up foreigner who believed that being one of the 20th century's greatest musical talents gave him the right to say things about people.

Most of all, though, the press industry erupted in response to Sinatra's comments about female journalists. The Australian Journalists Association, declaring that female journalists were worth much more than a buck and a half, demanded that he apologise to the women of the press. Other unions upped the ante: in solidarity with the journos,

---

* In Australian money, eight thousand dollars.
** *Citation needed.*

118

the Australian Theatrical and Amusement Employees' Association, the peak national body representing all varieties of oversensitive weirdos, announced that until Sinatra apologised, its members would not provide lighting, staging or backing musicians for his tour. The Waiters' Union joined in and terminated Sinatra's room service privileges, although if we're honest they were probably just looking for an excuse to slack off.

In response to demands for an apology, Sinatra politely refused, but did so extremely rudely. In fact, he demanded his own apology from the journalists' union, 'for fifteen years of abuse I have taken from the world press', which seems a bit unfair. The Australian Journalists Association, after all, can only reasonably be held responsible for the abuse given out by Australian journalists; abusive reporters elsewhere should give their own apologies.

Sinatra remained steadfast. He made it clear that he had come to Australia to do two things: sing, and tell Australian journalists to go fuck themselves – and right now he was resting his voice. Sinatra had never apologised to anyone in his life – not even to Marlon Brando for being such a jerk on *Guys and Dolls* – and he was not about to hand out his first-ever sorry to a pack of parasitical press hounds from a country that had only discovered movable type a few months ago.

The workers, united, would never be defeated, and to show it they doubled down. The Transport Workers Union, whose business, to be honest, it really wasn't, declared that Sinatra's plane would not be refuelled. Then came the development that, in any story about Australia, people know means shit just got real: Bob Hawke got involved.

In 1974, Bob Hawke was not yet prime minister, but he was the president of the Australian Council of Trade Unions, a role which in many ways is even better than PM, if you want to make visiting singers' lives uncomfortable – and who doesn't?

Hawke came out all guns blazing, telling Sinatra, 'If you don't apologise, your stay in this country could be indefinite. You won't be allowed to leave Australia unless you can walk on water.'*

Sinatra checked with his legal team and discovered that he could not, in fact, walk on water, and would have to make other arrangements. He considered calling in an American aircraft carrier from Japan to send a helicopter to pick him up, but dismissed this as, even for Frank Sinatra, too nuts. Finally he agreed to meet with Bob Hawke, the only man who could have the union ban lifted.

Hawke came to Sinatra's hotel room with fifteen union representatives, presumably to show that Sinatra wasn't the only one who could command the loyalty of shady thugs. In the ensuing conversation, Sinatra made a statement of regret and said that he had not intended 'any general reflection upon the moral character of working members of the Australian media.'**

This was not an apology, but everyone was tired by this point and Hawke hadn't had a drink for half an hour, so they decided that would do. The ban was lifted and Sinatra continued on his tour. Hawke went on to become the prime minister, and eventually the whole affair was seen to be worthwhile because it became the basis of a pretty bad movie that provided employment for many untalented Australian entertainment sector workers.

It's a strange reminder of the days when Australian society was very different indeed, but any lovers of weirdness will enjoy recalling the time when, just briefly, it seemed like Australia might be able to keep Ol' Blue Eyes.

---

* Of course, it is hard for modern readers to imagine a time when Australia would indefinitely detain people who came to our shores, but times were different then.
** If any members of the Australian media can be said to be working, am I right?

The Black Cats of the Bush

A ustralia is a beautiful country filled with fascinating and unique wildlife, but if it has a failing, nature-wise, it is the depressing lack of enormous scary predators roaming our lands. Outside of the saltwater crocodile, which tends to stick pretty close to the water due to its moisturising regime, Australia really comes up empty for the kind of ferocious beasts that other countries take justifiable pride in: your lions, your tigers, your bears, your honey badgers et al.

This said, it's no wonder that imaginations have been captured by the tales told of the Blue Mountains panther, sometimes dubbed the Lithgow panther, and other times called the Gippsland panther, the Otways panther or the Mitta Valley panther – although given how far these places are from each other, they are probably not all the same panther. Which is fantastic, because if there's one thing better than a panther, it is lots of panthers. Which isn't one thing at all, of course. If you see what I mean.

The mysterious Australian panthers are said to be large black cats, similar to domestic cats except much harder to get a decent photo of. The difficulty of getting conclusive proof of the Lithgow or any other panther has frustrated cryptozoology enthusiasts for many years, as every photo they produce of a black cat stalking through long grass gets dismissed as just a photo of a black cat stalking through long grass. There's no doubt it would be easier to prove the existence of Australian panthers if the average panther were pink or fluorescent or something.

Still, with over 500 reported sightings of panthers in regional Australia in the last twenty years, there can be no doubt that either the panthers are real or people in regional Australia need more hobbies.

Take the case of Amanda Dutton, who saw a panther while heading home from Mount Beauty* in Victoria's high country. Turning a corner on a dirt track, she saw the huge cat scamper from the road into a bush. 'It would have been as high as our kitchen bench,' said Ms Dutton, an utterly useless description for anyone who hasn't been in her kitchen. She also described the creature's tail as 'at least a metre long', which proves she either made an accurate estimate of the tail of a large black leopard, or looked up the length of a leopard's tail on Wikipedia afterwards. 'You can call me crazy, but I know what I saw,' Ms Dutton declared, so it's nice that we have her permission.

Then there was Alec McDonald, who was meditating** at Wahroonga, north of Sydney, when he saw a huge black cat and grabbed his phone, thereby gaining concrete proof that there was, in the Sydney region, either a panther or a cat that from a distance seemed large.

But where do these panthers come from? The stories have been around for decades, and the prevailing theory is that the ancestors of today's panthers either escaped from circuses or were released by American soldiers in World War II, who for some reason went around with large jungle cats.***

There are numerous problems, if you can believe it, with the theory that black panthers have been stalking the Australian bush for decades. First of all, the 'panther' is not a species of cat: black panthers are just melanistic leopards or jaguars – which is to say, they're regular big cats with a rare recessive gene. And this means it's extremely unlikely that multiple generations of the species could have been born with all of them being black: if the panthers are real, you'd expect to see at least the occasional spotted cat pop up. Unless, of course, it's just been the one

* Named by the Australian Tourism Commission as Australia's Most Ironically Named Landmark.
** Wink-wink.
*** Not that a panther wouldn't be useful in war, as long as it had been trained to distinguish between Nazis and non-Nazis.

panther every time over the years, which runs into the problem that that would be really stupid.

There's also the issue that, after all this time, we have still yet to see a photo or video taken during one of these sightings that can *definitely* be said to be a panther. There are many that *might* be panthers, but not one is so clear that there's no way it could just be a large domestic cat. And although many animals are rare and elusive, you would expect a beast as big as a panther to leave behind some definitive evidence of its existence. The bush where the panthers live is also mysteriously devoid of footprints and droppings, which is great for hygiene but not for those seeking proof.

However, there are also points in favour of the panther hypothesis. For a start, there was a sighting reported in 2018 by television personality Grant Denyer – and if you're calling Grant Denyer a liar, I will have to ask you to step outside.

Secondly, if there were panthers roaming Australia, it would be incredibly cool – and that alone is reason enough to believe it, in my book.*

---

* And this *is* my book, as by now you will have guessed.

The Day the Bat Clanged

We have already covered the propensity of the great Australian fast bowler Dennis Lillee to comport himself in an ungentlemanly manner on the field, with the tale of the day he kicked Javed Miandad to satisfy that lust for violence that all Australian men feel but few ever get to quench.

But although a white Australian physically assaulting a small Muslim in public is a great yarn, the height of weirdness in Lillee's career had come two years previously, also at the WACA ground in Perth – Lillee's home ground, and the place he felt most comfortable acting like a madman.

In 1979 Lillee was nearly a decade into his Test career and beginning to cast an eye towards the future, and when he cast that eye he found to his dismay that the future had very little money in it. Despite the World Series Cricket revolution, which had forced the cricketing authorities to distribute a modicum more of the game's largesse to the players, the founding principle of the game – worker exploitation – remained intact.

So it was that Dennis Lillee decided it was time to expand into the world of business, and the first business he decided to expand into was that of his friend Graeme Monaghan, who had begun to produce a line of cricket bats made of aluminium, which he called ComBats.

Now, the traditional way of manufacturing bats was to use wood,* preferably willow, rather than aluminium. But Monaghan had the bright idea that if he made them out of aluminium, he could save a buttload of

* For readers from the future, 'wood' was a substance derived from what we used to call 'trees'.

money on manufacturing costs and sell them to schools and people who were too poor to be fussy.

Test cricketers tend to be very fussy, but Lillee, having invested in Monaghan's metallic dream, had the even brighter idea that if people saw an aluminium bat being used in a Test match, by one of the world's greatest players, they'd rush out to the shops to snap up aluminium blades like nobody's business. In fact, like Graeme Monaghan's business, which was selling aluminium bats.

So it was that on the morning of the second day of the first Test of the 1979/80 season, Dennis Lillee walked out to bat on the WACA wicket with a ComBat, ready to get rich or belt someone over the head trying.

At first nobody realised he was packing metal, and the innings proceeded with appropriate Test match decorum. Indeed, everything was going swimmingly until Lillee made the fatal mistake of hitting the ball.

Facing Ian 'Meaty' Botham, Lillee played an attractive drive down the ground for three. An ordinary shot, but observers couldn't help but feel that when bat met ball, there had been a distinct *clang*, a tinny sound not at all like the conventional *thwack* of leather on willow.

At this point, all hell broke loose – or at least what passes for all hell breaking loose in Test cricket. The England captain, outraged by this offence against propriety, complained to the umpires that Lillee's bat was damaging the ball. Australian captain Greg Chappell, recognising that the ComBat had proved itself rubbish for hitting a cricket ball, sent the 12th man,* Rodney Hogg, out with a fine selection of nice willow bats for Lillee to choose from.

The umpires told Lillee to change his bat. Lillee told the umpires to shove it where the sun don't shine.** For ten minutes they argued, while the crowd pondered this exciting new form of the game and the Australian Cricket Board wondered if they could somehow monetise it.

Finally, Lillee received wise counsel from two old friends. First, Australian wicketkeeper Rod Marsh told him that with a wooden bat,

---

* Oh, you don't what that means either? Ignoramus.

** The MCG.

his shot for three would've gone for four. Second, Chappell came out onto the field himself and told his fast bowler to stop being such a tool. Lillee, seeing the sense of both, took a wooden bat from Chappell and, just to show that he was still a devil-may-care rebel with timeless style, hurled the ComBat into the outfield.

Everything turned out for the best. Australia won the Test. Lillee suffered no disciplinary action, the board making an official ruling of 'who gives a shit, really?'. Monaghan saw sales of the ComBat soar, and Lillee got a cut of the profits. And eventually the laws of cricket were amended to say that bats had to be made of wood. They were not, however, amended to say that you couldn't kick Pakistanis, so Lillee remained free to express himself creatively.

What would the game of cricket look like today if everyone in international games used aluminium bats? It would, of course, be absolute garbage. But, nevertheless, let us salute Dennis Lillee for his spirit of adventure.

Give Me a Home Where the Fluorescent Slugs Roam

Mount Kaputar is a peak near Narrabri in northern New South Wales. It's the remnant of an extinct volcano, with an elevation of 1489 metres. On its slopes can be found dry rainforests, dry eucalypt forests and heathlands. Stringybark and mountain gum trees abound. In winter the mountain occasionally gets a dash of snow.

For anyone wanting to climb Mount Kaputar, it offers several lookouts, cabins and camping facilities. All in all it is a reasonably pleasant mountain on which recreational activities for humans can be conducted with relative ease and comfort. It is therefore not very interesting, unless you count the slugs.

For Mount Kaputar is the only place in the world where you can find *Triboniophorus* sp. nov. 'Kaputar'* – also known as the giant fluorescent pink slug. This should not be confused with *Triboniophorus graeffei*, the red triangle slug, which is of course smaller and less pink, and don't you forget it.

The pink slug grows up to twenty centimetres in length, which just goes to show how everything is relative. After all, if you saw an elephant or a cruise liner that was only twenty centimetres long, you'd think it was fairly small. But when you see a pink fluorescent slug that is twenty centimetres long, you realise that twenty centimetres is in fact so large that it will haunt your nightmares for the rest of your life.

Why these horrifically big slugs, with their retro-80s aesthetic, choose

---

* Your guess is as good as mine.

to live on Mount Kaputar and nowhere else on the planet is unknown. There are plenty of more glamorous mountains they could have taken up residence on, but it's possible they just wanted a nice quiet life in a nice community where they need not fear the intrusion of the press.

On cool wet mornings on Mount Kaputar, the pink slugs can be seen in their hundreds, if you care to go and look, which frankly I would not recommend. Hundreds of slugs is not a sight anyone who wishes for good mental health should be exposed to. During the day they hide under leaf litter, coming out at night to climb trees, eat moss and plan their next move against the humans. In the morning they slither revoltingly back down to the ground, at which time they can be seen by masochistic early risers.

It gives one a creepy feeling at the back of the neck, does it not, to think that right here in our very country there is a mountain on which hundreds of giant pink slugs are at this very moment wriggling around subverting norms of civilised behaviour. It doesn't help to know that Mount Kaputar is also home to not one but three different species of cannibal snail. Although, to be fair, the instinctive revulsion one feels at the term 'cannibal snail' is a little misguided: if you hate snails – as all normal people do – cannibal snails are quite a blessing, acting as they do to keep the snail population down by eating each other.

All in all it can be said that Mount Kaputar is a great place to go if you want to experience the weirder and slimier end of the Australian fauna spectrum. Just be vigilant if you choose to make camp on the mountain: if you've yet to have the experience of putting on hiking boots in the morning only to discover a 20-centimetre fluorescent slug inside one, then you are extremely lucky. Pray that your luck never runs out.

The Great-Explorer Dust-up

A lot of people tend to assume that to be a great explorer you have to be good at exploring. It's strange that people assume this, because the evidence is quite to the contrary. For example, one of the most famous explorers in history is Christopher Columbus, who was wrong about absolutely everything. And then in our own country we have the cautionary tale of Hume and Hovell, the adventuring pals who hated each other's guts.

The names of Hume and Hovell are renowned in Australia: Hume gave his name to the Hume Highway, the City of Hume, the Division of Hume, Lake Hume and the Canberra suburb of Hume; whereas Hovell gave his name to some street somewhere that nobody has ever heard of. This reflects one of the painful truths about exploration: if you go exploring in pairs, one of you is always going to end up more famous than the other.

Not that Hovell knew this when he first started hating Hume. He thought he was a jerk pretty much before their expedition even started, and his feelings were warmly reciprocated by Hume. They had been put together to fulfil the wishes of the governor of New South Wales, Thomas Brisbane, to find new grazing land and discover where the colony's western rivers flowed, a mystery that had been tormenting Brisbane for years.

Hume and Hovell succeeded in discovering fine grazing land in the Western Port region, on the eastern shores of Port Phillip Bay, and made a strong recommendation that a new settlement be established there.

Accordingly this was done. Hovell accompanied the new settlers on their journey to found the new colony, resulting in an extremely awkward moment when it dawned on the explorer that this was not actually the place he'd been to with Hume. In fact, he'd never been there before in his life.

What had happened was this: Hovell, instead of measuring the expedition's longitude when they reached their destination, read it off the map, which they had made themselves. In fact, he never measured the longitude at all, which he blamed on Hume for his unsupportive attitude. As a result, they thought they were at Western Port but were actually near what would become Geelong, on the opposite side of the bay. This did not stop Hume repeatedly claiming that he had reached Western Port, until Hovell revealed the mistake and both men changed their stories.

From this, it can be seen that both Hume and Hovell were liars and idiots, and they received official reprimands for their terrible exploring, which had caused the government to spend a lot of money on putting a settlement in one place based on how rich and fertile Hume and Hovell said the land was in a completely different place.

It was no surprise that Hume and Hovell stuffed up, given how busy they had been squabbling the whole time. Earlier in the expedition they had, for a time, actually split up, after running into a big wall of rock, causing a heated argument as to the best way to proceed. Hume yelled at Hovell. Hovell yelled at Hume. Finally they decided that, as the dispute was insoluble, one half of the party would go with Hume and one with Hovell. They split up the expedition's belongings accordingly, which started another fight. Both men insisted on having the party's frying pan. Consequently there was seen the sight of two grown men in the Australian wilderness pulling angrily at either side of the pan. Finally, in zany sitcom style, the frying pan broke, and the argument was thus settled: one man would take the pan, the other the handle. It was a very Solomonesque solution.

Eventually the explorers reunited, Hovell realising that, as was fast becoming his brand, he had gone the wrong way. And so they were able to make their massive cock-up together. After their expedition they devoted most of the rest of their lives to sniping at each other in the press, showing that their sense of dignity was as strong as their sense of direction. Looking at the naming of various parts of Australia, you could probably say that in the end Hume won the argument. Then again both of them won compared with the other members of the expedition, as we don't know any of their names at all. Which just goes to show that, when it comes to history, stupidity has always paid.

The Yowie of Yore

What is a yowie? Is it, as some scientists have theorised, one of the top-selling chocolates in Australia in the 1990s? Well, yes and no. Although there can be no doubt the yowie is a delicious sweet snack, it is so much more.

The yowie is Australia's answer to Bigfoot, or perhaps the Australian branch of the Bigfoot franchise: the Hungry Jack's to Bigfoot's Burger King, if you will. For centuries tales of the yowie have abounded, and although there is little irrefutable evidence of its existence, there is plenty of refutable evidence, which is almost as good.

The yowie has been seen, heard and generally sensed in the depths of the Australian bush. Those who have seen it agree that it is somewhere between two and 3.5 metres tall, it either has enormous feet or it doesn't, and it may have a wide, flat nose possibly. All agree that the yowie is a ferociously aggressive creature, except for those who describe it as timid and shy. One thing that is certain is that the yowie is covered with thick hair or fur, which most experts believe is of some colour or other.

The legend of the yowie has its roots in the mythology of Aboriginal Australians. In 1842 it was reported in *The Australian and New Zealand Monthly Magazine** that the First Nations people believed in a being called a 'YAHOO', which was described as being similar to a man, but covered with long white hair, with 'extraordinarily long' arms, and with feet turned backwards so its tracks made it appear to be walking in the opposite

---

* 'Your number one source for all things monthly!'

direction. The detail of the backwards feet is confirmed by the 1980s short-story collection *The Squealies*, by Joan Flanagan, which independent research indicates that only the author of this book has ever read.

In the late 1800s the Australian media featured numerous reports of 'indigenous apes'. The *Australian Town and Country Journal** carried a story in 1882 from one Henry James McCooey, who claimed to have seen such a beast on the New South Wales south coast:

> I should think that if it were standing perfectly upright it would be nearly 5ft high. It was tailless and covered with very long black hair, which was of a dirty red or snuff-colour about the throat and breast. Its eyes, which were small and restless, were partly hidden by matted hair that covered its head. The length of the fore legs or arms seemed to be strikingly out of proportion with the rest of its body, but in all other respects its build seemed to be fairly proportional. It would probably weigh about 8st. On the whole it was a most uncouth and repulsive looking creature, evidently possessed of prodigious strength, and one which I should not care to come to close quarters with. Having sufficiently satisfied my curiosity, I threw a stone at the animal, whereupon it immediately rushed off, followed by the birds, and disappeared in a ravine which was close at hand.

So a picture of the yowie begins to emerge: hairy, ugly and a complete wuss. What better symbol for Australian identity could there be?

---

* 'Sick of having to choose town OR country? Your worries are over!'

The Midday Rumble

When asked in surveys what the biggest problem with Australian television is, respondents have for decades consistently said, 'There are not enough live fights between old men.' Perhaps they would thirst less for these spectacles if their appetites had not been whetted by what is widely agreed to be the greatest televised event in Australian – and possibly world – history: the time Normie Rowe and Ron Casey got in a fight on *Midday* with Ray Martin.

Part of our fondness for the memory of this epochal broadcast stems from the fact that, until he died, pretty much everyone harboured a secret desire to fight Ron Casey.* In his career as a radio and TV presenter, he distinguished himself by actions such as referring to Asians as 'little bastards', saying that Aboriginal Australians were 'disadvantaged because they won't get off their black arses and do some work', admitting to harassing women at work because 'if you are nice to ugly girls, it sort of helps them', and interviewing Holocaust denier David Irving. Perhaps Casey's finest hour was an unhinged rant about Japanese dive-bombers prompted by the fact that a rugby league award was sponsored by Nokia; he later apologised after being informed that Nokia was in fact a Finnish company, further covering himself in glory by referring to them as 'good Aryan boys'.

So we can see why anyone, even if not provoked, might want to punch Ron Casey in the face. And yet, in the end, it was Ron Casey who punched

---

* And, if we're honest, we still kind of want to even after he died.

Normie Rowe in the face, despite the fact that few had ever wanted to punch Normie Rowe – though after hearing his version of 'Que Sera Sera', several people said they wouldn't mind giving him a papercut.

The brouhaha arose on an episode of *Midday*, hosted by Ray Martin. This show was not usually a forum for violence: it was a program designed to showcase Martin's supreme talent for speaking in a pleasant voice and reassuring elderly Australians that the world was not as scary a place as they thought. Although watching Ray caused widespread sexual arousal among retirees, it generally did not provoke violence. But on this day things were different.

It was a special episode, devoted to a debate on the subject of whether Australia should become a republic. Among the guests were Casey, a passionate republican, and Rowe, a monarchist whose service in Vietnam had somehow led him to implicitly trust authority. Also present were monarchists Di 'Bubbles' Fisher and Bruce 'Tiddles' Ruxton, as well as republicans Barry 'Tedium' Jones and Geraldine 'Geraldine' Doogue.

From the beginning it was clear that Casey had come to needle Rowe, which was no surprise, given how much success he'd had over his career as the human equivalent of jock itch.

The panel boiled over when Rowe said that none of the others could understand his experience fighting under the Australian flag in Vietnam, something that, at the time, seemed to him to have some relevance to the republic issue. Casey responded by sneering, 'I'm so sorry, mate, you're a bloody hero, go on,' and to be fair he had a point, even if he didn't have to be such a jerk in making it.

Rowe responded, 'I really take exception to that, Ron,' taking his rhetoric to newly inflammatory extremes.

Casey doubled down on his general douchiness. 'Oh, we didn't bleed in Vietnam, I'm so sorry, mate.* You live with a badge and that's all you've got.'

This was too much for Normie. Casey assumed the badge he was

---

* And yet they weren't mates at all! Weird.

wearing was an RSL one, but it was actually a 3rd Cavalry Regiment (Vietnam) Association badge, commemorating Rowe's membership of a band of brothers, rather than his ability to get a discount chicken parma. The pop singer-cum-war hero stood and approached Casey, asking, 'Do you know what that is?'

Casey stood to confront Rowe, and at this point Rowe crossed his personal Rubicon. Declaring Casey's words to be 'bloody ridiculous', he gave the silver-haired bigot a fierce shove back into his seat. Casey, his blood well and truly up, immediately sprang up and landed a punch sweetly on Rowe's nose.

The story here takes a sad turn, as the *Midday* crew intervened to prevent the brawl from going any further, even though that is absolutely what everyone in the country wanted to happen. The show quickly cut to a commercial break, which, Casey reflected later, was a mercy as 'I didn't have two punches in me'. This makes the abrupt cutting-off of hostilities even more frustrating, as had it been allowed to continue, there was a real possibility we could've seen Rowe pounding Casey on the studio floor.

But as the old line goes, let's not ask for the moon as we have the stars. And in this case the stars were throwing punches on a respectable daytime talk show, something that had never happened before and hasn't again. We got to see Normie Rowe shove Ron Casey, and then Ron Casey whack Normie Rowe in the face, and that should be enough to give us a warm inner glow for the rest of our lives.

Activist and journalist Egon Kisch, cheerfully indicating the number of non-racists in the Australian government. (SAM HOOD)

The $100-a-head visitor encounter program at Victoria's Bunyip Sanctuary was discontinued shortly after this incident. (STATE LIBRARY OF VICTORIA, J MACFARLANE)

The *Torrens* limps into dock after hitting an iceberg, while a young James Cameron watches and takes notes. (John Oxley Library, State Library of Queensland)

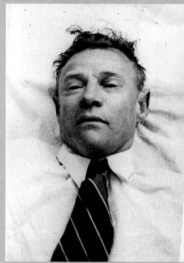

The notorious Somerton man, conveying by means of facial expression how unimpressed he is by his death. (Australian Police)

Taronga Zoo's Indian elephant Jessie in 1916, beginning to have doubts about the zookeepers' promise that they're taking her to live on a beautiful farm in the country. (Taronga Park Zoo)

The Great Emu War enters a grim new phase as the emus are shown their inferiority in hand-to-hand combat. (*THE LAND NEWSPAPER*)

The hanging of the Batavia murderers, the most wholesome and family-friendly event of 17th-century history.

An underground bedroom in Coober Pedy, complete with bedside shelf for head-injury treatment kit. (SHUTTERSTOCK)

An Australian black panther, seen here engaging in its favourite pastime of existing. (SHUTTERSTOCK)

A statue of Tony Abbott commemorates his greatest political achievement.

One of Mount Kaputar's giant pink slugs, luring its prey by imitating raspberry sorbet. (STITCHINGBUSHWALKER)

The mystery of Magnetic Hill, where Wile E Coyote has set up his most fiendish scheme yet.

The Big Pineapple, Queensland's least edible tourist attraction. (Shutterstock)

The Curse of the Ballandean Pyramid, according to legend, states that anyone who disturbs the structure will be afflicted with mild athlete's foot. (SHUTTERSTOCK/TIM RUMBLE)

Cooks' Cottage, where, to this day, the entire cast of MasterChef is imprisoned each year. (SHUTTERSTOCK/WORAKIT SIRIJINDA)

A Burke and Wills commemorative stamp, part of Australia Post's 'Heroes with No Sense of Direction' series. (SHUTTERSTOCK/NETFALI)

* FOR THE NEXT 120km YOU ARE IN LAND

OF the MIN MIN LIGHT

THIS UNSOLVED MODERN MYSTERY IS A LIGHT THAT AT TIMES FOLLOWS TRAVELLERS FOR LONG DISTANCES—IT HAS BEEN APPROACHED BUT NEVER IDENTIFIED

ERECTED BY THE BOULIA SHIRE COUNCIL IN THE INTEREST OF TOURISM

The Boulia Shire Council advertising its greatest asset: its thriving sign-writing industry.

The Moist Mystery of Harold Holt

On the corner of High and Edgar streets in Glen Iris, in Melbourne's leafy eastern suburbs, stands the Harold Holt Swim Centre. It is a wonderful place to relax, have a refreshing dip, keep fit or learn to swim, and former prime minister Holt would no doubt be proud of the fact his name is forever linked with such a fine facility, once he got over the discovery that the people who named the pool had perpetrated such a sick joke at his expense.

For the Harold Holt Swim Centre is no ordinary public leisure facility/monument to a national leader. In giving it that name, the Malvern Council acted with an instinct akin to inaugurating a John F Kennedy Memorial Shooting Range, or a Joan of Arc Barbecue Set. Naming public buildings according to a black comedy formula didn't really catch on, but the Harold Holt Swim Centre remains to remind us simultaneously of the ex-PM and what killed him.

Australian prime ministers don't tend to die in weird ways. We've never even had one assassinated, which has always made us feel a little insecure among other nations. There is a sense that you're not a proper nation until you've had a leader gunned down, and Australia has a well-developed inferiority complex as a result. But what we *do* have is one prime minister who died in such a weird way that even Abraham Lincoln* would raise his eyebrows and say, 'Damn, dawg.'

Harold Holt was not a particularly memorably prime minister while

---

* He of the Abraham Lincoln Memorial Murder Mystery Evening Fun Pack.

he was alive. He had assumed the position upon the departure of Robert Menzies, who had served as prime minister for most of the previous eight or nine centuries. As such, the Holt premiership was something of an anticlimax: in fact, the whole period 1966–1972 was quite a tedious one for Australians, who were just waiting around impatiently for Gough Whitlam to come along and go mental on everyone.

But what Holt lacked in charisma, policy boldness or any vaguely interesting personality traits he made up for in a willingness to go swimming at extremely inadvisable moments. Such a moment came along on 17 December 1967, when the prime minister and some friends* stopped at Cheviot Beach, at the southern tip of Victoria's Port Phillip bay, for a quick dip.

Cheviot was a remote beach where few pleasure-seekers ventured. There was no one else around and the sea was rough, but Holt claimed to know the beach 'like the back of my hand'. Tragically, nobody noticed that he was wearing gloves.

Holt plunged into the chilly waters and began flapping his limbs about in that comical manner which humans call 'swimming'. Wishing to show off to his lady friend, he swam out further and further, into deep water. Suddenly, a rip took hold of him. Being fifty-nine years old and flabby and wrinkly and gross, the PM found himself quite unable to fight the current, and was quickly carried away, in Marjorie Gillespie's words, 'like a leaf being taken out'. In the blink of an eye, he disappeared from view. He was never seen again.

A massive search was mounted for the unfortunate prime minister. It's one of the fundamental principles of the Westminster system of government that when a prime minister gets carried off by a rip, you should look for him for a while. But the sea was large and Harold Holt was small, and all efforts to locate him proved futile.

To this day, no trace of Holt has ever been found, leading to a proliferation of theories that he was not actually swept away by a rip, but

---

* Including his mistress, Marjorie Gillespie – so I guess the dude had something going for him.

was taken away by a Chinese submarine, or assassinated by the CIA, or that he dived to the ocean floor to assume his rightful place as Emperor of the Sea. More prosaically, some have suggested that he committed suicide, but this seems unlikely given he was the prime minister of Australia, with a wife *and* a girlfriend: life was going pretty sweetly for him.

No, sadly, the truth is most likely that Harold Holt simply fell victim to hubris: believing himself to be a fantastic swimmer, he found he was just a helpless old man flailing around in the water, and the sea took him in its usual merciless fashion. It's a sad story, but hopefully Holt is looking down somewhere, proud that in the Harold Holt Swim Centre, he has left a lasting and extremely tasteless legacy.

The Gay Blade of the Harbour Bridge

The crowd was gathered. The dignitaries were assembled. An atmosphere of excitement and festivity permeated the air of Sydney Harbour, as above them the colossal steel arch of the brand-new bridge shone in the early autumn sun.

Here was the culmination of a three-decade dream. The bridge had been discussed since the turn of the 20th century. Ten years ago, the government had passed the *Sydney Harbour Bridge Act*. Eight years ago, construction had begun. And now, on 19 March 1932, it was complete – and it was magnificent. That it would be an enduring symbol of the city – indeed, of the entire country – could be taken as read. Everyone present at the opening ceremony could feel the exhilarating electricity of history crackling through their bones.

The speeches had been made, the formalities observed. All that remained was the cutting of the ribbon, a task given to the premier of New South Wales, the Honourable Jack Lang. A man of strong principles and unflappable moustache, Lang gripped the ceremonial scissors tight and stepped forward to do his duty. The harbour held its breath, the immensity of the moment keeping all in tingling thrall. With apt gravitas, Lang parted the blades of the scissors and prepared to snip the momentous sash and give birth to a landmark.

And it was at that moment that, as the historians say, things went sideways. For those scissors never did get to taste the ribbon. Jack Lang never did get to do his duty. At the crucial moment, instead of the New South Wales premier officially opening the Sydney Harbour Bridge, something quite remarkable and undeniably weird happened.

For riding out of the crowd came a man on a horse.

This being 1932, this was not in itself so strange: cars had only been around for a few decades and riding horses was still seen as a respectable activity, rather than, as it is today, an affront to God Himself.

No, what was unusual about this fellow was not so much that he was on a horse as the fact that while on the horse, and dressed in full military regalia, he rode right up to the ribbon, drew a sparkling regimental sword and, with one swift slash, cut the ribbon himself.

'I declare this bridge open,' he bellowed, 'in the name of the decent and respectable people of New South Wales.'

The bridge exploded – not literally, but with shock and uproar. The carefully planned opening of Sydney's grandest monument had turned into a clusterboink of epic proportions.

Naturally, the man on the horse was immediately seized, and his sword taken from him. He was marched off in police custody, while Premier Lang sat and wept bitter tears over the loss of his crowning glory, consoled by the New South Wales governor, Sir Philip Game, and the minister for public works, Lawrence Ennis, who told him to cheer up – there would be other bridges.

The perpetrator of the outrage was revealed to be Captain Francis de Groot, an Irish World War I veteran who had moved to Australia after the war to become an antiques dealer, but had fallen into the well-known antiques-to-radicalisation pipeline. He joined the New Guard, a fascist paramilitary organisation whose raison d'être was opposing the extremist left-wing policies of Jack Lang, such as a minimum wage and preventing people from starving to death. The New Guard reasoned that allowing poor people to live was a slippery slope that might easily lead to allowing poor people to do other things, so they declared war on Lang, although only in a fairly stupid and pointless way.

It was in service of this war that De Groot had cut the ribbon, humiliating the premier and striking a blow for those aforementioned 'decent and respectable people', i.e. the people who had jobs, money, swords and so on. The thought that if you could get up close to the premier with a sword, you could actually stick that sword into the premier didn't seem to occur to De Groot, which frankly casts his 'paramilitary fascist' credentials into severe doubt.

In the end, no real harm was done. Jack Lang recovered from his grief and went on make everyone angry and lose his job, while the Sydney Harbour Bridge went on to become very famous and give birth to Paul Hogan.

As for Captain Francis de Groot, he was unexpectedly declared sane, tried for malicious damage and offensive behaviour, and fined £5.* He later sued for wrongful arrest and settled out of court for £69, so he made a profit from the whole business.** He died on 1 April 1969, which was later discovered not to be a prank. But his memory will live forever, as the man who proved that if you believe in yourself, and are a fascist, you can achieve something quite odd.

---

*   In today's money, $350,000.

** He sued on the grounds that the police had no right to arrest an officer of the Hussars, which is incredibly stupid, and the government really made fools of themselves by agreeing to settle.

The Amazing Disappearing *København*

I t's time for yet another tale of a lost ship – the kind of thing that happened so often in history that one starts to wonder whether boats were just a bad idea in the first place. Especially when it happened in the 20th century, which was supposed to be the century in which spooky, mysterious stuff stopped happening and was replaced by good, solid crimes against humanity that everyone could understand.

Anyway. The *København** was built in 1921 in Scotland for the Danish East Asiatic Company, a Copenhagen-based firm with an identity crisis. It was a five-masted barque, used as a naval training vessel for people who wanted to know how to sail old-timey ships that would soon be utterly obsolete, although it also had a diesel engine, in recognition of the fact that, as previously noted, it was that period of history in which engines existed.

At time of building, the *København* was the world's biggest sailing ship. Nicknamed 'the Big Dane' in honour of its resemblance to Scooby Doo, it made ten commercial voyages and circumnavigated the world twice before the fateful decision was made that it should sail from Buenos Aires to Melbourne and mysteriously vanish en route – although there is some disagreement among scholars as to whether the second part of the plan was explicitly laid out by the company.

The *København* left Buenos Aires on 14 December 1928 on its forty-five-day journey to Melbourne.** On 22 December the ship made radio

---

* Danish for 'Copenhagen' – so why do we call it Copenhagen in the first place? Weird.
** Today, of course, thanks to modern air travel, one can easily travel from Buenos Aires to Melbourne in just thirty-five to forty days.

contact with the *William Blumer*,* telling its fellow ship that God was in his heaven and all was right in the world, so to speak. Later the same night the *Blumer* gave the *København* another call but got no answer. Thinking this pretty rude, the *Blumer* sailed off in a huff. Nobody ever saw or heard from the *København* again, making the *Blumer* feel guilty for the rest of its life, driving it to drink and unemployment.

After contact with the *København* stopped, initially nobody gave the matter much thought. Captain Hans Andersen was known for going long stretches without communicating with anyone, as he hunkered down in his cabin and worked on his fairytales. 'It's just Hans being Hans,' they all said, imagining the skipper brooding silently in his room and gazing with handsome soulfulness out to sea, too lost in captainly thoughts to bother with the radio. It was only in April 1929, four months into the forty-five-day trip, that the Danish East Asiatic Company decided it seemed strange that the *København* hadn't arrived in Melbourne, or indeed anywhere else.

Sending a search vessel to Tristan da Cunha, a lonely archipelago in the middle of the South Atlantic, the company learned that back in January locals had spotted a five-masted ship with one broken mast, but it had sailed by without attempting to land. Several further months of searching were fruitless, until the Danish East Asiatic Company, beginning to get the impression that the ship was lost at sea, declared the ship lost at sea. Insurers Lloyd's of London officially announced the *København* missing on 1 January 1930, as a New Year's treat.

So, what happened to the *København*? Pirates? Krakens? A demonically possessed doll that murdered the entire crew and punched a hole in the hull to drag the ship to hell? Ah, we wish. The suggested explanations for its disappearance are far more prosaic/boring. Most believe it probably hit an iceberg, which since 1912 had been a popular activity for ships that wanted to look cool in front of other ships. Another possibility is that it was capsized by heavy winds, which would have come as a great surprise to the crew, wind being such a rare occurrence at sea.

---

* Named after William Blumer, who is so famous I need not tell you who he was.

But there are other, less popular but more fun theories. After the *København* disappeared, numerous sightings were made of a mysterious five-masted ship cruising about the open sea, spooking everybody out. In July 1930 the crew of an Argentine freighter claimed to have seen such a ship, their captain suggesting it may have been 'the wraith of the Copenhagen' because he didn't speak Danish. There were also sightings by Chilean fishermen, and at least one report that the *København* had been spotted transporting Johnny Depp to the set of his next film.

More materially verifiable evidence of the ship's fate came with wreckage discovered off Western Australia, the diary of a crewman found in a bottle in the Atlantic, and the remains of a lifeboat and its human ex-operators buried in the sand on the African coast. These sad remnants of the last voyage of the *København* stand forever as a cautionary tale for those who would sail among icebergs, and those reckless enough to want to go to Melbourne.

Get to the Chopper

In 1984, notorious criminal Marie Winter escaped from Melbourne's Wentworth Detention Centre by climbing a fence and leaping to cling to a helicopter that was hovering over the prison for exactly this purpose. It was a stunning act of outlaw audacity and very, very cool. The only thing that detracted from its general awesomeness was the fact that it didn't actually happen; it was just a plotline on the TV drama *Prisoner*.

Fortunately, there was one man who was determined to force life to imitate art – a man who refused to accept the confinement of helicopter rescues to the oubliette of fiction, and so set out to reify what had hitherto been only a dream.

That man was John Killick, and on 25 March 1999 he transcended the mortal plane and became, essentially, a god.

Killick had already writ his name large in the annals of history when, on Valentine's Day in 1966, he became Australia's first decimal currency bank robber. It was testament to his never-say-die attitude that he was still actively seeking innovations in law-breaking thirty-three years later.

Killick was in Silverwater Correctional Centre in Sydney, serving a sentence for armed robbery and wondering just how on Earth he was going to get himself out of yet another of his wacky scrapes. He was fifty-seven years old, and every year it got a little bit harder to summon the energy for another wild caper, but on this occasion he had a secret weapon: a slightly unhinged Russian girlfriend.

Her name was Lucy Dudko, and she was utterly devoted to the

veteran rogue – to the extent that when he suggested that she get a helicopter and pick him up from the clink, she jumped at the chance. Booking a helicopter joy ride over the Sydney Olympic Park on 25 March, she waited for a call from Killick to let her know he was heading into the exercise yard – but with a very different kind of workout in mind! Ahem. As you have probably surmised.

Not long into her chopper ride, Dudko pulled out a gun and told the pilot there had been a sudden alteration to the planned route. Directing him to Silverwater, she instructed him to land on the prison's playing field, where Killick hopped on board and the happy couple flew off into the sunset. Or, as it was morning, just generally into the sun. But not literally, obviously.

The story doesn't end there: indeed, if it had done it would've been a gross violation of the law of gravity. As the chopper flew away from the prison, guards opened fire on it, but failed to bring it down or even get a lucky headshot in. Killick and Dudko forced the pilot to land, tied him up and went on the run. For forty-five days they stayed on the run, until they made the crucial error of stopping being on the run.

The couple were arrested on 8 May at the Bass Hill Caravan Park in western Sydney, having checked in as 'Mr and Mrs MG Brown', a devilish bit of subterfuge that somehow failed to fool the authorities. And so it was off to jail again for Killick, and for the first time for Dudko.

While in prison, Dudko sent 4500 love letters to Killick, who began to feel that he really needed his space. Their relationship ended when the Russian discovered the Bible and found out that springing armed robbers in a helicopter is, surprisingly, specifically forbidden in Leviticus.

Lucy Dudko was released in 2006 and moved to the Blue Mountains. John Killick left prison in 2015. He wrote three books about his life as a criminal and later expressed deep remorse for his crimes, and even deeper remorse for making money from writing books about them.

A condition of Killick's parole was that he have no contact with Dudko, without permission from his parole officer. It is unknown whether such permission has ever been sought or given. Dudko's decision to cuddle up to Christ threw a spanner in the works as far as their romance was concerned, but it would be nice to think, after all these years, that the once-lovestruck couple could get together now and then, to reminisce about the old days, when they would hijack a helicopter, bust out of jail and ride high through the skies, feeling just as cool as Marie Winter from *Prisoner*.

Looking Through a Raw Onion

Most people reading this book will be old enough to remember that time in Australian history known as 'less than ten years ago'. It was a magical time: today it is hard to believe how hopeful and joyous and disinclined to crawl underneath our houses and let cockroaches eat us we all were. And a big part of the joie de vivre of that era was down to one man: part-time prime minister and full-time loose unit Tony Abbott.

Now, you knew Abbott was coming into this book. It's a book about weird stuff in Australia, and Tony Abbott is to weirdness as Charlemagne is to the power structures of medieval Europe. Abbott doesn't just epitomise weirdness, he shaped the very concept and made us think about weirdness in a whole new way. Until Abbott came along, we thought we knew what weird meant. We were wrong.

There are as many examples of Abbott's weirdness as there are pictures of him in tiny Speedos, i.e. thousands upon thousands, cursing all who look upon them. The time he commended his daughters' physical attractiveness to the cast of *Big Brother*. The time he knighted Prince Philip. The time he answered a question from a reporter by staring intensely at him in complete silence for thirty seconds on live television. And of course, just generally, the way he sort of vibrated oddly whenever talking about anything to anyone.

But nothing encapsulated the weird essence of Tony Abbott better than the day when, despite being in no way compelled to do so by either contractual or constitutional obligations, he publicly ate a raw onion.

It was March 2015, and it was in Tasmania, though it should be stressed that this was no excuse. On a visit to Charlton Farm Produce, the then prime minister (though not, it should also be stressed, the very-much-longer prime minister) was privy to a display of the fine produce that Charlton Farm Produce produced, which included brown onions. This was a perfectly normal thing for a farm produce business to have around the place, and nothing to be ashamed of. Nobody is blaming the good people at Charlton for what happened next; the Australian people should be able to expect their prime minister to see an onion without losing control of himself.

For upon seeing the onion, Prime Minister Abbott grabbed the onion. And upon grabbing the onion, Prime Minister Abbott bit into the onion. Having bitten into the onion, Prime Minister Abbott chewed the onion, and he swallowed the onion, while a shocked nation looked on, scarcely able to believe how much evil there was in the world.

It should be made clear that this onion was not cooked. It was not sliced or diced. It was not even peeled. No onion preparation had taken place. It was a raw, fully intact onion, and nothing about it would've suggested to a reasonable person that it might have actually been an apple or a banana or a club sandwich.

Abbott knew it was an onion. He knew he was in public. He knew television cameras were on him and the press gallery was watching. Nevertheless, he persisted. He chowed down on that onion with an absence of shame not seen in an Australian prime minister since Edmund Barton unzipped and did his elephant impression in the House of Representatives.

Nobody quite knew how to react to Abbott's revolting act. There was no precedent for it, in Australia or anywhere else. No US president had ever publicly eaten a raw onion. No British prime minister had either. No European monarch had, even though most of them were clinically insane. Neither experience nor historical awareness could help us understand how to respond to a prime minister who had gone so far off the rails that he would eat an onion and damn the consequences.

Of course, the PM's enemies had a field day. 'Eating an onion is a pretty good metaphor for the Abbott government overall,' tweeted Labor MP Tim Watts, though he did not elaborate on exactly what he meant. That the government was crazy? That it had no sense of taste? That it didn't know what onions were? It wasn't clear, but it was certainly rather cruel of Watts to stick the boot into a man who was obviously unwell.

Most others responded with kindness and compassion, recognising that when a man eats an onion, it is a cry for help. By September the same year, the Liberal Party had relieved Abbott of the prime ministership in order to allow him to rest and recuperate. Happily, this seemed to work, and as far as we know Tony Abbott has not eaten any onions on camera since.

A happy ending in Australian politics! Now that's rare enough to celebrate.

Running Up That Hill

There are many places in the world that make you go, 'Wow!' There are also many places in the world that make you go, 'Yuck!' But there are relatively few places in the world that make you go, 'What the fuck just happened?' Such a place is Magnetic Hill, in the Flinders Ranges.

When you head to Magnetic Hill, driving along Black Rock Road, you will know you're there because of the huge magnet by the side of the road. Do not be alarmed: this is purely a decorative magnet and will not suck the iron out of your blood like in X-Men. The weirdness here takes a different form.

As well as the big magnet, you will find on Magnetic Hill a sign that instructs you to:

- Turn the ignition off
- Put the car into neutral
- Release your brakes

Upon following these instructions, you will naturally find your car begins to roll. But – and this is very much the point – it will begin to roll *uphill*.

Whaaaaaaaat?

How is this possible? What strange sorcery is at work, so that gravity reverses and pulls objects up rather than down? There's a lot to unpack here.

Some people think the big magnet is what pulls cars uphill, which just goes to show that some people are extremely stupid. In fact, Magnetic

152

Hill is just one example of a 'gravity hill': perplexing phenomena that exist around the world where the laws of physics seem to duck out the back for a smoko, leaving vehicles rolling and water running up instead of down. Sadly, there is a perfectly rational explanation for the mystery of Magnetic Hill, and it does not involve the reversal of gravity: rather, this is one of those oddities that can be explained by the fact that human beings' brains don't work properly.

In general, we can tell whether a road is sloping up or down by reference to the horizon, and to other features around us. But in some places, the horizon can't be seen, meaning we lose a crucial reference point. Also, objects like trees or fences may lean, creating the impression of the ground being at an angle. Without the horizon to orient our visual sense, our hapless ape brains may decide that a road is sloping up when it is actually flat or sloping down. It can also go the other way, where the brain is tricked into thinking an uphill slope is flat, making your walk a lot less pleasant than you expected.

So Magnetic Hill is explained, and there's nothing to worry about. But when you take friends and family out to the hill, there's no need to tell them all this. Just set the car in neutral, let it roll, and watch as their brains leak out their ears. There's no harm in allowing people to believe, every now and then, that there are places in the world where the nature of reality itself has gone mental. It adds a little spice to life – and who knows? Scientists are wrong all the time, and if one day it's discovered that actually gravity hills aren't optical illusions at all but spells placed on the ground by leprechauns, who'll be having the last laugh?

The Rough End

What is your favourite Big Thing? I don't mean, like, do you prefer elephants or the Ministry of Defence? I mean, of the wonderful array of bafflingly large objects scattered around this country for people to gawp at, which is the Big Thing that most rouses your affections?

There are plenty to choose from: the Big Banana, the Big Prawn, the Big Merino, the Big Potato, the Big Lobster ... you could write a whole book just on Australia's Big Things. In fact, people have done just that, and without wanting to blow my own trumpet, none of their books were as good as this one.

But in this one, there is only room to wax lyrical about one Big Thing, and so let us examine what I like to think of as the Grandaddy of Big Things – the Elvis of Big, if you will* – the Big Pineapple.

One of the greatest things about the Big Pineapple is that it's *really* big. It has this over, for example, the Big Banana, which while very big for a banana doesn't have the truly epic scale of the Big Pineapple. While the Big Banana could definitely crush your car if it fell out of a Big Banana Tree onto it, the Big Pineapple is on another level: it is the kind of pineapple that can make a person think that fruit has become a god.

The Big Pineapple was built in 1971 at Woombye on the Sunshine Coast. As a marker advertising the adjoining plantation, it immediately achieved its desired effect, viz. telling people, 'Oi! There are pineapples here!'

---

* Elvis was quite a Big Thing himself by the end, of course.

The other great thing about the Big Pineapple is that it's not just a big pineapple – if indeed you could ever refer to a big pineapple as 'just' a big pineapple, given how truly wonderful the very idea of a big pineapple is. But anyway, the point is that the Big Pineapple comes with an entire thrilling pineappley complex surrounding it: a wonderful place to take the kids and leave them in the car to play on their phones while you go exploring.

Set on 165 hectares of pure excitement, the Big Pineapple complex includes pineapple plantations, subtropical rainforests, a restaurant, shops, a koala enclosure, a lagoon and much more.* There is also the jewel in the crown of the Big Pineapple, apart from the actual Big Pineapple: the Pineapple Train.

On the Pineapple Train you can cruise in comfort around the whole complex, taking in the sights and learning about the reality of life in a fruit-themed tourist attraction. Or, rather, you could do so, and you hopefully will be able to again, but at time of writing the Pineapple Train was closed for maintenance. It is uncertain when it will return to service, as it can be difficult to source pineapple parts.

Unfortunately, you can't go inside the Big Pineapple at the moment either. When I was a nipper, my family went to the Big Pineapple and viewed all kinds of fascinating exhibits about pineapples. These days you have to admire the mighty structure from the outside only. And mighty it is: sixteen metres of fibreglass on a steel frame that looks good enough to eat – albeit you would never try to, for that would be disrespectful to the grandeur rising to the sky before you.

The Big Pineapple is a magnificent part of Australia's heritage. It reminds us simultaneously of the potential of humanity to create monumental beauty, of the value of effective marketing and of the importance of a healthy diet. But more than anything, it is perhaps the most perfect of manifestations of that divine spark within us all: that divine spark that is represented, to greater or lesser extent, in all our Big

---

* Okay, maybe not *much* more. A bit more.

Things. The divine spark that whispers in our souls, 'Hey! Why not build a big frigging pineapple? What's stopping you?'

Nothing is stopping us, except our own timidity. Thank God that in 1971 that timidity was overcome, to spectacular effect.

Pyramid Scheme

The country with the most pyramids in the world is Sudan. The country with the tallest pyramid in the world is Egypt. The country with the biggest pyramid by volume in the world is Mexico. But, ladies and gentlemen, I hereby humbly submit that the country with the weirdest pyramid in the world is Australia.

The Ballandean Pyramid is located near Ballandean, in the Granite Belt of the Darling Downs in southern Queensland. It is quite near a series of natural rock formations called The Pyramids, which is needlessly confusing and something that definitely needs to be sorted out by someone asap.

The Ballandean Pyramid is most definitely *not* a natural rock formation. Indeed, few rock formations throughout history have been less natural. Queensland is not a normal place for pyramids to be. They don't quite fit in with the overall decor of the place. Big pineapples? Sure, that's as Queensland as can be. Pyramids? Not so much. Which is why the man who built the Ballandean Pyramid was such a visionary, an artiste with a willingness to defy convention that is rarely seen nowadays.

This man is Stewart Morland, owner of Henty Estate, a vineyard that up until the early 2000s was known in the area mainly for its complete lack of pyramids. One day Morland was mooching around the estate, squishing grapes or whatever, when he suddenly had a startling revelation: there was a big bunch of rocks lying around on his land.

The rocks were plentiful, and they were big. The Granite Belt is well named: it is full of granite, and if you pick a bit of it up you can really belt someone with it. Stewart Morland sat down among his vines and had a good long think about what to do with his rocks. This already shows the mettle of the man: most of us are pretty happy to do nothing with our rocks, but Stewart was simply not the kind of guy who just leaves rocks be.

Stewart's friend Peter Watters wandered along and noticed the rocks. 'What are you going to do with those rocks,' Peter asked in that jocular way of his, 'build a pyramid?'

Stewart leapt up as if electrified. 'You're damn right I am!' he yelped, and quickly called up local contractor Ken Stubberfield. 'Ken,' he cried. 'I've got a bunch of rocks. I will pay you a *thousand dollars** to make them into a pyramid.'

'Sure,' Ken replied. 'I've got nothing better to do.' And the rest is history.

Today the Ballandean Pyramid stands proudly as Australia's only real pyramid, as far as I know, and I am certainly not going to check. It took Ken Stubberfield eight months to build, weighs 7500 tonnes, stands 15 metres tall and is 30 metres wide at the base. This should give you some idea of just how many rocks were lying around Stewart Morland's property. It's a wonder there was any room for the grapes.

It is a truly magnificent structure, easily visible from Jacobson's Lane, Ballandean. It is forbidden for the public to climb the pyramid for any reason, but of course this prohibition carries within it its own loophole: if you do climb it, nobody is allowed to come up and get you. So feel free (as long as you're not planning to come back down).

More than anything, the Ballandean Pyramid is a wonderful testament to the magic and mystery of the human species. Pyramids in other lands have been built for many reasons: as tombs, as tributes to the gods, as astronomical markers. But only Australia has a pyramid that was built purely for the hell of it. That's something we can all be proud of.

---

* In the early 2000s this was a lot of money.

Billy Runs Out of Puff

It's easy to laugh at Billy Snedden. So let's get to it. In many ways, Snedden was the archetypal Australian politician: staid, serious and dull enough to bring anyone forced to endure his company to tears. But the man had hidden depths, which were sadly only revealed upon his death.*

Up until his death, Billy Snedden had been quite active in the living community. He had been a member of parliament for twenty-eight years and had served as both minister for labour and treasurer, before becoming leader of the Liberal Party in opposition between 1972 and 1975, fighting the good fight against Gough Whitlam's attempts to build a socialist utopia, and losing the job just before the Liberals were blessed by the Dismissal. After this, Snedden served as speaker of the House of Representatives from 1976 to 1983, leaving parliament when the Fraser government was defeated.

Although plagued by ill health in his retirement, Snedden remained active as chairman of the Melbourne Football Club, a director of the Victorian Football League and a loyal supporter of the Liberal Party. This was not the only thing he did in defiance of his ill health, and time was to show that perhaps, if he'd been a tad less active, he could've benefited by it. And thus let us cut to the chase.

Billy Snedden had two sons and two daughters, and that was his first mistake. Or, rather, just one of them was his first mistake: his son Drew. If it hadn't been for Drew, the unfortunate events of 27 June 1987 may

---

* Much like Harold Holt – although it would be very crass to make a 'hidden depths' joke about Holt, wouldn't it?

never have happened – although with a pants man like Snedden, you never can tell.

That was the date of the election campaign launch of John Howard, and Snedden left the function in high spirits because he didn't know how the election was going to turn out. Full of beans and certain other substances, the happy Liberal headed for the Rushcutters Bay Travelodge, the classiest accommodation available in 1980s Sydney. But he did not go alone.*

Snedden was accompanied to the motel by a good friend: his son Drew's ex-girlfriend. This, Drew later declared, was 'a coincidence', although one suspects that perhaps it was not that much of a coincidence. Who would've suspected the stuffy old Tory leader from the 1970s would be the type to go about scooping up his son's exes? And yet it was perfectly understandable: if you're on an adrenaline high from a banging do with the Howard posse, you're naturally going to be looking for a wild time with a young lady – and what better way to find young ladies than to thumb through your youngster's address book?

It could've been such a beautiful story: old man retires from politics, scores with hot girl, learns true meaning of happiness. Instead it became a disturbing cautionary tale: old man retires from politics, scores with hot girl, has fatal heart attack. The Snedden legend was cut off – in a very real sense – in its prime.

'SNEDDEN DIED ON THE JOB' blared the headline of the *Truth* newspaper, in its typically sensitive way. *The Sydney Morning Herald* reported that Snedden had died while wearing a condom, and that 'it was loaded' – which phrasing united the nation in a simultaneous cry of 'Yuck'.

It was a sad end ... but on the other hand, who among us does not hope that if we have to go, we go in just that way? Not in exactly that way, of course – none of us is hoping to pop off in a Travelodge – but in a general sense, we all want to die doing what we love, and Billy Snedden definitely did that.

---

* Frankly, if he'd been going to the Rushcutters Bay Travelodge alone, this would be an even sadder story.

'I'm sure the old man went out happy,' said Drew Snedden. 'Anyone would be proud to die on the job.'

Whether 'proud' is exactly the right word here is unimportant – the point is that when the son of a great man says we should celebrate the fact his father died while penetrating said son's ex-girlfriend, we should listen. And we should reflect on whether, like Billy Snedden, we are truly living *our* best lives?

Now We're Cooking

Australia is a country full of tourist attractions, from the Sydney Harbour Bridge to Newcastle KFC. But although attractions abound in this country, there have always been those who've insisted that we simply don't have enough, and that it is vital we import some from overseas if we are to maintain our reputation as a place where people can go to look at things.

And so we come to Captain James Cook. Captain Cook was one of the greatest of all Australians, an achievement made all the more noteworthy for the fact that he was actually English and died before the word 'Australia' was even invented. As all schoolchildren know, Captain Cook not only 'discovered' Australia but also won the battle of Gallipoli almost single-handed, so it's fitting that some kind of memorial should stand here in the country that he never really knew existed.

The story of Cooks' Cottage begins with Cook's parents. James Cook was notable among 18th-century navigators in that he had not one but two parents. In 1755 these parents, being slaves to convention, decided to build a house and live in it. At some point during the next couple of decades, their son James probably visited them there. And thus was an epic story spawned.

In 1933, all of the Cooks were dead. The owner of the cottage at this time, finding it a bit smelly, decided to sell it, but made it a condition of the sale that the cottage remain in England. Is it just me or is this a pretty weird condition to put on a house sale? Don't most people, when they sell houses, just kind of assume the house is going to stay more or less where it is? You get the feeling this lady had definitely received a tip-off from someone.

The Australian industrialist and philanthropist Russell Grimwade* came to the cottage owner and made a suggestion. 'When you think about it,' Russ said, 'isn't Australia basically just another part of England?' As the owner was considering this, Grimwade added, 'Oh, and by the way, I will give you more than double the asking price.' At this, the owner agreed that, yes, Australia, as part of the British Empire, was basically as English as tea and genocide, and he told Russell that he was free to take the cottage.

So it was that Russell Grimwade got to fulfil his long-held and extremely odd dream: to pull Cooks' Cottage into little pieces and ship it to Australia. Why did he want to do this? Nobody knows. He just occasionally had these funny little ideas, and his family and friends didn't like to say anything.

Cooks' Cottage – which let's remember was called Cooks' Cottage because Captain Cook's parents lived in it, not because Captain Cook ever did – was placed into 253 cases and 40 barrels** and put on the ship *Port Dunedin*. It was put back together in Melbourne, where in October 1934 Grimwade presented it to the people of Victoria as a gift for the centenary of the settlement of Melbourne. 'Uh ... yeah ... thanks,' the people of Victoria said uncertainly.

Several years later the Lego corporation began manufacturing its interlocking plastic bricks. I leave it up to you to decide who stole whose idea here.

Today Cooks' Cottage remains a popular tourist attraction, depending on how you define the word 'popular'. Visitors can explore the little house, enjoying a variety of antiques and accoutrements that did not belong to the Cooks but are sort of the same as the stuff they might have had. Also the guides are dressed in period gear, so you can have a bit of a laugh at the things people will do for money. There is also a cottage garden, which

---

* Founder of the Russell Grimwade Prize, which you will naturally have heard of.

** A lot of the cottage turned out to be made of wine.

is information potentially of interest to someone.

Cooks' Cottage is one of Australia's weirdest historical destinations. Not that it's strange to preserve the home of a significant historical figure so future generations can see it. But it's definitely strange to preserve the home of the parents of a significant historical figure, break it up, sail it around the world, then rebuild it in a different country so future generations can see it. Nothing you see in Cooks' Cottage will ever be as fascinating as pondering the mentality of the man who said, 'That's a pretty house. Let's take it on tour.'

Getting to the Bottom of Things

There are many interesting things to see in the historic town of Richmond, Tasmania. You can view the picturesque old colonial bridge, where resides one of the state's most distinguished ghosts.* You can stuff yourself with sugar at the wonderfully well-stocked candy store.

Or you can go look at some poo.

The Pooseum – the hilarious pun in the name capturing its unique mixture of whimsy and disgustingness – is a museum dedicated to all things faeces. You may question the need for such an institution, but then if we didn't have things just because we didn't need them, there wouldn't be a Tasmania in which to have a Pooseum in the first place.

The Pooseum was created by Karin Koch, an event manager who one day found out that there is a species of caterpillar that can launch its excrement up to 1.5 metres from itself. Most of us, when we learn this fact, are able to move on with our lives, but the fact haunted Karin. She found herself unable to break free of the idea that, with fascinating facts about poo out there to be learned, it was her responsibility to bring them to light.

And so was born the Pooseum, a place where people can go to find out about animal droppings and the unproven allegation that they are in some way important to our lives.

'Humans too often feel embarrassed talking about bowel movements,' Karin Koch has written, although there is a fairly well-supported counter-thesis that states that humans don't feel embarrassed

---

* See *100 Tales from Australia's Most Haunted Places*, Affirm Press, 2022, thank you very much.

often enough talking about bowel movements.

Some say the Pooseum is the weirdest museum in Australia. Others say that it's merely the most unpleasant. Either way, it's certainly an experience you won't get at more conventional edutainment venues, which is a selling point as far as we can tell.

At the Pooseum you can learn about poo via more than fifty information panels and forty videos. Seriously, you can. If you really really want to, you can absolutely do that. You can watch forty videos about poo. They will let you. There is of course a kids' corner, which seems a little redundant. If this entire thing wasn't built purely for the amusement of children, it is very difficult to justify. You can also see models of various animals' digestive systems and, of course – crowning glory of the Pooseum – view actual carefully preserved stools from numerous different species.

From these diverse exhibits you will learn a lot, including:

- Why poo doesn't always smell bad
- How animals use poo to their advantage
- How people make electricity using poo
- How long it takes an elephant to do a poo
- The limits of your own mental fortitude

The Pooseum is possibly Australia's greatest example of Pobjie's Law:* if there is a thing, there is a museum about that thing. Around the world, you'll find museums of food, of garbage, of torture, of dirt and of penises. But we are indeed fortunate that here in Australia we don't have to go far to find a museum that is entirely shit. So to speak.

Like many great Australians, Karin Koch had a dream. It was a gross dream and a dream that many wish she had never allowed to see the light of day, but a dream it was, and if you hold your nose, it just might be possible to admire that.

That doesn't mean you should actually go, though.

---

* ™Ben Pobjie 2023.

Where There's a Wills, There's a Burke

There is a lot that was weird about the legendary doomed Burke and Wills expedition. The fact that a major mission of exploration was launched under the charge of a man who was very bad at exploring is not necessarily one of them: this was, after all, the Golden Age of Idiot Explorers.* The British Empire, having built itself on the principle of putting men in positions for which they were hopelessly unqualified, had yet to see any reason to change the policy. So allowing Robert O'Hara Burke, a policeman with no exploring experience, to lead the expedition made perfect sense, as did the fact that, under Burke's leadership, the expedition failed and seven men died.

Second-in-command was the British surveyor and surgeon William John Wills, and it was the conclusion of Burke and Wills's story that was truly bizarre, finishing a fiasco with an episode of dark farce.

Burke and Wills left Royal Park in Melbourne in their attempt to cross the continent from south to north on 20 August 1860. One wagon broke down before they left Royal Park, two more broke down at Essendon on Melbourne's edge and they spent the first month or so throwing large amounts of their supplies away to lighten the loads. Despite this, by April 1861, a forward group of the expedition composed of Burke, Wills, John King and Charles Gray had managed to get to the Gulf of Carpentaria and the northern coast of the continent – well, not really, because of swampland, but almost – with only a

---

* See the earlier chapter on Hume and Hovell.

moderate-to-severe level of misery, stupidity and death.

But all these things ratcheted up when it came to the return journey. After reaching the Top End, Burke turned back to return to Cooper Creek, where he'd left the rest of his men, pausing along the way to beat Gray for being sick, and subsequently to bury Gray for being dead.

Burke had instructed the Cooper Creek party to wait there for thirteen weeks, but they actually waited for eighteen, having been tipped-off by Wills that Burke had no idea what he was doing. However, with food running low, everyone getting scurvy because Burke had forgotten to pack any orange juice, and the increasing likelihood that Burke et al. were never coming back, they decided to go home before they all died as well. Before leaving, they buried some provisions and carved a message on a tree so Burke and Wills could find the supplies, in case they did return.

Which, of course, they did. In fact, Burke, Wills and King reached Cooper Creek just *nine hours* after the rest of the men had left for home. After resting and consuming the buried provisions, the three men decided to travel 240 kilometres south-west to a cattle station near the aptly named Mount Hopeless. Or, rather, one of the men decided to do this. Wills and King had wanted to do something less suicidal, but Burke had overruled them, and the other two, being Englishmen with a strong sense of duty to obey obvious cretins, did as he said.

They left a message buried in the same place as the provisions, telling anyone who came back to Cooper Creek where they had gone. However, in yet another of Robert O'Hara Burke's wacky tactical masterstrokes, they did not change the mark on the tree in any way.

Accordingly, when the rest of the expedition met up with a relief party bringing supplies north, and together they returned to Cooper Creek in the hope of rescuing Burke's party, they saw no evidence that anyone had been there. In a stroke almost as brilliant as one of Burke's, the others didn't think to dig at the tree to check whether the provisions had been disturbed, instead shrugging their shoulders and going home again.

So to recap the sequence:

Group One leaves.

Group Two waits for them.

Group Two leaves.

Group One comes back just after Group Two leaves.

Group One leaves.

Group Two comes back.

Group Two doesn't check to see whether Group One came back.

Group Two leaves.

There's an elegance to the sheer imbecility of it all.

Having decided to cross the desert to Mount Hopeless, Burke, Wills and King discovered they didn't have enough water to do so, and therefore had to stay near the creek. It occurred to them at this point that the expedition had developed a definite theme, and it was not a pleasant one. Exhausted and malnourished, they sat by the creek and awaited the inevitable. The local Yandruwandha people gave them some food, but they stopped doing so when Burke shot at one of them, reasoning that if he'd stuffed everything up consistently so far, why stop now?

Eventually, Burke and Wills succumbed to starvation and thirst. John King managed to meet up again with the Yandruwandha and, without Burke around to shoot at them, survived with their help.

Maybe the weirdest thing of all is how revered and respected the Burke and Wills saga tends to be in Australian history. From the comical beginning to the depressingly pointless end, the whole thing was a disaster, and a valuable lesson to all: you too can go down in history if only you have the courage to be a complete moron and die.

Morrison's Multiplicity

Scott Morrison is* a man of extraordinary talents. As a young lad in Bronte,** he used to look up at the night sky, take in the glittering blanket of stars and dream that one day he would complete a demographical analysis of Christian Brethren assemblies. The odds were against him, but somehow that dream came true.

Morrison had other dreams too, but as he grew older it became more and more obvious to him that although a man might dream big, he has only a finite span of years in which to fulfil those dreams. Even as he ticked off the items on his bucket list – become managing director of Tourism Australia, get fired as managing director of Tourism Australia, become immigration minister, buy a tiny boat to put in his office, become treasurer, make Malcolm Turnbull cry – he knew that the list was long and life was short.

So it was that when he became prime minister, Morrison bethought himself, 'Well, this is all very fine, but where does this leave my lifelong ambitions to also be health minister, resources minister, finance minister and home affairs minister?' Not only was the prime ministership not helping him achieve these goals, it was actively preventing him from doing so.

At this point, two significant things happened: first, Morrison saw the word 'multi-tasking' in a copy of *Take 5* magazine; and second, the Covid-19 pandemic devastated the entire world. Both of these things proved to be godsends for the prime minister, whose energetic ways had

---

*   Or, depending on when you're reading this, was.

** A suburb of Sydney named for its unusual number of madwomen in attics.

led him to be dubbed 'the human French bulldog'.

Morrison, mind ticking into overdrive, realised that the pandemic provided him a unique opportunity to live his best life. If, on the pretext of preparing for a coronavirus-struck cabinet, he appointed himself as all the ministers that he wanted to be, he could also kill two birds with one stone: simultaneously achieving both his ambition to be multiple ministers and his ambition to play a clever prank on the governor-general.

And so it was that Prime Minister Scott Morrison made himself resources minister, finance minister, home affairs minister, health minister and, because he'd quite enjoyed it the first time, also treasurer again. How did one man have the energy to perform all these roles while also carrying out his duties as prime minister? Quite simple: he ensured he was always fresh and alert by sleeping fifteen hours a day.

A lot of people criticised Morrison for these actions, but these critics ignore several key points:

- If five cabinet ministers all died of Covid on the same day, and Morrison had not already given himself their jobs, the country would've been paralysed for up to two hours.
- Morrison deliberately kept the self-appointments a secret so that people would not lavishly praise him as a national hero, which was incredibly selfless of him.
- Nobody knows who the resources minister is anyway, so does it really matter?
- Who are we to deny a man his dream?

Nobody had ever been five ministers plus prime minister at the same time before, and at time of writing nobody has since, although it really only just happened, so don't assume anything. You could call Scott Morrison a trailblazer. Or you could call him a wild maverick with the guts to do what's right, no matter what makes sense. But I prefer to view him simply as a man with a dream: a strange, strange dream that, come hell or high water or democracy, was going to come true.

If you can't find inspiration in that, maybe it's *you* who needs to take a good long look inside your black heart.

The Ineffability of Yeast

Is there anything more Australian than Vegemite? Racism and mammals with multiple vaginas? Yes, perhaps. But when it comes to yeast extracts, there is none that can claim to be more inextricably entwined with the Aussie way of life than the thick brown goo that millions of us smear over our stomach lining every morning.

Vegemite was invented by Cyril Callister in 1919 to deal with the growing mountain of spare yeast that was starting to impinge on Australians' quality of life – and it might be said that the very existence of Vegemite is weird enough to qualify for inclusion in this book. Realising that all good food originates in a laboratory, Callister took a heap of brewers' yeast and severely punished it for its sins. Adding celery and onion extracts and salt, he produced a sticky black paste that was very obviously inedible, but it was after 5pm so he told his bosses he'd done it and went home.

The taste of Vegemite is so unusual that it can only be described by reference to other weird made-up gloops like Marmite or Promite or Cenovis.* Other countries are often baffled by Australians' love affair with Vegemite, but given that in Iceland they eat rotten shark meat, in Turkey they eat tripe soup and in the United Kingdom they elected Boris Johnson prime minister, I don't see what right any of them have to be so freaking judgemental.

Having developed the substance, all Vegemite needed was a name.

---

* A Swiss spread invented to save lives during the fondue famine of the 1870s.

Originally it was called 'pure vegetable extract', but this made people less inclined to eat it and more inclined to burn the shops selling it down. A contest was held to find a catchy name, but nobody could think of one, so they went with 'Vegemite', to signify that it was made with VEGEtables, and that it MITE not be poisonous.

But though Vegemite is a weird food, even weirder have been the various attempts to market it over the years – and the fact that despite these campaigns people keep buying it.

Early on, Vegemite was not selling well, due to the public's knowledge of how it was made. Thus was launched the Kraft company's first vaguely lunatic marketing stab, as they renamed the spread 'Parwill'. Because there was already Marmite, right? You see? If 'Marmite', then 'Parwill'. You see what they did there?

Yeah, so they changed the name back pretty soon.

A slice of luck then befell the makers of Vegemite with the outbreak of World War II. This enabled Kraft to slip Vegemite into the rations of the defence forces, to remind them what they were fighting for. This resulted in terrible shortages of civilian Vegemite, and the snappy ad slogan: 'Vegemite fights with the men up north!* If you are one of those who don't need Vegemite medicinally, then thousands of invalids are asking you to deny yourself of it for the time being.' Amazingly, to this day many people still eat Vegemite despite not needing it medicinally.

Of course, Vegemite really took off with the post-war unleashing of the 'Happy Little Vegemites' ad campaign. With its implicit promise that if people bought Vegemite the children would stop singing, Vegemite quickly overtook foie gras as the nation's favourite spread.

However, as with all wildly popular things, there came a time when it was necessary to change Vegemite for no apparent reason. This led to one of Australia's strangest ever marketing gambits, when Kraft, realising that everyone was pretty happy with the product the way it was, decided to do something about it.

---

* This would've made a great story arc on Game of Thrones.

The result was 'iSnack 2.0', a new spread that combined Vegemite with cream cheese to produce a substance that not only tasted terrible but also had an idiotic name. The name was chosen on the basis that young people in the 21st century love iPhones and iPads, and do not know the difference between electronic devices and food. After an enthusiastic public response along the lines of 'What the hell is wrong with you?', Kraft announced that iSnack 2.0 was dead, only four days after announcing its birth. Instead the new product would be termed 'Vegemite Cheesybite', which is still a terrible name but not so terrible that it would distract consumers from the main point: its awful flavour.

Somehow, despite every obstacle – its taste, its appearance, the numerous advertising campaigns clearly concocted by internal industrial saboteurs – Vegemite thrives to this day. Studies estimate that over eight million Australians spread Vegemite on their toast every morning, and almost half of them go on to eat it. If Australia is a weird country, Vegemite is the symbol of that weirdness: a shining example of this country's steadfast refusal to be normal. Makes you proud.

The Yowie Today

It may come as a surprise that the public enthusiasm for yowies remains as high as ever – indeed, recent polls have seen yowies outpointing eighty per cent of LNP candidates in marginal seats. The home of modern-day yowie lore is Dean Harrison's Australian Yowie Research, which can be found at yowiehunters.com.au. The site states that 'files begin in the late 1700s to this current day', and the web design makes it easy to believe that the site first went online in the 18th century.

Head to this website if you need to either report a yowie sighting yourself* or read about others. For example, you could learn about the sighting at Mulgoa in 1994. Two friends who had been for a bushwalk were driving home when 'a monstrous, black, upright creature appeared on the track up ahead'.

It's easy to imagine the two friends' terror: nobody is ever really prepared for the day when a monstrous black upright creature appears in front of them. To make things worse, not only was the beast upright and ten feet tall but it 'took up the width of the track' and had no neck. Also, 'it had no definite form', which does raise the possibility that this thing was less a yowie and more a low cloud. Then again, who knows? Just because all the animals currently known to zoology have had definite forms doesn't mean yowies have to.

The two friends quickly wound up their windows, looked up and saw that the yowie had vanished. In the words of one of the friends,

---

* Go on. I dare you.

'For something that big to disappear is strange,' which is both true and somewhat suggestive that it was, indeed, a cloud.

A more recent yowie sighting was at Bara in 2018, when a man driving on Bara Road to Mudgee saw something that 'looked like a caveman/ Neanderthal' standing in the road holding a chicken. This confirms speculation that yowies enjoy a) standing in roads and b) chicken.

The Bara monster was around two metres tall, covered with thick coarse hair, had long arms and, like the Mulgoa creature, no neck. It was 'barrel chested, no discernible waist, sort of a cone head or egg shape, broad shoulders, flat nose'. It's a relief to learn that there are yowies that do have definite forms, at least, although possibly the Bara sighting goes too far the other way: while the Mulgoa yowie might've been a cloud, the Bara one may just have been a really ugly bloke.

If you head over to the AYR website, you'll find loads of testimonials like these two. In the face of such overwhelming evidence, it's difficult to deny the fact that yowies definitely exist, or at the very least that there are lots of people who have seen a weird thing in the bush. From these accounts we can deduce that the yowie is ten or six feet tall or somewhere in between, covered in long or short hair that is black or brown or reddish, walks upright or on all fours, has no neck, smells bad, and is either an ape, a caveman, an ancient spirit or something else. There are many tales attesting to all of these facts. So many. Seriously. It will make you so tired.

Whether the persistence of yowie sightings is proof of the monster's existence or simply of the enormous amount of spare time available to people under late capitalism, there's no doubt the stories enrich our culture and keep the desperate hope alive that somewhere out there, there is something interesting happening.

Blood on the *Boyd*

Since time immemorial, wise heads have agreed that one of the weirdest things anyone can do is go from Australia to New Zealand. Unless one is doing so in order to play rugby, there seems no good explanation for such behaviour. You don't necessarily need the threat of murder to prevent you from being so mad and reckless, but if ever a friend of yours expresses a desire to go wandering off across the Tasman Sea, it's probably a good idea to remind that friend of the Boyd Massacre, the day that a jaunt to the Land of the Long White Cloud proved incredibly ill-advised for the crew of the brigantine *Boyd*.

The *Boyd* had transported convicts to New South Wales, but its past employment in bringing torturous misery to the most marginalised and wretched of society gave no hint that its fortunes would take a depressing turn. After dropping its unhappy prisoners off in Sydney, in 1809 the brigantine turned south-east and headed for Whangaroa, on New Zealand's Northland Peninsula, where the sailors were to gather kauri spars, once they had found out what kauri spars were. There were about seventy people on board, including a young man named Te Ara – or, as the crew, who had extremely limited cultural literacy, called him, George. Te Ara was the son of a Māori chief, but was expected to work his passage on the *Boyd* in a manner most unbefitting of royalty. The treatment of a Māori chief's son as a common deckhand was a powder keg ready to explode, as were the several powder kegs on board.

Whether Te Ara refused to work because he was a chief's son or because he was feeling under the weather (or because he was wrongly accused of spoon theft, or because he was pulling the sailors' pigtails), one way or another the boy blotted his copybook, and Captain John Thompson ordered him flogged as punishment. Te Ara was tied to a capstan* and whipped with a cat-o'-nine-tails.** This was momentarily satisfying for Captain Thompson, but he would live to see his desire for short-term pleasure conflict with his long-term life goals – for example, his goal to have a life.

When the *Boyd* landed at Whangaroa Bay, Te Ara, outraged at his treatment, told his tribe just what the white men had been doing to him. To the men of the *Boyd*, it had seemed a minor thing: English people were always being whipped for minor infractions, and many of them had come to quite enjoy it. Māori people, on the other hand, had strict rules about how a chief's son should be treated, and one of those rules was that if white people flogged him, those white people were seriously going to get it.

First, the Māori told Captain Thompson they could show him where the best kauri trees were, and led him and four of his men to the entrance of the Kaeo River, where they killed them all with clubs and axes. Some of the killers then put on the victims' clothes, while another took the bodies home to eat. Yes, you read that correctly.

The disguised Māori sneaked onto the *Boyd* that night, called their comrades to attack and killed all the crew, before starting in on the passengers, cutting them to pieces on the deck. Survivors escaped along the beach but all but one were run down and murdered. Just five people were spared in the massacre, although one of those was killed and eaten later.

Having finished the killing, the Māori grounded the *Boyd* near their village, ransacked its stores and tried to get its muskets to work. Unfortunately, this exercise was unsuccessful and instead resulted in the explosion of the ship's supply of gunpowder, and the consequent deaths of ten Māori. The ship burnt up and sank down, and that was, in a very

---

* A device consisting of a cap attached to a man called Stan.
** A device consisting of a cat with nine tails.

real sense, the end of the *Boyd*. On the bright side, the mistreatment of Te Ara had very definitely been atoned for, and the Māori and the British could now call it quits.

Except, of course, they didn't. In 1810, sailors from five whaling ships undertook a revenge attack on the village of Te Pahi, a chief who had tried to rescue the survivors of the *Boyd* and whom the sailors had confused with Te Puhi, Te Ara's brother. This wacky mix-up resulted in the deaths of as many as sixty Māori. Realising that he had been mistaken for a leader of the massacre, Te Pahi then attacked Whangaroa and was killed. So, in the end, you might say the whole affair ended absolutely horribly for everyone.

Anyway, you can definitely see now just how bad things can get when people get it into their heads to go to New Zealand.

The Mystical Land of Atlantium

We have already touched on the Principality of Hutt River, a proud nation whose magnificence is only slightly tainted by the fact it never technically existed. Hutt River was a weird occurrence in Australian history, but even weirder is the fact that it is by no means Robinson Crusoe – and in fact if it were Robinson Crusoe, it is difficult to discern exactly what that would even mean. The point is that in founding the Principality of Hutt River, Prince Leonard I seemingly kickstarted a movement, albeit a strange and sort of pathetic one.

One devotee of this movement is George Cruickshank, known to his subjects as George II for reasons which, given he is the first monarch of his country, surpass understanding at this time. George II is the founder of the Empire of Atlantium, an empire founded in his suburban Sydney backyard in 1981 which now covers 0.76 square kilometres in the Lachlan River Valley, making it one of the 21st century's fastest-growing empires.*

Atlantium's Lachlan River holding, known as the Province of Aurora, is, however, only the material geographical manifestation of the empire. It's a self-declared 'secular, pluralistic, liberal, social democratic republican monarchy', so the first thing many people notice about Atlantium is that it makes no sense. But its nonsensicality is just one of Atlantium's fascinating aspects: the truly unique thing about the empire is that, although it claims sovereignty over Aurora, it does not actually have any

---

* Just behind Taylor Swift's.

geographical location. And not in the way that most micronations have no geographical location because they're not real: Atlantium is also not real, but even the people who say it's real don't say it has a location. See what I mean? No, of course not. Neither do I.

Just because there's no physical location doesn't mean it's not a real country, of course. After all, Belgium is a real country, and nobody has ever been able to find it. Atlantium has its own flag, constitution, judicial system and website, and that's enough to make a country in any fair-minded person's estimation.

The point is that to George II and the 3000-odd citizens of the empire, Atlantium is not a place so much as an idea – and they mean this literally, rather than in the phoney dumb way Americans say it about their country. According to the Atlantium website – which is itself a masterpiece of 2003-vintage web design – 'Atlantium recognises that the days of nation-states founded on fixed geographical locations or majority ethnic identities are numbered.' To which one might respond with two observations: 1. If those days are numbered, it is still an extremely large number; and 2. The Atlantium website also says, 'There's nothing funny about Atlantium,' which is untrue to such an overwhelming extent that it casts into doubt everything else the Atlantian government says.

The main point is this: even if you do not reside in the Province of Aurora, or in George Cruickshank's backyard, you can actually become a citizen of Atlantium. All you need to do is fill out the online application and pay the US$25 processing fee, and if you think I'm not doing just that as soon as I finish this chapter, you simply do not know me at all.

Citizens of Atlantium enjoy many benefits, including having Latin as their official language, using a decimal calendar and use of the official Atlantian post office. Most importantly, you will be under the protection of the benevolent George II, who rules his subjects wisely and well, and spends a lot of time sitting in open-topped cars wearing colourful ribbons, which is all you really want from a king.

It's amazing to think that this glorious empire, with its grandeur, pomp and vision for a better world, was born out of one bored teenager's desire to do something stupid in his backyard more than forty years ago. It gives hope to all the people of the world: if Atlantium can make it, anyone can. Even New Zealand!

La-la-la-la Lola

Eliza Rosanna Gilbert, Countess of Landsfeld, was, in the vernacular of the day, quite a gal. Born of prominent Irish gentlefolk in 1821, at an early age she began pursuing her passion for romping around the world messing with people. At the age of sixteen she eloped with an army officer. At the age of twenty-one she left him and took up dancing in Calcutta.* By 1843 she was enthralling audiences in London as Lola Montez, a name which captured the imagination of a world that, at the time, had an extremely easily captured imagination.

Lola danced all around Europe,** getting mixed reviews as a dancer but solid five-star raves for her work as a celebrity mistress. Affairs with Franz Liszt, Alexandre Dumas and King Ludwig I of Bavaria cemented her reputation as that very special kind of woman: the kind that men liked to have sex with. Sadly, after several years of sexy times with Ludwig and unofficially directing Bavarian government policy, Lola was forced to leave Europe as the Bavarian people took exception to both of those things. And so it was off to America, where once again she took the Lola show on the road. She married a journalist, had an affair with a doctor, divorced the journalist, waited for the doctor to be murdered and then buggered off.

Having heard that there was no better place in the world for a passionate Irish-Spanish dancer with saucy outfits and athletic mattress moves than Australia, Lola headed down under in 1855, determined to take the Gold Rush by storm.

---

* Professionally, that is. She wasn't just killing time.
** Again, as her job – it wasn't her form of transport.

Her determination paid off: Lola was an immediate hit in Melbourne with her famous Spider Dance. This was a complicated dance in which Lola would imitate the actions of a spider, during which she would lift her skirts up so as to prove to the audience that her dance was authentic: just like a spider, she was wearing no underwear.

Opinion on the moral propriety of the Spider Dance was divided. The Melbourne *Argus* editorialised: 'We feel called upon to denounce, in terms of unmeasured approbation,* the performances in which that lady last evening figured.' To the disappointment of all *Argus* readers, the editor went on to say, 'We do not intend to enter into details,' but he did add that Montez's display had been 'utterly subversive of all ideas of public morality'.

Lola claimed her right of reply to this attack: 'I throw back with scorn the insinuation of *The Argus* that I in this dance come forward to pander to a morbid taste for indelicate representations.' Strong stuff! Lola angrily averred that the Spider Dance was a traditional Spanish one, and that it had been 'witnessed with delight in Spain by all classes and both sexes, from the Queen to the pensioner'.**

If the response of the respectable press was less than glowing, Lola could take heart in the views of the ordinary man on the street, who was heard to opine, 'Whoa!' and 'Bloody hell!' on the subject of her dancing. Taking heart from this, when the Melbourne box-office takings declined due to the refusal of the stuffy middle classes to come to her show and risk more of an eyeful than they felt ready for, Lola took her dance to the regions, heading out to the goldfields to entertain the diggers, who tended to be somewhat more liberal-minded, or at least more sex-starved.

It was out at the Victorian diggings that Lola Montez performed her most notorious act – even more infamous than showing her bits or manipulating the King of Bavaria to persecute Jesuits. Arriving in Ballarat, she set hearts and groins aflame once again with the Spider Dance, but ruffled the feathers of Henry Seekamp, editor of the *Ballarat Times*.

---

* How you would measure approbation anyway is a mystery.
** The pensioner in question being Mr Eugene Cressborn, retired wool classer.

Whether he was a spiritual brother to the editor of *The Argus* or he just had high standards when it came to spider dances, Seekamp gave Montez a big thumbs-down in his pages.

Lola was outraged. Couldn't she go anywhere without snivelling little newspapermen bitching about her erotic gyrations? A woman could be insulted only so many times, she thought, before she must needs cut loose and show the world what she was made of.* The time for articulate letters to the editor was over: direct action was now called for.

So it was that she bailed up Henry Seekamp in the street outside the Ballarat theatre, and set about him mightily with a horsewhip. It was the first recorded public flogging of a journalist, and tragically also the last. Although a trendsetter in many ways, Lola did not start a craze for whipping editors, even though it would've been the greatest gift she'd given the world.

Seekamp, duly chastened, went back to his office and resolved from now on to never be heard of by almost everyone. Lola, meanwhile, having made her point forcefully, went back to her Spider Dance and reached a pinnacle of artistic achievement in April 1856, when she performed to a wildly enthusiastic crowd in Castlemaine – who she then told to go fuck themselves, which dampened the applause somewhat.

Shortly after alternately wowing and insulting Castlemaine, Lola Montez set sail for America again, her Australian sojourn over. We shall not see her like again. But in these staid and censorious days, when public whippings are rare,** don't you wish she'd come back?

---

* Although obviously she'd already given them a pretty big clue during the Spider Dance.
** But public vulva airings less so.

Moomba Boom

As the saying goes, some are born weird, some achieve weirdness and some have weirdness thrust upon them. And then there is the city of Melbourne, which simply chases after weirdness like a hunter after a man-eating buffalo, never at peace until weirdness has been captured, subdued and absorbed into its very being.

Which is a long-winded way of saying it's time to talk about Moomba.

The origins of the word *Moomba* are somewhat disputed, but it's believed by some linguists to be a word from an Indigenous language meaning 'up your arse' – although when the City of Melbourne decided to name a major cultural festival after it, they thought it meant 'let's get together and have fun'. As it happens, both meanings apply in equally profound ways to the Moomba festival itself. Except for the having fun bit.

The first Moomba was held in 1955. It was a fifteen-day festival intended to celebrate the fact that people in Melbourne had very little going on in their lives. The Church of England attacked Moomba as hedonistic and depraved, but in reality it was nowhere near that good.

These days, Moomba, contrary to popular opinion, is still a thing, but only lasts four days, over the Labour Day weekend in March. This shortening of the timespan has been extremely effective in enabling the people of Melbourne to close their eyes and pretend it's not happening.

There are a lot of weird things about Moomba, even if you don't count the fact that it still exists. One is the Moomba Parade. According to organisers, 'since 1955 this spectacular parade has charmed Melburnians with its fantastical floats, giant puppets, dance troupes and bustling community groups'. To which one cannot help but respond by asking, firstly, who the hell is charmed by community groups, and, secondly, if the numbers were crunched, just what would be the ratio of people charmed by the giant puppets and dance troupes to people terrified by them? Certainly the attractions of the parade run the gamut from 'what the hell is that?' to 'why would anyone spend their time on this?' to 'Oh those poor people'. In the latest Moomba Parade, participants included the Ambulance Victoria Pipes and Drums band – and isn't it good to know part of the emergency services budget is going to this – the Confident Kids Performing Arts School, Folk Group Bulgari and something called 'emotion21' that could be god knows what kind of nightmare. There is also what seems to be every currently operating dance studio in Australia, to the extent that the parade comes off less as a celebration and more as a peculiarly aggressive complaint from several hundred dance students about how badly they've wasted their money.

But if you don't like the parade,* you can catch the inline skating, or the silent disco, or the 'hoops, thighs and buttocks' dance workshop, or the event that is termed simply 'Bees', and involves dressing up and playing with three human-sized bees. Why would anyone want to do any of these things? Only because they have found life to have developed a stale and acrid quality that they can endure no longer. Which is why the festival is held in Melbourne.

There is also the crowning of the 'King and Queen of Moomba', which has been named by UNESCO as the most pointless exercise in human history. Many prominent people have been Moomba Monarchs, although they'll deny it if you ask them. These include Robert Morley, Johnny Famechon, John Farnham, Bert Newton, Cathy Freeman, Lucy Durack, Bert Newton again, Shane Warne, Con the Fruiterer, Mickey Mouse and, perhaps most famously of all, Community and Emergency Services.** The job of the Moomba Monarch is to sit on a parade float for a bit and

---

* And I use the word 'if' loosely.
** All of these really were Kings or Queens of Moomba, and no, there is no rational explanation.

then go home and tearfully attempt to scrub the shame from their skin.

Should you wish to experience the magic and wonder of Moomba yourself, it's easy enough: head down to Melbourne in March and wait for the horror to begin. Just don't be surprised if you find yourself somewhat alone.

The Batsmen's Boardroom Brawl

Cricket has always been a sport with an uneasy tension at its centre: a game capable of arousing passions far beyond the human norm, it nevertheless has striven always to cultivate an atmosphere of decorum and gentlemanly fair play. In recent years standards have slipped somewhat, to the extent that not only are women allowed to wear trousers while playing, but Test players have numbers on their backs like common rugbyites. This is fairly disgusting, but it's important to remember that the Good Old Days of cricket, while involving more genteel on-field proceedings, also involved a certain amount of off-field bloodshed.

This is not a metaphor: there was a time when emotions ran so high in the stately boardroom of Australian cricket that actual human blood spattered the fittings.

It all began with the devious machinations of one Peter McAlister. McAlister had played eight Test matches for Australia, displaying a talent that many good judges described as almost existing. However, what he lacked in playing ability McAlister made up for in being a complete douchebag, and other players developed a well-justified loathing of him, based on three factors:

- He was a jerk to pretty much everybody.
- He was a suck-up to the Board of Control, and had wheedled his way into being sent on the 1909 Ashes Tour for the purpose of spying on the rest of the team.

- On that tour, as chairman of selectors, he had appointed himself vice-captain, ahead of others who knew which end to hold a bat by.

Thus, the relationship between McAlister and the human race was already at quite a low ebb when the selectors met to pick the team for the fourth Test of the 1912 season. It had been further soured by McAlister's bitchy comments, in private and in public, about the Australian captain, Clem Hill, who unlike McAlister was a bona fide legend of the game. Moreover, the board and the players were already feuding over the choice of team manager for the impending 1912 tour of England: the players wanting to choose their own manager and the board wanting to appoint their choice, in order to make sure the players didn't do anything outrageous like earn a living wage.

It was amid this atmosphere that the selection panel met. Things got off to a bad start immediately, with McAlister telling Hill that his captaincy in the previous two Tests had sucked. Hill responded that McAlister was 'no judge of cricket', which was an observation fairly well supported by the evidence. McAlister retorted that he himself had been quite a super captain, to which Hill shot back that perhaps McAlister should captain the team himself – not that ridiculous an idea, for although McAlister was retired, his batting output was only slightly worse than it had been when he was playing.

The heat kept rising. 'You are the worst captain in living memory,' snapped McAlister.

Hill stood up, the steely forearms which had made his cut and pull shots the envy of the cricketing world twitching beneath his shirtsleeves, eager for a good workout. 'You've been asking for a punch all night,' he snarled, 'and I'll give you one.'

He was as good as his word. Lunging forward, he landed a stinging blow across McAlister's chops. McAlister responded with a hefty swipe of his own, and the game was most definitely afoot.

The pair grappled with each other, staggering around the room for a good twenty minutes, which frankly sounds exhausting. Hill, a robust man of great strength, and of course still an active professional athlete, was generally agreed to have come out on top: in fact, at one point the other officials present had to restrain the skipper from hurling McAlister out of the third-floor window. Opinion is now divided over whether they did the right thing or not.

Finally Hill left, with McAlister on the floor, covered in blood, shouting, 'Come back and fight, you coward ... It's only a flesh wound ... I'll bite your leg off,' and so on. The meeting continued without further incident, and Hill was selected in the team and remained the captain – which may be the oddest part of the whole incident.

These days, when players are routinely expected to be willing to shed their own blood for the team cause, it's strange to think there was a time when players were willing to shed other people's blood for it. But it also makes one slightly wistful, as most would agree that Australian cricket in the 21st century could do with a few more players willing to punch selectors in the face and/or throw them out a window. So let's salute Clem Hill for his principles and his courage: we will not see his like again.

The Singular Saga of the Scareships

There was something about 1909 in Australia. While other countries sedately dealt with mundane matters like Panamanian independence and the beatification of Joan of Arc,* Australia leant fully into the bizarre. Not only did the year see Australian rugby league's first one-team grand final *and* the creation of the Australian Capital Territory, which has been the source of vast amounts of rich natural weirdness over the last century or so, it was also the year in which this country was gripped by the terror of the 'scareships'.

Scareships – the name derives from the fact that they were airships which were scary – were reported as having been sighted over other nations, but the tone of the Australian press had been entirely dismissive. Scareships, we believed, were the sort of nonsense embraced by credulous fools elsewhere. Here in God's Own Country we were made of sterner, more realistic stuff.

But as it turned out, we were made of the same stuff as everyone else. On 9 August 1909, Melbourne's *Argus* newspaper reported that the Reverend B Cozens** had seen something most mysterious at Kangaroo Ground,*** east of Melbourne. Cozens testified that he saw 'two beautiful revolving lights high up in the air above the Dandenong Ranges'. The lights whirled, spun, rose and fell, changing colour from white to red to blue in quite a patriotic manner. The lights were also seen by Cozens'

---

* Took you bloody long enough, Catholics.

** An important detail given members of the clergy never lie.

*** So named because the local kangaroos tended to be on the ground.

neighbour J Swain, a reliable witness despite not having a first name, and by other *Argus* readers from elsewhere in Melbourne's surrounds.

You could easily write the whole thing off as just another symptom of the insanity known to afflict all residents of Victoria, were it not for the fact that the very same night a similar eldritch visitation was experienced by people in the famously sensible state of New South Wales. At Moss Vale, south-west of Sydney, the locals gathered in the main street and gaped in wonder at the huge object hovering in the sky, a bright light reflecting from its shiny surface. Even stranger, thousands of miles distant, at Bundaberg, Queensland, folks spotted what was said to look like 'a balloon floating in midair with a powerful lamp suspended from it'.

Now, a balloon with a lamp hanging off it is not necessarily a supernatural entity, but in 1909, much like today, seeing a massive lamp-bearing balloon floating above you could not be said to be in any way normal.

After the sightings of 9 August, scareship fever gripped the nation. From every corner of the country came more reports of eerie craft with menacing lights bobbing about the night sky. A 'lighted airship' was seen over Victoria Park, Perth, shortly after lights were seen whizzing about above Pingelly, 150 kilometres to the south-east. White lights were spotted over Zeehan, in Tasmania, and to put the seal on the whole bizarre business came a report from Bulli, on the New South Wales south coast.

The Adelaide *Advertiser* of 17 August, sticking its nose in non-Adelaide business for some reason, reported that 'several inquisitive residents of Bulli' had the previous evening peered through telescopes at the lights floating above their town, and seen something quite remarkable, to wit:

It looked like a distant world, on which they could plainly see a group of gigantic creatures illuminated and adorned by a celestial radiance quite foreign to anything on this earth. They appeared to be trying to signal to the earth, and one in particular, who seemed to have control of the others, was so enthusiastic about it that he wanted to jump right off to this planet, whilst the remainder of the group were doing their best to restrain him.

The paper said that the residents of Bulli believed themselves to be the recipients of a visit by Martians. Today, in less superstitious and/or stupid times, we have a decision to make. Either 1909 saw Australia – and other nations – visited by beings from another world, possibly including one reckless individual who really wanted to come down for a closer look; or 1909 saw a bunch of idiots making up dumb stories about lights in the sky.

I know which version I'd rather believe. How about you?

Mowing Down Tyranny

Many of us over the years have said to Jim Penman, 'Jim, you are the king of lawn care!' But how often have you wished that Jim could also be the actual king of us all?

Never, of course. Nobody would ever wish this. It is completely mad. And yet, the line between genius and madness is a thin one, and one which the founder of Jim's Mowing defiantly straddles with his every utterance.

The first thing to know about Jim Penman is that his name is not Jim. His name is David, but he rightly believed nobody would engage with a business called David's Mowing, so he transformed himself into Jim. Thus he became so rich that he could publish books about how changes in our genes have doomed Western civilisation to destruction.* But it was in 2023 that Jim Penman proved that there was more to him than grass and race science, and achieved what some might say is his true final form. For it was then that Jim Penman finally seceded, declared independence and made himself King.

The mowing monarch didn't take this action due to dissatisfaction with the nation of Australia, which remains one of his very favourite nations. It was purely out of anger at the state of Victoria during the Covid pandemic, which as Penman noted had turned into a less tolerant version of Ceaușescu's Romania. In protest, he created the independent state of Jimland.

---

* *Biohistory: Decline and Fall of the West*, by 'Jim' Penman.

Yes, it's called Jimland, and according to the man himself it's going to be a real proper country, with all the accoutrements of a genuine sovereign nation as imagined by an old man who doesn't know how to navigate away from the one website that he's found. 'I'm going to be the king,' he says. 'I'm going to be starting knighthoods and citizenships, we're gonna have our own stamps and our own flag. We're gonna raise money for men's sheds.'

So Jimland will have knights, stamps, a flag and men's sheds, and most people would agree that's basically all a country needs. Some get by with even less – there are no men's sheds in the Vatican, for example.

But what is involved with creating a new country where previously there was only a home-services franchise? Well, as Jim says, 'We just declare independence. It's like when the United States colonies declared independence from Britain in 1776. If you've got unjust and tyrannical government, you can secede.'

Now, constitutional scholars are divided on this. Some have opined that, in fact, this is not much like when the United States colonies declared independence from Britain at all. And if it is, then Jim Penman should possibly start preparing for a protracted and bloody war. Because right now he's got Jim's Mowing, Jim's Cleaning, Jim's Dog Wash and even Jim's Insurance; but I'm pretty sure there's no Jim's Musketeers or Jim's Artillery. And even the Australian Defence Force should be capable of taking down a regiment of dog washers.

The carnage of revolution could be avoided, however, by one simple act. All that Victorian Premier Dan Andrews has to do is apologise for locking the state down during Covid and making himself into a Stalinist monster, and Penman will stand his legions down and agree to put Jimland on ice.

However, at time of writing such an apology is not forthcoming, and so there is no way to know whether, by the time you read this, man and mower are once again living side by side in harmony, or whether you are reading in the blighted wasteland of a once-prosperous nation devastated by the violence between the foot-soldiers of despotism and the freedom-loving lawn folk.

All we can do is pray.

The Wild World of Wurdi Youang

In south-west Victoria, north-east of the You Yangs, off the Little River–Ripley Road at Mount Rothwell, there lies a bunch of rocks.

This, in and of itself, might not be enough to excite you. But as is so often the case in life, it's not the fact that there are rocks that matters, but rather what *kind* of rocks they are. And as it happens, the rocks under discussion are particularly intriguing ones.

Officially registered as the Mount Rothwell Stone Arrangement, but known in the Wadawurrung language more attractively as Wurdi Youang, this group of ninety basalt stones is arranged in a roughly egg-shaped formation about fifty metres across, aligned east–west, with three particularly tall ones at the western end.

In scientific terminology, Wurdi Youang is what is called 'very very old'. The age is not known for certain, but some estimates put it at 11,000 years, which would make it older than Stonehenge and Mick Jagger put together.* It would even make it older than the Egyptian pyramids, although to be fair the pyramids are bigger, so let's call it a draw. The Wurdi Youang rocks certainly date to the period before European settlement of Australia, when the original inhabitants of the continent were forced to live without all the benefits of genocidal white people. It must have been awful for them.

The great question of Wurdi Youang is just why the stones were placed there. Of course, a group of stones doesn't necessarily need an explanation:

---

* It'd be pretty cool if Stonehenge and Mick Jagger *were* put together.

sometimes people just put stones around the place for fun, and there's nothing wrong with that. If young people today spent more time arranging stones and less time shooting pensioners in the head, it would arguably be a better world. Nevertheless, it seems likely that Wurdi Youang came into existence for reasons other than simple wholesome recreation.

It has been noted that the straight sides of the arrangement nearly perfectly align with the position of the setting sun at the summer and winter solstices, while at the equinoxes the sun sets over the three high stones at the western end. What does this mean? Beats me, but I'm assured it's extremely significant, and something that is extremely unlikely to have happened by chance. It also shows that the people who assembled the Wurdi Youang stones were pretty on the ball, intellectually speaking. I mean, I consider myself reasonably smart, but if you asked me to arrange some stones to track the solstices, I admit I would not know where to start.

What all this means is that Wurdi Youang could be the oldest astronomical observatory in the world, and evidence not only of First Nations people's knowledge of the heavens, but also of the sophistication of their agriculture, as a system for tracking the seasons would be most useful for anyone planting crops. Backing this up is evidence near the site of 'gilgies', which are terraces used for farming. Experts believe that the rocks are situated near what were permanent villages, which makes sense: if you're going to go to the trouble of dragging ninety great lumps of basalt around so they match the positions of the sun, you'd want to hang around to get the benefits.

This is, of course, quite difficult to prove, but just as the stones of Wurdi Youang give a good approximation of the setting sun's position, it can be pretty confidently asserted that when something is clearly both thousands of years old and deliberately placed in significant position, something quite clever was going on – something that could upend assumptions about the ancient Australian way of life, and annoy all kinds of prominent media commentators.

The Precocious Frenchman

As everyone who went to school with or before me knows, Australia was discovered by Dutch explorer Dirk Hartog in 1616, a historic event marked by Hartog nailing a plate to a post for want of anything better to do. Of course, even back when I was in school, we were taught that by 'discovered' it was only meant that Hartog was the first white man to stumble on Australian shores, and that quite a lot of non-white people had already discovered Australia by being born on it. Years later, of course, that same generation of students was left with a hollow sense of betrayal when they found out that Hartog wasn't the first white guy to come here, as Willem Janszoon had landed at Cape York in 1606.

As it turns out, it doesn't matter anyway, because neither Hartog nor Janszoon got here before any other European, and the Dutch can suck it. The actual first European to reach Australia was Binot Paulmier de Gonneville, a French navigator, which came as a shock to everyone at the time, who had assumed that the French weren't really up to much.

Unless, of course, he wasn't. Perhaps we should explain.

In 1503 the sea route from Europe to India was under Portugal's policy of *mare clausum*, meaning only Portuguese ships were allowed to sail around in it and steal stuff from the places they found. However, countries that weren't Portugal differed in their opinion of whether this was okay, and so it was that Captain de Gonneville said, 'Up yours, Portugal!' and set off to sail to India.

It was when rounding the ironically named Cape of Good Hope that

De Gonneville's ship, *L'Espoir*,* ran into a terrible storm, which blew it off course and onto the shores of a strange and alien land, sailing down a river which he described as similar to France's Orne, i.e. wet and brown. He took refuge in the new country for six months while he repaired his ship, which shouldn't have taken that long really, so clearly he was having a great time.

De Gonneville met the natives of the strange land and made friends with them. He claimed they were a happy people, because their land was so rich that they didn't have to work. This does sound nice, although it also sounds a little bit like a lie, but maybe the natives just told De Gonneville they didn't have to work so he didn't ask them for a job.

De Gonneville called the land the 'Southern Indies', in accordance with the fashion of the time to call absolutely everywhere the Indies. He left in July 1504, taking with him two of the inhabitants of the southern land, and returned to France, where he wrote a report of his journey that was met with a stunning explosion of indifference.

This all changed 160 years later, which was obviously way too late to be of any good to De Gonneville. In 1663 a book was published under the title *Memoirs Concerning the Establishment of a Christian Mission in the Austral Land*, written by Jean Paulmier de Courtonne, who claimed to be a descendant of one of the natives brought back to France by the explorer.

The book caught the imagination of the French public, who saw it as evidence that France had a claim to the legendary Great Southern Land pre-dating that of the English and the Dutch. (It didn't pre-date that of the people who lived there, but, as had been scientifically proven during the Renaissance, they did not technically exist.)

The sticking point, however, was the question of exactly which country De Gonneville had landed in. Many believe he had reached Madagascar, which would make sense given it's quite close to Africa and might easily have been in *L'Espoir*'s path when it was caught in the storm around the cape. To this day, in De Gonneville's hometown of Honfleur,

---

* French for 'The Hope', which, aptly enough, was all you had to rely on if you wanted to sail to India.

he is celebrated as the first European to arrive in southern Brazil, which is certainly possible, though you'd think that if he'd gone *that* far – sailing all the way past Australia's southern coast, across the Pacific, around the tip of South America, and then north up the east coast of that continent to Brazil – he might've noticed. Surely even in 1504 Frenchmen had some ability to gauge the passage of time.

Many historians believe that it is likely De Gonneville landed in north-western Australia. His description of the land and the people are consistent with the Kimberley region of Western Australia; the river he found could've been the Glenelg or the Prince Regent. Furthermore, there are cave paintings in the area that indicate that white men may well have encountered the local people in the 16th century and left their mark: some paintings depict strange figures with weird clothing, which most would recognise as an accurate description of the French. Then there's the old story of the people of the Napier Broome Bay: of white men in armour who came, fought the locals, ate some snails and left in an unusually sardonic and aloof manner.

If De Gonneville and his men were the first Europeans to see Australian shores, it wouldn't be the first time that we who went to school in this country found out that everything we were taught is wrong. Of course, if the story is ever confirmed, it will probably then turn out that actually De Gonneville was beaten to it by the Portuguese or the Vikings or the Welsh or something. But, as any good historian knows, learning you were wrong is half the fun.

The Lofty Land Rover of Keith

One school of thought has it that the town of Keith, in south-eastern South Australia, represents one of history's most terrible PR miscalculations. Originally, the area was named Mount Monster, after a granite hill outside the town. It should be a truth universally acknowledged that any town which is offered the chance to be called Mount Monster should grab that chance with both hands, and yet the people of Keith fumbled it. In the most pathetic act of nomenclature since the burghers of Batmania decided they'd rather be dubbed 'Melbourne', the Mount Monsterians plumped for Keith, and their descendants have rued it ever since.*

People who drive through Keith** tend to think, as they see the 'Welcome to Keith' signs, 'Hmmm. A town called Keith. Bit weird.' But within minutes their idea of 'weird' is expanded further than they could've dreamed.

For Keith is not just notable for choosing objectively the wrong name for itself. Its crowning glory is a pole in the middle of the town. And the main point of interest about the pole is that it has a Land Rover on top of it.

No, I am not using a random word generator. By the side of the road in Keith, there is a Land Rover. On top of a pole.

'Well, why not?' you might ask. 'Why not put a Land Rover up a pole?' Okay, fine. But you could also ask, 'Why not put a squid in

---

*   Presumably. I mean, I haven't asked them. But come on!

** And, I suppose, theoretically, people who actually drive *to* Keith, although that's hard
     to imagine.

a baptismal font?' and although there's a certain logic to it, it doesn't explain anything.

The explanation is actually remarkably simple, while also being kind of ridiculous. It seems that in the 1940s, Keith was a dusty speck in the middle of the Ninety Mile Desert, and like many places in the middle of deserts, somewhat dry. That was until an insurance salesman* named Hugh Robinson bought the worthless land around Keith and made an offer to farmers around the country: come and work the land for ten years, turn it into viable farming land and at the end they could buy a piece of it at a bargain rate.

The farmers flocked to take Robinson up on his offer, clearing the scrub and sowing the soil as hard as they could. To do so they used a range of machinery, and part of that range was the trusty Land Rover, a useful vehicle to have if you needed to get around a region whose terrain tended to rather overstress its 'sand or mud' motif.

The scheme was a success and Keith thrived as the hub of a vibrant farming district. And so it was that in the 1990s an idea was hatched to erect a memorial to the hardworking pioneers who had made the desert bloom.

The first idea floated was to put a bulldozer up a pole, but this met with some resistance. Interestingly, the resistance was not along the lines of 'Why do we have to put anything up a pole?' but rather 'Yes, obviously we need to put something up a pole, but a bulldozer would be silly.'

Striking the people of Keith, somehow, as *not* silly was the idea of instead shoving a Land Rover up the pole. Colin Mayfield, one of the original 'AMP settlers', said it was perfectly logical: 'If you sat it flat on the ground it wouldn't look real good, so we stuck it up a pole.'

The pole itself was as significant as the vehicle, as back in the day it had been used as a landclearing device, strung between two bulldozers. It wasn't very good for this purpose, but for the purposes of being a pole it was outstanding.

---

* Nature's heroes.

And so, on the basis that a Land Rover on top of a pole does, in fact, look real good, the Keith Land Rover Pole was inaugurated in 1995, and ever since has stood there as a testament to man's ability to conquer nature through hard work and innovation, and also his ability to have extremely odd ideas about historical monuments.

Today, as you pass through Keith, make sure you stop to drink in the Land Rover – or, as the locals call it, the 'truck on a stick' – and think with admiration of the tough country folk who tamed the dusty wilderness and then put a Land Rover up a pole, because being tough country folk is no barrier to also being really strange.

The Terrible Tiger of Bulli Mountain

You've heard of the Lithgow panther, but do you know the Bulli tiger? Ah, the mystery of the tiger may not be as widely known as that of Australia's various hypothetical panthers, but it is just as exciting a tale to ponder. What's more, it might even be true!

Picture the scene. It's February 1903, and a young schoolteacher is riding his horse towards Marulan, in the Southern Highlands of New South Wales. As he rides, he hums a merry air and counts his blessings: he is young, he is fit, and he is a citizen of a young and vibrant nation still revelling in the euphoria of Federation and blessed with two of the greatest characteristics any nation can possess: an abundance of natural beauty and a total absence of enormous wild predatory cats.

How naive the young schoolteacher was to be thinking such thoughts! For, six miles from Marulan, the merry air was suddenly snatched from his lips as a huge beast loomed out of the bush and pounced upon his horse.

The young teacher spurred his steed on and managed to escape with no greater injury than severe shock and some extremely nasty scratches (on the horse). It was a strange and frightening occurrence, made all the more so by the fact that the young man swore blind that the creature that had attacked him was a tiger.

'A tiger? In Australia?' people scoffed, in an inadvertent paraphrasing of *Monty Python's The Meaning of Life*, which would not be released for another eighty years. Indeed, ever since tigers had been discovered by the Duke of Wellington in the late 1600s,* one of the most prominent characteristics of the species had been the fact that they do not live in the Southern Highlands of New South Wales. And yet ...

Had the incident been an isolated one, it could've been written off as the ravings of a demented educator. But the tiger did not melt into obscurity. A local settler by the name of John Field came forward to declare that the day before the attack on the teacher, he had seen the tiger lounging about four miles out of town. More Marulan locals soon came forward to say that they, too, had seen an animal which could be described as bigger than a wombat, stripier than a cow and more cat-shaped than a kangaroo.

Having terrorised and thrilled the people of Marulan, the tiger now made its way east to the Illawarra, possibly seeking a beach holiday. In April it was seen swimming across a creek near Lake Illawarra, and then in Balgownie Heights wandering along the road in the moonlight. Here it was known as the Albion Park tiger rather than the Marulan tiger, but presumably it was either the same tiger or a close friend. But then, all of a sudden, the Albion Park tiger underwent another transformation and became the Sherbrooke tiger, when it was seen near Sherbrooke on the Bulli Mountain.

Here the tiger disturbed the campsite of two Sherbrooke locals, who were interrupted during a card game by the sight of the gigantic cat sitting on a log a few metres away, looking at them with what might've been avuncular fondness but what was understandably interpreted by the lads at the time as intense and malicious hunger.

The press at the time reported on the tiger sightings with some level of scepticism, upsetting the Sherbrooke campers, who wrote to *The South Coast Times* to correct the record. Yes, they bloody well had seen a tiger, they said, and no, contrary to the paper's insinuations, it was *not* just a big dog.

That was the end of the tiger sightings until, oddly, six years later,

---

* *Citation needed.*

in the – as previously noted – particularly weird year of 1909. AJ Hill, a bank manager, was stopped on his drive home from Kiama by a tiger, which stalked across his carriage's path, passing within a few feet of him before slinking off into the scrub. *The Kiama Independent* reported 'much merriment' resulting from stories of tigers, and said 'the whole matter is generally treated as a joke'. But those who pooh-pooh the Bulli Mountain tiger ignore the principle that if a whole bunch of people in the same area report seeing a tiger, you can't assume that they're *all* mad.* Also, unlike the legendary panthers of Australian folklore, it's a lot harder to mistake a house cat for a tiger, what with the stripes and all.

Some have suggested the tiger was actually a leopard: apparently there was a fellow in the Marulan area who had brought one back from South Africa, which had subsequently escaped. This is an interesting theory, though it does raise the question of whether, though people in the past are known to have been very stupid, they can have been quite so stupid as to not know the difference between stripes and spots.

It will never be known for certain whether the Bulli Mountain tiger truly existed, or was just a leopard or a dog or an unusual gumtree. But I for one would far rather it existed than not, so consider me Team Tiger for life.

---

* I mean, you *can*, but it'd be a bit rude.

The Wailing Waterhole

It was in the 1890s that two shearers came to camp by the waterhole at Wilga, near Ruthven Station, in western Queensland. They lit a fire, ate their supper and drank their tea, and were just about ready to lay down their heads when the tranquillity of the night was ruffled by a distant noise.

It was a soft wailing, a sad keening wafting in as if on the breeze, from far away. And then from not so far away. And then really quite close. It was growing louder and louder, and from a soft wail it became a loud scream, and then a deafening, agonised, demonic shrieking, assailing the shearers' ears and echoing like the calls of banshees around the bush. The noise, as far as the petrified shearers could tell, was coming from the waterhole, though the water was still. Eventually the shrieking diminished, grew soft again and finally fell silent again, leaving the men shaking, gibbering and generally what-the-helling.

When the shearers told the story back at the shed, some of their colleagues laughed at them, and you can see their point. But others shook their heads and said that it was well known there was something horrible at the waterhole: the Indigenous locals avoided it, horses were scared of it and cattle driven there stampeded at sundown.

The shearers were, in fact, only the latest in a long line of people to experience the horrors of the Wilga waterhole, where animals and birds dared not go and where night-time brought screams that seemed to emanate straight from the fires of hell.

Once, a station hand from Ruthven built a hut by the waterhole, bringing his wife – a sensible country woman, by all accounts – to live there. One night the man arrived home late to find his wife 'in a state of collapse', telling him of the unearthly shrieks she had heard coming from the waterhole. Her husband told her it must have been the screeching of nocturnal birds, but when, some time later, after two nights away, he returned to find her hysterical, it was clear that something, not to put too fine a point on it, was up. Half-crazed with terror, she cried as she told her husband of the nightmarish screams from the waterhole that had caused her to 'almost lose her reason'. The station hand made what seems a very wise decision and moved out of the hut. Nobody ever moved into it: word spreads pretty quickly when it comes to disembodied screams from a haunted waterhole that quite a lot of evidence suggests may be the mouth of hell on Earth.

The stories have come in thick and fast over many years, from numerous sources and periods from the mid-19th century to the 1940s. Always the tales are the same: a soft, ghostly wail that increases in volume until the listener finds their head ringing with horrifying shrieks, as if a horde of unhappy souls are being tortured somewhere beneath the undisturbed serenity of the water.

Some have latterly suggested scientific explanations for the screaming waterhole: subterranean passages and rushing water that might create spooky noises under the right conditions. Others have suggested less scientific explanations that involve rather more murder, restless spirits and Satanic presence.

The only thing we can do, when faced with irrefutable evidence that something weird is going on but no satisfactory evidence as to what that something is, is to go find out for ourselves. So I encourage all readers to head out to Wilga and camp by the waterhole. If you make it through the night, let me know.

The Mournful Mystery of the Madagascar

On 12 August 1853, the frigate *Madagascar* sailed out of Melbourne under damp winter skies, bound for London. On board, in addition to the crew, were more than 150 passengers and, more importantly, almost three tons of gold, valued at around £250,000.* But the *Madagascar* never made it to London. It never made it anywhere at all. The onlookers who waved it off as it exited Port Phillip Bay turned out to be the last people to see the ship at all.

The journey had been drama-packed before it even began. It was understaffed, because fourteen crew members had quit as soon as they arrived in Melbourne, skittering off to the goldfields to make their fortune and/or starve to death in a mudpit. At the same time, demand for passenger berths to London was soaring, because unlike those who had just arrived in Australia, people who had been there for some time already were willing to pay top dollar to get the hell out.

These included some who had more reason to want to migrate than a simple hatred of the climate or a longing for a decent theatre scene. The *Madagascar*, scheduled to sail on 10 August, was delayed when police boarded the vessel and arrested the bushranger John Francis. The next day, two more men were arrested, which did nothing for the *Madagascar*'s reputation. One detective, Mr J Tuckwell, observed while carrying out the arrests that the ship was harbouring 'drunken men and women, swearing and fighting ... like wild beasts'. The crew, in Tuckwell's

---

*   In today's money, seventy quadrillion dollars.

estimation, was 'the most villainous motley lot that had ever signed articles on a capstan's head'.* The detective feared greatly for the fate of the *Madagascar*'s innocent passengers, given the presence on board of an array of dangerous escaped convicts, who for some reason the police failed to detain, presumably thinking that the movie that would result from letting the *Madagascar* sail would be worth it.

Anyone wishing to write that movie, however, would be forced to make extensive use of their imagination, because what actually happened after the motley crew, the drunken brawlers and the massive pile of gold left Victorian shores remains unknown.**

Many theories have been advanced: a freak wave that sent the ship to the ocean floor; an iceberg with a grudge; or even the spontaneous combustion of the ship's cargo of wool, which apparently is something that happens sometimes to wool and should cause all of us to reassess our attitudes towards jumpers.

Of course the more exciting possibilities of the *Madagascar*'s demise are those involving skulduggery. It is possible that the crew, packed with criminals as they were, had mutinied and taken the ship for themselves, sailing it and its precious cargo to an unknown location, just like Mel Gibson.

Even more likely, though, is the theory that the ship was taken by pirates, who took the gold and sunk the ship afterward. If true, this would be a terrible tragedy – but then every possible outcome would be a terrible tragedy, and at least this one involves pirates.

The only actual evidence ever found in connection with the *Madagascar* is a collection of objects discovered in 1997 by researcher Gerald Crowley on the Polynesian atoll of Anuanuraro: knives, spoons and nails that Crowley claimed were from the ship. Crowley swears blind that somewhere in the atoll there is a shipwreck, but swearing blind is not

---

* Makes you wonder how villainous and motley a crew that had NOT signed articles on a capstan's head would've been. Such monumental evil hardly bears thinking about.

** Indeed, when the movie did come to be made, the story turned out to be quite fanciful, involving a talking lion and his friends.

considered conclusive proof in the scientific community.

In the end, we are unlikely to ever know the fate of the *Madagascar* for sure, and this might make it the best kind of story of all: the kind you get to write your own ending to.

The Mystifying Min Min

All around the world there are told stories of mysterious lights. From England's will-o'-the-wisp, defying explanation, to the Aurora Borealis, which has an explanation I can't be bothered looking up, weird shiny bits of sky have captivated humanity for millennia. Australia – and I bet you saw this coming – is no different.

The min min were spoken of in Indigenous legends long before white people stepped onto Australia's shores, and the lights' existence has been attested to many times since then. Nobody knows where they come from or what they are. Nobody even knows why they're called min min. Some say it's a term from an Aboriginal language. Some say they're named after the Min Min Hotel, near where the lights were seen in 1918.* Some say they're named after the character Minnie Bannister from *The Goon Show*.**

The min min lights have been spotted from northern New South Wales to north Queensland, as well as in South Australia and Western Australia. It is clearly a widespread phenomenon: the only question is whether it is a widespread phenomenon of unusual meteorology, a widespread phenomenon of supernatural entities or a widespread phenomenon of people who need eye surgery.

The lights are usually described as disc-shaped and white, but sometimes they change colour. The brightness of the min min varies

---

* Of course, if that were true, it would just raise the question of why the hotel was called that, given it's a very silly name for a hotel.
** No, they don't.

between different accounts. Some stories claim the lights will follow you home, or come up close to you and then retreat, as if they want to ask you out but are too shy.

The lights do not harm anyone, but just scare the bejesus out of them – although one legend claims that if you chase the lights and catch them, you will never return to tell the tale. This seems highly dubious, however. First of all, if you never return to tell the tale, then who first told the tale of how this happens? Secondly, what does 'catching the lights' even mean? The people who have spread this story around really need to clarify their allegations if they expect to be taken seriously.

Speaking of being taken seriously,* there have been many attempts by show-off spoilsports to explain the min min through purely rational means. One suggestion is that the lights are swarms of insects infected by glow-in-the-dark fungi, or a particular kind of bioluminescent owl. This theory is generally rejected because there is no known bioluminescent source bright enough to account for the min min, and also – come on, an owl? Do you think we're idiots, science?

It's also been theorised that the lights could be marsh gas, which would be plausible except lots of people have seen them in places that are nowhere near any marshes, so I don't know who the genius was who thought to say that out loud.

Perhaps the most likely scientific explanation is that the min min lights are an example of a Fata Morgana mirage. This is an illusion caused by temperature differences between layers of air, causing the bending of light so that objects beyond the horizon appear to sit above the horizon, although they're often distorted so as to be unrecognisable. If this were the case, it would not only explain the lights themselves, but also why earlier accounts speak of stationary lights (campfires) and later ones describe them as moving (car headlights).

This is certainly a very plausible explanation for the min min lights, and seems very likely to be true. But when you think about it, isn't it *as*

---

* Not, you understand, a phenomenon I'm greatly familiar with.

likely that Australia is home to menacing light-generating ghosts, or under surveillance by aliens? Who are we to say?

The Devil and the Gravedigger

It's hard to believe that a place called the Isle of the Dead could be home to unsettling experiences, and yet sometimes the least likely locations produce the creepiest stories. So it was with Mark Jeffrey, aka 'Big Mark'.

Mark Jeffrey was said to be a man of admirable principle, who 'always fought against injustice'. Unfortunately, he frequently did this in a very literal sense, and his tendency to respond to injustice with his fists would cause him much trouble. Mark's father had been a violent alcoholic, which is one of the worst kinds. Mark and his brother became burglars in order to get away from their father's beatings, and it worked a treat, as after being caught in 1849 they were sentenced to fifteen years' transportation to Australia, which took them as far away from him as anyone could hope.

Mark was an intimidating fellow: in prison he ran into the man who had testified against him at trial and yelled at him so much the man had a fatal heart attack. This was a pretty neat trick, and it's surprising that when he got to Australia, he was frequently punished for misbehaviour and insubordination – the authorities were clearly risking their own lives by disciplining Big Mark, as he could've given them a fatal scolding at any time.

After his fifteen years were up, Mark Jeffrey was free, but he had suffered leg injuries while a convict and was unable to work. In colonial Australia, having sore legs was considered a serious crime, so Mark was sent back to prison at Port Arthur, Tasmania.

After he spent four years in Port Arthur's Separate Prison,* the authorities believed he'd learned his lesson, so he was let out, whereupon he killed a man in a pub fight and went back to Port Arthur, this time for life. Long stretches in leg irons caused him terrible pain, so he wrecked his cell and tried to kill his doctor, but this didn't seem to make his legs feel better at all. By this time, the powers that be were getting kind of sick of Big Mark Jeffrey, so they gave him a new job: he was to be the gravedigger on the Isle of the Dead, and if that didn't shut him up, nothing would.

The Isle of the Dead used to be called Opossum Island, but people found that nowhere near spooky enough, so it was renamed in honour of the fact that the colonial government had designated it as a cemetery. You might think it was quite a depressing place, but given it was used to bury convicts from the Port Arthur prison, it was actually as cheerful as a cemetery could be, because pretty much everyone buried there would've been hugely relieved at being allowed to die.

The only non-deceased inhabitant of the island, Mark kept busy digging many graves, including his own, which he apparently tended with great care and attention to detail. Ironically, he didn't end up getting buried on the Isle of the Dead, but in Hobart, so that was a waste of effort. But the most notable experience that Big Mark had on the island did not involve a spade: it was the night he met the Devil.

Exactly why Satan should choose to visit Mark Jeffrey is unknown. To encourage him to repent, perhaps? Or, as it was Satan, to encourage him to stop repenting? Maybe he came to give him gravedigging tips, or a leg massage? All we can be certain of is that one night, in his hut, Mark Jeffrey saw the devil** – calling him 'His Satanic Majesty' and thereby inspiring a classic Rolling Stones album – and was so terrified by the experience that he begged to be transferred off the island.

Although the government didn't like Mark much, they still had some

---

* So-called because, with twenty-three hours a day in solitary confinement, it separated you from your sanity.

** I mean, we can't *really* be certain of that, of course. We can actually be pretty certain it never happened at all. But please, go with it, for my sake.

218

sympathy for a man whose home address was known to Lucifer, and they granted his request. Jeffrey was sent to Hobart, and then to the Invalid Depot at Launceston, before gaining his freedom one more time. In his later years Jeffrey began annoying people in a new way, becoming extremely religious and expressing deep regret for his lawless past. In his book *A Burglar's Life*, Big Mark tells the story of his troubled life and his complicated relationship with the Devil, as well as his hope that God would give him a pass on the robbery and assault and manslaughter and so forth, and let him come upstairs when the time came.

What passed between the unhappy convict and the Prince of Darkness that frightening night on the Isle of the Dead, only they know, but there's nothing like meeting Satan to turn a fellow's life around.

The Citadel of the Central Highlands

What is the worst thing about Australia? If you answered, 'Not enough medieval architecture,' you are dead on. Oh, it's not to say that our country doesn't have many excellent features, but when you compare it to, say, Scotland or Germany or Liechtenstein, you can't help but notice that our landscape is depressingly devoid of keeps and portcullises and moats and all that kind of awesome stuff from the movies.

Luckily, there have been a few people in Australian history who not only noticed this glaring lack in the nation's aesthetic tapestry, but decided to do something about it. One of these visionaries was Keith Ryall, a plucky body armour salesman who figured that if a man can make a living selling body armour in the 20th century, why shouldn't he build a castle? And so he did.

Thus, in 1972, did construction begin on Kryal Castle, named after its founder and intended to bring the magic of medieval Europe into the Victorian countryside. In 1974 Kryal opened to the public, and to this day it continues to give thousands of Australians a taste of the Middle Ages that is as awe-inspiring as it is historically inaccurate. But then, if you want historical accuracy, go to Normandy. Don't have the airfare? Didn't think so. Take a drive to Ballarat and enjoy yourself instead.

Kryal Castle is in fact eight kilometres outside Ballarat, looming over the picturesque country with an air of forbidding festivity. As tourist attractions go, it is one of Australia's more unexpected: most visitors to our shores are probably unsurprised by the number of places where they can meet koalas and crocodiles; the fact they can wander around a castle may be less predictable. It's like going to France and finding a Vegemite museum.

The journey of Kryal has not always been a smooth one. As unlikely as it seems, there have been times when the profitability of a regional Australian medieval castle theme park was in doubt. In 2007 the castle was put up for sale but struggled to attract interest from the cashed-up. Talk turned to the possibility of turning it into a medieval-themed brothel, which on the one hand would've been quite distasteful, but on the other hand kind of alluring.

The brothel plan was scotched in 2011, when Kryal was sold to a couple who intended to continue running it as previously. This couple then almost immediately gave it back to Keith Ryall, having found that they had bought the castle without checking whether they had any money. The following year it was sold again, to Castle Tourism and Entertainment Pty Ltd, a company which, having named itself 'Castle', considered it a matter of honour to keep all its ventures on-brand. A few years later, Castle sold it, which was a bit anticlimactic. However, before selling, they revamped and upgraded the site, so that today, under its current owners, Kryal Castle exists in a state of exquisite anachronistic glory.

Anyone going there today will find four-star accommodation, functions, murder mystery evenings, day and night tours ranging from the educational to the supremely creepy, and a cornucopia of medieval entertainments, from open-air comedy skits, to magic potion lessons, to archery and sword-fighting sessions, to spectacular jousting displays.

Keith Ryall died in 2015, and his funeral was held at Kryal Castle. It is to be hoped he died knowing that, thanks to his utterly bonkers decision, generations of Australians have experienced, and will continue to experience, one of the coolest, oddest and undeniably maddest tourist experiences to be found anywhere in Australia – or, indeed, the world.

A Most Cunning Man

In 1970 an extremely uninteresting notebook came into the possession of the State Library of Tasmania. For forty years it lay dormant, like a Ring of Power on a hobbit's mantelpiece, with nobody bothering to probe deeply into its contents because of how dull it looked. Only after this long stretch of indifference from library staff did a Dr Ian Evans, fresh from discovering traditional English magical markings at the Shene Estate and Distillery in Pontville, come to the library and suggest that the little book in its leather pouch was more than it appeared: for here was the *Almanack* of William Allison, cunning man.

William Allison arrived in what was then known as Van Diemen's Land in 1828 to work for Lieutenant Arthur Davies, as overseer of Davies' property 'The Lawn', on the north bank of the Derwent River. He left 'The Lawn' in 1832 and was later licensee of the British Hotel in Liverpool Street, Hobart, from 1845 to his death in 1856. But it is less his employment history that marks Allison as a man of peculiar interest than what might be termed his extracurricular activities.

Allison's *Almanack** was an 1811 edition of *Vox Stellarum* ('The Voice of the Stars'), one of the era's most popular volumes, with additional pages inserted by Allison and bearing his own notes. These notes bear witness to Allison's career as a 'cunning man', a practitioner of folk medicine and magic.

---

* Almanacs were annual volumes of useful information, such as weather forecasts, crop planting dates, rising and setting times of the Sun and Moon, sporting results that Biff Tannen can bet on and so on.

The cunning folk operated in Britain from medieval times to the 20th century, providing useful services to the general public that included fighting the evil spells of witches, finding stolen property or treasure, and general healing by use of both herbal remedies and magical charms. Or to put it another way, they didn't really do much at all, but believing that they did seemed to make people happy, so we shouldn't judge.

The discovery of Allison's *Almanack* was proof that the cunning folk tradition had made the journey from England to Australia, exploding the conception of white colonial Australia as an unmagical place entirely concerned with sheep and genocide at the expense of more spiritual pursuits.

In Allison's notes can be found valuable cures for ailments such as rheumatism and burns, as well as 'sacred charms' to protect against fevers, and, of course, a recipe for sherry.* How reliable his remedies are – Allison's prescription for 'pain in the head' involves soap, rhubarb and '1 scruple of aloes', which as far as I know is not even a thing – must be left to others to judge. What cannot be doubted is that while Allison was managing property and serving drinks, he was also using his learning in the ways of folk medicine and general woo to help the Van Diemen's locals at least have a bit of hope that their aches and pains might be relieved.

Several of the recipes that Allison wrote down – for example, his treatment 'for the gravel', which was the old-timey euphemism for kidney stones – are credited to one Benjamin Nokes, a fellow cunning man who was transported to Van Diemen's Land for burglary and went on to be a publican and one of the founders of Methodism in the colony. Another, for a 'witch bottle' to protect against evil spells, is credited to Moses Jewitt of Durham. These are further proof not only that cunning folk knowledge was imported from England to Tasmania, but also that there was an active cunning community in the latter, with wisdom and weird assumptions about the power of rhubarb circulating among the colonials like rock cake recipes at the CWA.

---

* It begins with ten gallons of water and thirty pounds of sugar, and I don't see why we shouldn't just stop right there.

The little slice of magic to be found in that unprepossessing little book in the State Library may be only a footnote in the voluminous tale of brutality and horror that was colonial Tasmania, but it does at least show that this country's history was weirder than we usually think – and that's something to be grateful for.

Birdman, or the Unexpected Virtues of Wetness

Melbourne's Moomba Festival warrants another tale in this book owing to the strangest of all its traditions: the Birdman Rally. This began in 1976, inspired by the observation that the previous two decades of Moomba had been sorely lacking in wet lunatics. The Moomba Birdman Rally is not the world's only Birdman Rally, but it is definitely the one watched by the greatest number of people who are experiencing a strange and worrying mix of exhilaration and despair.

According to the Birdman Rally website, 'the Birdman Rally is a competition for home-made gliders, hang gliders and human-powered aircraft'. According to anyone who has ever seen it, the Birdman Rally is an inexplicable ritual wherein grown adults put on idiot costumes and jump in the river. The costumes are, theoretically, 'aircraft', in that they usually include some form of wings, although not the kind of wings that prevent you from falling in the river. Many competitors add feathers or other avian accoutrements to their getup, in the belief that this somehow makes it more fun. If you really wanted to make the Birdman Rally more fun, you'd have a line of riflemen on the shore trying to pick the jumpers off as they leapt into the air.

However, the rally is for charity, so it's a good thing really. Although how the charity aspect works is a little uncertain. Are people giving these maniacs money to jump into the river? Are they promising to, say, donate a hundred dollars to leukaemia* if a Birdman manages to stay airborne

---

* Leukaemia treatment, I mean. Not to promote it.

for 100 metres, and/or suffers a permanent spinal injury? It's hard not to think that just giving the money directly to the charity of your choice would both be more efficient and not encourage people to jump into rivers.

Moomba is a lot less popular than it used to be. Its cachet probably started declining after one of the Kings of Moomba turned out to be a child molester – or maybe it was after the internet was invented and people found out they didn't have to leave their houses if they didn't want to. Whatever the case, it may be that one day soon Moomba is just a memory, and a vague and indistinct one at that.

But until that day comes, it seems, there will always be people willing to jump in the river to avoid dealing with their emotional problems. And, in a way, that sums Melbourne up perfectly.

The Persistent Poltergeist of Guyra

The film *The Guyra Ghost Mystery* was released in 1921, to near-universal indifference. Although *Smith's Weekly* ran a review that promised it '[s]hould interest those who believe in ghosts,'* it would seem that such did not constitute a large enough portion of the population to generate a box-office smash. Perhaps it was a problem of promotion, for though the movie's advertising campaign promised 'five reels of laughter', the real-life story it was based on was far from a jolly one. Audiences might not have approved of the light-hearted treatment of a tale that, at its heart, was one either of chilling paranormal horror, or of a little girl who was a complete douchebag.

The story begins in April 1921 – making the fact that the film about it was released in June 1921 a savage indictment of the slowness of modern Hollywood – in the quiet New South Wales country town of Guyra. The Bowen family found their peaceful existence shaken by an invisible presence that thumped loudly on the walls of their weatherboard cottage, shaking the little house to its foundations. Even more alarmingly, rocks were thrown at the house, shattering all the windows: a terrifying experience for anyone living in 1921, when science had not yet determined any explanation for rock-throwing apart from ghosts. The disturbances seemed to be targeting William and Catherine Bowen's twelve-year-old daughter, Minnie.

It got so bad that the local police, who had some spare time,

---

* This review was only two sentences long. The first sentence said, 'Photographed on the spot' – which probably just confused people.

surrounded the house to keep watch, but they could neither prevent the attacks nor identify their source. One officer was forced to take leave due to the distress he suffered from witnessing the phenomena. The Guyra locals became terrified of the Bowen poltergeist, many of them taking to sleeping with guns* for protection, seemingly believing that ghosts were vulnerable to bullets.

At their wits' end,** the Bowens called in spiritualism student Ben Davey, being unable to find anyone with a real job. Davey came up with a working hypothesis, based on the fact that, three months earlier, May, Catherine Bowen's daughter from a previous marriage, had died. Davey believed that May was trying to communicate with, and/or murder, Minnie. He said to Minnie, 'If the knock comes again, ask if that's your sister May.'

'I can't speak to my sister, she's dead,' said Minnie, who was incredibly slow on the uptake. But Davey kept nagging her until Minnie finally agreed to talk to her dead sister. 'If that's you, May, speak to me,' she said, and then began to cry. Davey asked if May had spoken. Minnie confirmed that she had, and that she had said to tell their mother that she was in heaven and happy.

And so everything was settled and everyone moved on with their lives.

Ha ha, of course they didn't! The Bowens, who just couldn't leave well enough alone, decided to start holding seances to contact May, who objected to being nagged in this way and so resumed her wall-banging, window-breaking activities. The police continued their investigations, grilling the Bowens and their friends and searching all around the house, but could find no clue as to any earthly source of the disturbance. The family put up heavy shutters to protect their windows, but one day found they had been smashed and piled on their verandah.

The Guyra Ghost became famous, not just in Guyra and not just in Australia, but around the world, where the haunting was reported in

---

* Sleeping with guns nearby, I mean. They weren't having sex with them.

** Not necessarily a lengthy journey.

myriad countries whose citizens, under normal circumstances, considered it the height of bad manners to acknowledge Australia's existence.

Finally, the affair reached crisis point, with the arrival of Harry Jay Moors. Moors was a close friend of Arthur Conan Doyle, the idiot creator of Sherlock Holmes who believed that fairies were real. Staying three days in the Bowen home – presumably with the Bowens' permission – Moors left convinced that there was a poltergeist present. He also told *The Sydney Morning Herald* that Minnie Bowen was 'normal', a judgement that remains arguable.

The matter of the Guyra poltergeist has never been entirely resolved. Later, Minnie confessed to having thrown some stones on the roof, but denied any other part in the happenings. Indeed, it is difficult to see how she could possibly have been responsible for the noises and wall-shaking, or for throwing rocks at the house while she was inside it. Then again, it is difficult to see how ghosts can be real, so we're back where we started.

Only one thing can be stated with any certainty: the Bowen family starred as themselves in *The Guyra Ghost Mystery*, so if they made the whole thing up to get a start in showbusiness, it was at least a partial success.

The Island That Isn't

Many people* say that the most mysterious island in Australia is Australia itself, given that it is populated by bizarre wildlife and eccentric people, and that there is no really conclusive proof that it actually exists. But in the freezing waters between Australia and Antarctica lies an island that may be even stranger than the Australian mainland.

Emerald Island was first sighted by the sealing ship *Emerald* – this was not a coincidence; they named the island after the ship – in 1821. From a vantage point on Macquarie Island, navigator Christopher Nockells wrote: 'At 11am we saw the semblance of an island bearing east by north about 25 miles from our position. It appeared high with peaked mountains – about 30 miles long – the longer axis direct northeast and southwest.'

According to the men of the *Emerald*, the island was located at 57°30'S 162°12'E, right in what scientists term 'the diamond-nipple zone'. And that was fine. They had discovered a new island. Great news. The *Emerald* gathered up its massive pile of dead seals and headed for home, satisfied with the knowledge of a job well done.

It was not until 1840 that a problem was discovered: that when the American Exploring Expedition sailed south to confirm the existence of Antarctica,** Emerald Island wasn't there. At least, nobody on the expedition could see it, and given the expedition comprised four whole

---

* Well ... me.
** It was 1840 and they still weren't sure? Unforgivable tardiness.

ships full of people with more or less functioning eyeballs, you'd expect them to be able to.

So it had to be assumed that the island didn't really exist, and that the crew of the *Emerald* were either liars or nuts, as cruel as that is to say of professional seal-clubbers. That was that.

Except it wasn't, because fifty years after the American expedition failed to see Emerald Island, another captain sailing out of Port Chalmers in New Zealand *did* see it, exactly where Nockells had said it was and matching his description perfectly. This captain sailed around the island but found nowhere to land. Emerald Island, once more, was a thing.

And then, once more, it wasn't, because in 1909 Ernest Shackleton, while messing around in Antarctica for reasons that we can only ascribe to masochism, sent his ship the *Nimrod* to have a look around and see if it could find Emerald Island. When the *Nimrod* reached the relevant coordinates, it sailed straight over them with no problem. There was no island there.

So what are we to think? Emerald Island has been definitively identified, and also definitively debunked. Today the consensus is that there is no island there, although as late as 1987 there were maps that still showed it. But if it's not there, what did the people who saw it see? Did they just imagine a great lump of rock with mountains sticking out of the sea?

Phantom islands are a quite common phenomenon. There are a number of them in the region of Emerald, which the *Nimrod* also failed to find on its search. Another is Sandy Island, between Queensland and New Caledonia, which has frustrated cartographers for years with its habit of constantly disappearing and reappearing. But the question of what the freak is going on has not been entirely resolved. Maybe Emerald Island was an optical illusion. Or maybe those who found it made a mistake in their measurements, and it's actually in a different location than was recorded.

In which case, it's out there somewhere, waiting to be found! Why not hop on a boat today and give it a go?

A Hard Road to Hoax

Australia loves a poet. Or at least it used to, back when poets were mostly drunks writing rhyming couplets about wild horses and explosive dogs rather than pale waifs in hand-knitted slacks mumbling incomprehensibly about the Liberal Party. And although neither of these stereotypes is at all accurate, it's nonetheless true that the status of the poet in Australia has been in decline for many years: a decline that perhaps started with the 20th century's greatest literary hoax. For what this hoax effectively implied was that poetry, when you get right down to it, is stupid.

It began with *Angry Penguins* – doesn't it always? *Angry Penguins* was a literary journal founded in 1940 by Max Harris, an 18-year-old surrealist poet who believed in the power of poetry to tell people that you're better than them. The title was taken from the phrase 'drunks, the angry penguins of the night' from Harris's poem 'Mithridatum of Despair', and if that doesn't tell you all you need to know about *Angry Penguins* you cannot be helped.

In 1944 Harris received a letter from Ethel Malley, who had enclosed a collection of poems written by her late brother Ern Malley, a passionate Modernist poet who had tragically died at the age of 25 the previous year. Harris was stunned by the poems, of which there were seventeen, the entire sequence titled *The Darkening Ecliptic*. He showed them to his friends, who were equally stunned. Malley's poetry was fierce and vital, powerful and emotionally wrenching: exactly the kind of impenetrably pretentious nonsense that Harris valued above all things. He immediately rushed the poems of Ern Malley into the autumn 1944 edition of *Angry Penguins*, thrilled to be introducing an unknown poet of major importance to the Australian public.

The Australian public, upon viewing the poems, responded by asking Max Harris if he was, in fact, having a laugh. Critics certainly were: the poems were widely derided as hilariously inept claptrap. How this differed from *Angry Penguins'* usual output was not revealed.

On Dit, the student newspaper of the University of Adelaide, suggested that Harris had written the terrible poems himself as a hoax. They were half-right: *The Darkening Ecliptic* was indeed a hoax, but one perpetrated upon Harris rather than by him. Less than a month after the poems came out, the *Sunday Sun* revealed that Ern Malley was a fictional character invented by writers James McAuley and Harold Stewart.

McAuley and Stewart had set out to trick Harris by writing the first thing that came into their heads, opening books and picking words at random, and generally deliberately writing terrible, meaningless poems with the aim of exposing *Angry Penguins* and the avant-garde-poetry movement as a ridiculous sham.

It worked. Not only was Harris shown up as a man who could not distinguish fake from real or good from bad, he was prosecuted for publishing obscene materials by the South Australian police, who had no idea what the poems were about but were sure it must be rude. Harris was found guilty and fined, *Angry Penguins* folding soon afterwards.

More than the downfall of the penguins, Ern Malley had the effect of dealing a terrible blow to the push in the Australian literary scene to make poetry denser and harder to understand. It took many years for the scene to recover to the point where poets could deliberately aggravate people again.

In later years critics re-evaluated the work of Ern Malley, suggesting that McAuley and Stewart had accidentally written poetry that was actually good, proving that picking random words out of books and purposefully trying to be bad was a valid method of artistic practice. Which might be true, as a lot of writers seem to do that anyway.

But what Ern Malley taught us above all was that publicly humiliating snotty artistic types is enormous fun and should be done as often as possible. If there's such a thing as a distinctively Australian literary tradition, surely taking the piss out of literary traditions has to be a huge part of it. Or, as the great Ern Malley himself put it:

> Princess, you lived in Princess St.,
> Where the urchins pick their nose in the sun
> With the left hand. You thought
> That paying the price would give you admission
> To the sad autumn of my Valhalla.

I rather think there's something in that for all of us.

The Lost Whalemen

Ever since mankind made the game-changing discovery that whales were soft and squishy, sticking sharp things in them has been one of the world's most popular pursuits. Even today, though much of the world has grown squeamish, gutsy countries like Japan and Norway continue to derive enormous pleasure from traditional whale-stabbing activities.

Australia tends not to go in for harpooning much anymore, but there was a time when our ancestors were enthusiastic practitioners of the cetacean-puncturing arts. Tasmania, being surrounded by water, the substance in which most whales prefer to live,* was particularly prominent in the whaling trade – between 1828 and 1838, it's estimated, Tasmanian whalers killed about 3000 southern right whales.** This was a very productive time for the industry, but also demonstrated the truth of the old whalers' aphorism: 'If you kill all the whales, the whales won't be there anymore.' Declining whale numbers forced whaling ships to head further out into the open ocean to find their quarry, and it was this that led to the mysterious tale of the *Grecian*.

The *Grecian* was a brig that sailed in 1859 from Hobart, or, as it was then called, Hobart Town, because up until 1881 the residents were not confident that anyone visiting Hobart would know at first sight what it

---

* Despite not being able to breathe underwater; just one of many reasons that whales are stupid.
** In whaling circles, considered much preferable prey to the southern wrong whale, which, when harpooned, releases a powerful stream of horribly inappropriate jokes.

was. On 5 November the *Grecian* sighted whales off South West Cape and set off to nail one.

Drawing near to one colossal specimen, the *Grecian* lowered its small boat, containing mate* Bob Marney and five hardy men trained and experienced in the art of slaughtering enormous wet things.

The whale fled the hunters, but they would not be denied. Marney and his crew ran the beast down and struck true with the harpoon, but as is so often the case with these rebellious young whales, this one refused to accept its fate. With the harpoon buried deep in its flesh and the boat attached with rope, the whale took off, dragging Marney and his men behind it.

This was not an unusual occurrence in whaling: generally, the harpooned whale flees for a while, until it becomes exhausted from the effort and the blood loss, and the whalers are able to finish it off, hack it up and haul the huge slimy bits of dead flesh out of the churning bloody sea and onto the ship. It's truly one of nature's most touchingly beautiful spectacles.

But not on this occasion. This time the whale proved to have staying power far beyond the capacity of most mammals with a giant spear stuck in their side. In scenes reminiscent of Moby Dick, presumably – maybe if one of you has read it you can confirm this – the whale just kept going and going. As night fell over the ocean, the *Grecian* lost sight of the boat, and the six whalers disappeared in the cold darkness of the Southern Ocean.

More than three weeks later, on 30 November, the *Grecian* returned to port – whereupon, according to local press, 'Captain Clarke reports that all his endeavours to find the boat's crew which missed the vessel while killing a whale on the evening of the 5th, have proved ineffectual'.

Clarke remained hopeful of his men's survival, but the crew were never seen again. The mystery is why, as the whale dragged them out of sight, they did not cut themselves loose. Perhaps they did, and drifted in open water, evading the search until the searchers gave up. Perhaps the

---

* As in ship's mate, not just a friend. Although I'm sure he was great company too.

236

boat capsized and they were tipped into the icy ocean. Or maybe, caught in their own ropes, they were pulled to a watery grave when the persistent whale dived. There is no way of knowing their fate for sure, and no way of imagining it that doesn't end with 'Hell of a way to go'.

The six lost men of the *Grecian* were Robert Marney, John Gray, Joseph Walton, Joseph Kemp, George Jacson and John McFarlane. After the tragedy, they were commemorated in a popular ballad, which goes in part:

> With all his crew he sailed away
> Lost in the darkness one stormy day
> Off yon green island out far from here
> Where we lost Marney and his boat's gear
> We cruised east and we cruised west
> Around Sou'west Cape, where we thought best
> No tale or tidings could we ever hear
> Concerning Marney and his boat's gear

The Missing Mace

When the Westminster system of government was devised, one thing that all the founders of the system agreed on was that it would be necessary for the speaker of the parliament to have a lethal weapon on hand. Thus was born the tradition of the speaker's mace, a bejewelled medieval club that symbolises the authority of the chamber and may be used by the speaker to murder anyone who breaches standing orders.

The mace is a powerful symbol of the majesty of democracy, and so to steal it is a heinous crime against humanity – not in a real way, but in a bad vibes sort of sense. But in the wee small hours of 9 October 1891, just such an outrage was committed against the heart and soul of the Victorian parliament in Melbourne.

When the Legislative Assembly rose the night before, the mace had been in the best of health. The sergeant-at-arms* had placed it in its oak box in the antechamber leading to the speaker's private quarters. This box was locked and the key placed in a secret location known only to the sergeant and the speaker's messenger, whoever that was.

Yet just after noon the following day, an attendant dusting the room noticed marks on the box that indicated someone had tried to pry it open. He reported this to the sergeant-at-arms, who quickly determined that the mace was gone. Immediately, all of parliament – indeed, all of Melbourne itself, because it was a deeply politically engaged city and there

---

*   A character from *He-Man and the Masters of the Universe*, hired to provide security for Parliament House.

was very little else to do – flew into an uproar. Detectives moved in to discover the truth of the matter.

Clues were quickly identified: a window had been opened and black fingermarks left on the frame, but whose fingers they could not tell, except that they clearly had not washed their hands lately. No other valuables had been taken, and the police considered the theft an amateurish kind of job – possibly even a prank. Of course, it was all very well for the coppers to call the thieves amateurish, but they'd got away with the mace and the police had no idea who they were.

A suspect did suggest himself early on: parliamentary engineer* Thomas Jeffery had been seen running from Parliament House carrying a large package, and his tools were found to match the markings on the mace's box. However, Jeffery claimed the package was firewood, and since the detectives could neither find any evidence of the crime at his house nor establish any kind of motive, they had to let him drop.

Parliament was for a time forced to use the old mace, an unsatisfying small and dowdy item, before a new one was crafted in 1901, and this is the one used today. Amazingly, to this day the stolen mace has never been found. In more than 130 years, despite intensive investigations and the offer of lucrative rewards, what happened to it remains as much of a mystery as it was in 1891.

There is, however, a story that has long done the rounds concerning what really happened to the mace – and it falls very decidedly into the category of 'God, I hope that's true'. According to the rumour, certain members of parliament, on the night in question, had got drunk and taken the mace to a brothel in Little Lonsdale Street, where they acted out a 'mock parliament' ceremony that would have necessitated the use of fainting couches across the colony had the details been publicly revealed. They never were, though, so it must be left to our imaginations just what can be done with a large and valuable mace in a brothel. Anyway, according to this story, the mace was left at the brothel and

* Why did Parliament House need an engineer? Just another of the intractable mysteries of this case.

never recovered. Another version has it that, after sobering up, the MPs cleverly decided that rather than risk sneaking it back into Parliament House, they'd pay someone to throw it in the river.

A board of inquiry convened to determine the fate of the mace declared that this story was complete rubbish – but they would say that, wouldn't they?

The Boy Anzac

The young men of Australia flew into a state of high excitement in 1914 when World War I broke out. *Finally*, they thought, *a chance to go overseas and get shot!* There could be no higher calling than to die for one's country, it was generally thought, but if one could not manage that, then dying for the imperial ambitions of a European power was almost as good.

As a rule, it was only adult males who were allowed to go to war, which chafed badly with the younger generation, who didn't see why just because they hadn't attained their majority, they should be denied all the fun and excitement and adventure and exit wounds of warfare.

Such a youth was Walter Dunn, who at the age of thirteen found himself filled with a powerful urge to kill Germans, and so set off to live out his dream, despite the fact that this was an absolutely horrifying idea. The details of Dunn's life are both fascinating and somewhat hard to pin down, due to the fact that – unsurprisingly, for a boy who chose to mix puberty with shell shock – he had a habit of making up all kinds of nonsense about himself. Still, some of what follows is almost certainly true.

Dunn claimed to be an orphan, his mother dying in 1912 and his father in 1914, which made his escape to foreign climes a little easier. Alternatively, he claimed that his father was an officer in Princess Patricia's Light Infantry, which was almost certainly untrue, although Princess Patricia's Light Infantry is a real regiment that only sounds made-up.

Even in the bloodthirsty days of 1914, a thirteen-year-old was not going to be accepted for military service through the normal channels, so

Dunn stowed away on an apparently poorly guarded troop ship, travelling either from Australia to Colombo and then to Egypt, or with the 1st Canadian Contingent to England and then France. In Egypt* or possibly France, he was discovered, and as the only sane and rational course of action was to send the boy home immediately, the Light Horse** adopted him as a mascot.

Many regiments had mascots – often bears or monkeys or the like. Having a human mascot was a slight departure from usual practice, but so was allowing thousands of your own men to be slaughtered in trenches, so it wasn't really the time to be carping about breaches of convention.

Giving him the job of bugler so as to make it seem at least sort of normal, the Light Horse let young Walter join in all the fun of the Gallipoli campaign, which was a marvellous lark for all concerned. According to the lad's account, he was present at the Gallipoli landing and helped tend the wounded, which is entirely possible and a real demonstration of how kids today have gone soft.

Dunn was wounded in the arm at Gallipoli and invalided to London, where he stowed away again and went to France to quench his thirst for unspeakable living nightmares. Finally, in 1916, the Allied forces grew sick of Dunn hanging around, refusing to clean his trench and asking officers to 'watch what I can do' in the middle of battles. He was discharged for being underage and sent home to Australia, where he went to the papers and told them his unbelievable – some might say literally so – story. Dunn said he would like to return to the front, which should've been enough to have him sectioned there and then. But then he also said a lady in Adelaide had promised to adopt him, which may have explained his desire to go back to the Somme.

When Dunn reached the age of eighteen, he enlisted legitimately, but was waiting in South Australia to be deployed when the tragic news that the war was over arrived. What happened to him after the war is

---

* Or, as the Sydney *Mirror*, reporting on the story, called it, 'Gypoland'. Yeah. So stop complaining about the modern media.

** The Light Horse Brigade, that is. Not just a really skinny horse.

unknown: like the Beatles, he had peaked young and his later work was of little interest. But whatever occurred in his adult life – with or without the lady from Adelaide – Walter Dunn will forever hold a place in history as the youngest Anzac, not to mention the bravest teenage lunatic this nation ever produced.

The Hanged Man

In 1962 a man was found hanging from a tree on an Adelaide golf course, presumably a suicide. It was a reasonable presumption: it's almost impossible to play golf without at least thinking about killing yourself, and nobody blamed the man for finding it all too much. The fact that there were bruises on the dead man's face didn't change anyone's mind: golf is a rough game. The world moved on.

It was more than half a century later, in 2020, that the truth was revealed: this was no suicide, and the man – a Polish immigrant named Stanislaw Kilanski – was the victim of something much more sinister than a difficult bunker. The story begins not with Kilanski but with a young divorced mother named Kay Marshall.

Marshall was working at the British High Commission in New Zealand in 1958, processing passports, when she was hit on by a Russian diplomat named Lutsky. New Zealand intelligence, recognising that the diplomat was trying to turn her to the Soviet cause, à la Senator Palpatine to Anakin Skywalker in *Revenge of the Sith*, encouraged Marshall to pursue a fake affair with Lutsky so they could screw with the Russians. Marshall, who thought she could use a change in her routine, said sure, why not, and her career as a double agent was begun.

After a couple of years of passing fake intelligence to the Soviets on behalf of New Zealand, Kay Marshall, as all New Zealanders eventually do, moved to Australia. In Sydney, the Russians looked to kick things up a notch. In 1960 she was introduced to Ivan Skripov, first secretary of the Soviet embassy in Canberra. He was also a KGB officer, which was very naughty of him and something that the Australian government did not approve of at all.

After carrying out numerous test errands for Skripov over the following two years, Marshall won the Russians' trust and was given an important mission: she must go to Adelaide and meet a bespectacled man with combed-back hair and a black briefcase. She would then give him a hair dryer, which was a nice thing to do, but it turned out it wasn't a hair dryer at all but a secret radio messaging device.

Marshall carried out her part of the mission, but after she waited a while at the designated place, nobody showed up. The exchange never took place. Some time later, Skripov was exposed as a spy and kicked out of Australia. Kay Marshall was sent to San Francisco by ASIO to protect her from the Soviet agents after her blood. Later she returned to Australia and lived a quiet life until she died in 1992, not from a poisoned umbrella.

It was assumed that the agent whom Marshall was meant to meet in Adelaide in 1962 had slipped through ASIO's fingers and remained at large. Until ...

In 2020 filmmaker Peter Butt made a documentary about Kay Marshall and the Skripov affair. In the course of this he reviewed footage from the ASIO cameras that had been trained on Marshall while she waited for the rendezvous that never happened. While doing so, he noticed something that flipped everything on its head.

Across the road from the meeting point, a wedding had been taking place. One of the surveillance cameras captured the event: in particular, it captured the arrival of the wedding photographer: a bespectacled man with combed-back hair and a black briefcase.

The man took a photo of the wedding party, then looked around. The footage shows that, after scanning the area, he catches sight of the ASIO cameras, upon which his face assumes a stricken look. 'His face dropped,' said Peter Butt, 'as if to say, "I'm a dead man."'

He wasn't wrong.

Doing more research, Butt discovered the existence of Stanislaw Kilanski, the unhappy hanged man from the golf course. He also discovered a photograph of Kilanski, which revealed his perfect resemblance to the wedding photographer, and film of the Polish immigrant at the State Communist Party Conference in Adelaide six years previously.

And that, it would seem, was that. There was not, and never will be, official confirmation of what happened to Stanislaw Kilanski, but we can make a fairly secure surmise. Abandoning the rendezvous with Marshall because he knew he was being filmed, he had communicated this to his Soviet masters, who decided that rather than risk their agent being identified, arrested and interrogated by ASIO, it would be much less trouble to string him up.

And that, as anyone who ever read a John le Carré novel knows, is how it goes in espionage. One day you're a successful wedding photographer, the next day you're a Christmas bauble. Probably best to just stay away from the KGB. That's my advice.

The Ghosting of the *General Grant*

By this point in the book, canny readers might be beginning to believe that for most of history, the worst decision anyone could make was to get on board a ship. Indeed, in specifically Australian history, the only thing that could be said to be more lethal than trying to sail to Australia was trying to sail away from Australia. In the case of the *General Grant*, it was the latter that was its fatal error.

The *General Grant* – named after General Ulysses S Grant – had been built in Maine in 1864 and, like all things that come from America, it was doomed to miserable failure. In 1866 it found itself in Melbourne, waiting excitedly for Grant to become president so the ship could get a promotion. It's a cruel element of the ship's tragic fate that it never got to see Grant's inauguration and died a mere General.

On 4 May 1866, the *General Grant* left Melbourne for London under the watchful but apparently not watchful enough eye of Captain William H Loughlin. On board were fifty-eight passengers, twenty-five crew, 2576 ounces of gold,* nine tons of zinc spelter ballast,** a big bunch of wool, and additional cargo referred to only, ominously, as 'skins'.

At 11pm on 13 May, the *General Grant* sighted the Auckland Islands dead ahead, and the captain realised, with a cold chill down his spine, that if he was not careful he would soon be in New Zealand. There was little wind present, and the crew, unable to invent the internal combustion engine in time to avoid the cliffs, smacked straight into them. Drifting

---

*   In today's terms, eighty-seven cents.
**   A technical nautical term for ballast that is made of zinc spelter.

into a cave *Goonies*-style, the captain ignored the clear opportunity for an exciting pirate adventure, and instead the damaged ship bobbed about for a bit with its mast banging against the cave roof. As it happens, a mast hitting a roof is what nautical people call 'inadvisable': eventually the impact caused the mast to plunge through the hull. A large hole opened up and the ship, in accordance with the inexorable laws of gravity and seawater, went down. Sixty-eight people drowned, with only fifteen surviving the wreck.

As the ship sank, boats were launched, one of them quickly sinking itself, proving that little boats aren't necessarily any easier to keep afloat than big ships. The other two boats made for Disappointment Island.* After making it to safety, they then moved on to Auckland Island, where they spent the next nine months learning what real disappointment felt like. Finally, on 22 January 1867, four of the survivors of the *General Grant* decided to make an attempt to reach New Zealand. They had no compass, chart or instruments, but managed to overcome these handicaps to disappear and never be seen again.

Later in 1867, another survivor died, and the last ten restless souls, bursting with wanderlust, moved on to Enderby Island, where they stuffed their faces with seal meat until finally, on 21 November, they were picked up by the *Amherst* and forced to try to reintegrate into normal human society.

Though the victims of the wreck of the *General Grant* were soon forgotten, the gold it had carried wasn't, and the temptation of it quickly attracted treasure seekers, who frequently found themselves punished for their greed in conveniently poetic ways. The wreck itself has never been found, leaving only the story of the *General Grant* to warn those who allow hubris to impel them to get on boats.

---

* Named by its discoverer after his children.

The Misplaced *Mikiri*

The Simpson Desert is 176,500 square kilometres of sand and rock and heat in the middle of Australia. Named after industrialist Alfred Allen Simpson, in recognition of his astonishing personal dryness, it is an inhospitable expanse that, though a nice place to visit, is a really awful place to collapse and die of thirst in.

For millennia, though, the Wangkangurru people made their home in the Simpson, finding the heat only a mild inconvenience and overcoming the arid landscape with masterly ingenuity. For underneath the desert, water can be found, and the Wangkangurru long ago figured out how to find where the water was and bring it to the surface, digging deep narrow wells called *mikiri*. Some of these wells were as much as seven metres deep, but no wider than a man's shoulders, all dug by hand.

When white people came to Australia, the ingenuity of the Wangkangurru proved helpful. Explorer David Lindsay made use of the *mikiri* to survive during his crossing of the desert in 1886. He visited the wells with an Indigenous guide, which was fortunate, because as a proud bearded white man, he had very little idea what he was doing and would've died very quickly without help.

At the beginning of the 20th century, during the so-called Federation Drought – which despite the name was not a drought actually caused by Federation* – the Wangkangurru left the Simpson, leaving behind the *mikiri* scattered throughout the land. Abandoned

---

* Not as far as we know, anyway. It's entirely possible that God hates the unification of self-governing colonies. It'd explain all the rain when the cricket's on.

to the desert, the wells filled with sand.

But the *mikiri* were not forgotten. Songs and stories kept the memory of the wells alive. In the 1960s, Mick McLean, a Wangkangurru man from the generation that walked out of the Simpson during the drought, told stories of the *mikiri* that were recorded for future generations by the linguist Luise Hercus. In this way the *mikiri* came to the interest of many, who began to head out into the desert to find out just where they were.

It was adventurer Denis Bartell who, in the 1980s, uncovered the eight wells used by Lindsay on his expedition, later using them himself when he became the first white man to cross the Simpson unaided from west to east – a remarkable milestone in the still-developing story of white people's struggle to learn how to do things for themselves.

But many more than eight *mikiri* exist in the desert, and more were found by archaeologist Mike Smith when he travelled into the desert in 2019 with a camel train, having not heard about cars. Smith was invited by Don Rowlands, a Wangkangurru man and head ranger of the Munga-Thirri Simpson Desert National Park, to survey the desert and reveal the incredible secrets of his ancestors to the world.

Thanks to people like Smith, Rowlands and Bartell – but especially to the old Wangkangurru like Mick McLean, who ensured the old stories and songs survived – we are blessed to have knowledge of the extraordinary achievements of the first inhabitants of the Simpson Desert, who found a way to thrive in land that is as hostile to human life as it is inviting to compilers of landscape photography coffee-table books. Around the *mikiri* can be found the remnants of ancient homes and cooking sites, where the Wangkangurru lived and worked, sustained by the water from the well. Some of the recently rediscovered *mikiri* had been untouched for centuries, their original users having left even before white men ventured into the desert.

The *mikiri* are powerful reminders not just of the marvels of Australia's First Nations civilisations, but of the fact that when you take the time to look around this place, there are whole worlds out there you never even suspected.

The Baffling Face

George Grey was born, through no fault of his own, in Lisbon, Portugal, but managed somehow to be English anyway. After joining the British Army, he was sent to Ireland, where he committed a severe breach of protocol by liking the Irish people. Having noticed that the Irish were, to put it mildly, having a hell of a time in Ireland, he got the idea that maybe they'd have a nicer time if they weren't in Ireland. And so it was that he crossed the world in 1837 to try to find a nice empty space in north-west Australia where they could put all the Irish people so that the British could stop worrying about them.

As it turns out, Grey's explorations did not result in the establishment of an Irish homeland – which may have been just as well, considering that there already was an Irish homeland,* and north-west Australia is far too dry to do a decent impression of it. He did, however, find plenty of very interesting things on his travels, so all in all he could consider it time well spent – apart from the parts where they got shipwrecked or flooded or ran out of food, or the time Grey himself got speared and nearly died. It was what one might call a mixed holiday.

Grey managed some notable achievements in his exploring career, including discovering the Glenelg River, which came as a huge relief to everyone as they'd been wondering where it had got to.** He was also the first known European to see the Wandjina figures, depicted on the rocks

---

* Ireland.

** Mind you, since then we've lost track of it again. Nobody knows whether it's in Western Australia or Victoria.

of the Kimberley. He drew pictures of these artworks and took them back to white society, which was very impressed even though they had no idea what they were. The nature of the Wandjina only became clear later, when a clever white person had the idea of asking the Indigenous people about it.

However, Grey also discovered something in a Kimberley cave that was even more mysterious than the Wandjina. Here follows Grey's own account of the discovery:

> We observed the profile of a human face and head cut out in a sandstone rock that fronted the cave ... the head was two feet in length, and sixteen inches in breadth in the broadest part, the depth of the profile increased gradually from the edges where it was nothing, to the centre where it was an inch and a half ... the only proof of antiquity that it bore about it was that all the edges of the cutting were rounded and perfectly smooth, much more so than they could have been from any other cause than long exposure to atmospheric influences.

Grey was stunned by the discovery, as the Indigenous peoples were not known to have any tools capable of carving such hard rock to this extent. Moreover, the sketch Grey made of the stone face is not in a known Aboriginal artistic style, and appears to depict a European man. This, given Grey and his troupe were, as far as anyone knew, the first Europeans to see these caves, was what might be termed perplexing.

It was an intriguing mystery, and as soon as George Grey got back to Perth, he made it a priority to forget all about it. Rather than investigate further, he got married and became the governor of South Australia, which just goes to show that some people's priorities are just pathetic.

The mystery of the stone face persists, but there is a theory which is rather fun and cool and only a little bit awful. Although Grey had made the first official exploration of the area by Europeans, long before there were two other white men who were known to have fetched up on the coast nearby: Wouter Loos and Jan Pelgrom, two of the mutineers of the *Batavia*, who were marooned in Western Australia in 1629 as punishment for all the murders they had done. Pelgrom, who was saved from hanging because he was only 18, and Loos, spared because, I don't know, people found his name amusing or something, were put ashore by the Hutt River with a boat and tools of survival, and it's possible they made their way north to where the stone face was found.

Of course, why the two guilty Dutchmen would've chosen to carve a face in the rock is anyone's guess. Maybe just out of boredom, or maybe one of the pair had died and the other tried to carve himself a friend. Or maybe it wasn't the mutineers at all, and at some other long-ago time someone else had arrived in the Kimberley, by luck or shipwreck or poor directions, and left a mark of their presence in the shape of the face.

Whoever it is, it's to be hoped they are proud of the immortality they have achieved. Unfortunately, that is very unlikely because they've been dead for centuries. Life sucks sometimes.

Where There's Smoke, There's an Orangutan

Mollie was an ape, and by that I mean no disrespect – she was literally an orangutan. As a baby, she was given a gift that few infants ever enjoy: a free trip to Australia. Hardly believing her own luck, Mollie discovered that the news got better: she was going to Melbourne, the fashion capital of the nation. Even better, she would get to live there permanently, in a beautiful, clean, modern cage, never having to endure the privations of the horrible, smelly, wet jungle again.

Some would say that the conditions of the typical zoo in the early 1900s were cruel, but is it cruel to give an animal a home? To tend to its every need? To force it to live a lonely life in a tiny, confined space? Well, yes, obviously. But this was a long time ago and pretty much everything was cruel back then. Orangutans were certainly not treated in an enlightened way, but then neither were the poor, and at least Mollie got fed.

In fact, Mollie got more than fed. Recognising that an animal needs more than basic nutrition to lead a happy and fulfilling life, the Melbourne Zoo's management supplied her with lemonade, ice cream and, of course, cigarettes and alcohol.

It was the cigarettes that really made people fall in love with Mollie. From 1901 to 1923 the zoo-going public learned that there are few things more adorable than a smoking ape (assuming it is smoking a cigarette and not just on fire). And Mollie didn't just smoke them: she learned to light her own smokes from watching visitors, and would often light the pipe of Mr Wilkie, the zoo director, who liked to pop round to Mollie's cage to hang out with someone intelligent for a change.

Mollie's skill with a match was not always a boon. At times she would light her hessian bedding on fire, either accidentally or in protest. She was moved from a wooden enclosure to a concrete one lined with iron to make it non-flammable and ensure both that Mollie was safe, and that she was never exposed to anything even remotely resembling her natural environment.

It's important to note that there was a lot more to Mollie than respiratory risk-taking. She was an ape of great intelligence and not a little defiance. Back in the early 20th century, zoos were not, as they are now, pleasant places where people are content to gaze raptly at the wildlife. Back then, it was common practice for visitors to enjoy a more interactive experience, specifically by tormenting the animals.

Mollie's fans would often step up to the bars of her cage and offer her food, and then pull it away at the last second, gaining endless amusement from this very clever trick. Mollie enjoyed the game too, and would join in by reaching through the bars and grabbing hold of her tormentor, the bars alone preventing her from ripping them very literally into pieces. It is something of a shame she never got a full workout on a zoo patron, as that would've been one hell of a show. Especially when Mollie had been on a bender.

These days, there are still primates in zoos around the world that enjoy the occasional smoke, but in Australia you'll find only smoke-free apes – in fact, they're not even allowed lemonade and ice cream anymore. To some, this probably seems a bit of a shame, whereas to those who like animals it's something to be extremely thankful for.

Nevertheless, when you see a picture of Mollie with one of her bags sitting on her head like a scarf, and look into her calm, dark eyes, it's hard not to wish you could've met her. You get the feeling Mollie would be a great person to hang out with, share a drink and a smoke, look out at the zoo and agree on a plan to burn the whole damn place down.

The Prince's Perilous Plunge

Anyone who has ever been to the great city of Melbourne and taken a look at the glorious brown ribbon of the Yarra that wends through it knows just how inexplicable it is that anyone would deliberately jump into that water. Those who have done so are true heroes, risking life and genetic mutation for nothing but the glory of being wet in an urban setting.

Of all the tales of wilful Yarra penetration, perhaps the greatest, or at least the most interesting, is that of the prince who made a world-record dive into the river. It's a cracking yarn, despite the fact that he wasn't a prince and didn't make a world-record dive. In fact, it's possible these details make it even more compelling.

Prince Wikyama, for that was not his name, was born in Solomon Islands in 1886. At that time his name was Alick Wickham, and he quickly grew into a young man of unusual strength, athleticism and attractiveness. At the age of fifteen he was sent to Sydney to finish his schooling, and in Sydney he decided that, one way or another, he was going to make a splash.*

The first way in which young Wickham made his mark was while swimming laps at the Bronte Beach sea baths. Here he used a stroke that he had learned in his island home, but which stunned onlookers, who had been using a less effective stroke known as 'white man's flail'. The Australian champion swimmer Dick Cavill adopted Wickham's style,

---

* Double meaning, you see? Clever.

which was thereafter known, quite racistly, as the Australian crawl. It became the preferred stroke for freestylers worldwide.

Not content with revolutionising the swimming world – and, let's be honest, who would be? – Wickham continued to catch the eye with his aquatic exploits. In 1903 he equalled the national 100-yard record. In 1904 he broke the world record for fifty yards, which was impressive even though hardly anyone ever did the fifty yards. He broke numerous records over the next few years. In addition to his racing, he made a living performing tricks and stunts for an awestruck public who had never seen a man get wet in such creative ways.

But youth fades and fame is elusive. By 1918 the reputation Alick Wickham had won as the heartthrob of Sydney swimming was a relic – but then he received an offer he couldn't refuse from John Wren.

John Wren was a colourful Melbourne racing identity, by which is meant he was very rich and extremely dodgy. But he balanced his criminal side with his philanthropic one, supporting many charitable causes, one of which was the Deep Rock Swimming Club on the Yarra. In 1918 he decided to hold a swimming carnival at Deep Rock to raise funds for the Returned Soldiers' Fund. The showpiece of the carnival would be a world-record high dive from the cliffs opposite the club, into the disturbingly brown depths of the Yarra.

A combination of patriotism and a wistful longing for past glory made Alick Wickham accept Wren's offer to be the perpetrator of the high dive, and to be billed as 'Prince Wikyama', an exotic member of the Solomon Islands royal family visiting Melbourne who had decided to jump off a cliff for a lark.

With the promise of action, excitement, royalty and possible bloodshed before them, 60,000 people crowded the banks of the Yarra on the appointed day to see Prince Wikyama dive to death or glory. They paid six shillings* each, raising a total of 360,000 shillings for the soldiers' fund, which was quite possibly a lot.

---

* In today's money, one-eighth of a cent.

At 5pm Alick Wickham climbed to the wooden platform set up for him on top of the cliff. Stepping to the edge, he took a deep breath and ... climbed back down. He was seen speaking earnestly to carnival officials, who assured him that absolutely nobody had died jumping off that particular cliff in the last few weeks. Eventually, he ascended once more, stepped up ... and plunged in.

The crowd gasped as the 'prince' swooped gracefully down to the water before disappearing below the surface. Then cheered as he emerged, alive and not particularly maimed. If they were honest, a few of them were probably disappointed that he had survived, but they took it in good humour and didn't ask for their money back.

John Wren paid Wickham £100 for his dive, and claimed the prince had broken the world record by diving from a height of 205 feet.* Later measurements indicate the distance was more like 135 feet. Wickham had definitely not broken the world record, but he had still dived a hell of a lot further than normal people would consider sane, so he deserves credit for that.

After his diving days were done, Alick Wickham was reduced to driving a cab in Sydney, before returning to Solomon Islands and making a hobby of unsuccessful marriages. Today he is mostly forgotten, while John Wren is remembered as one of Australia's greatest corrupt scumbags. It would be nice if we could correct that injustice by bringing to light that great day when tens of thousands lined the river to see a prince defy death from the clifftops.

---

* In metric, 165.8 kilograms.

Castle of the Dolls

At Bli Bli, on the Sunshine Coast, 100 kilometres north of Brisbane, the castle still stands. Its flags still fly above the turrets, and the great stone walls still look down imperiously onto David Low Way and the Right Hook picture-hanging service.

Yes, Sunshine Castle is still an imposing edifice. Arguably the most magnificent example of Norman architecture in south-east Queensland, it was built in 1973 by Ian and Marcia Hayne, a couple who truly believed in the ideal of a modern Australia bristling with medieval attractions. Over the years it passed through the hands of different owners, who continued expanding and improving its offerings.

Thousands flocked to Bli Bli to experience the majesty of Sunshine Castle's Great Hall, its magnificent array of medieval shields, armour and weaponry, and its displays on Middle Ages history and culture. Parties, weddings and other functions were held there. Most of all, people came to see the dolls.

When the castle was originally built, it was called the Fairytale Castle, and it housed eight fairytale dioramas, along with a collection of dolls. Over time the doll collection increased, to the point that the castle's Doll Museum, with its more than 2000 dolls, became a major part of the experience. There were myriad dolls in hand-sewn national costumes from all around the world, fairytale dolls acting out familiar children's stories and dancing dolls on a moving mechanical display. People who visited the multiple levels of dolls were dazzled by the craftsmanship on display, not to mention unnerved by the innocent yet somehow accusatory gazes of the dolls' lifeless eyes.

Sunshine Castle was a place of magic, of knights and ladies, swords and sorcery, delightful displays and gorgeous Queensland sunshine that the Normans could only have wished to experience in their real castles back in the day.

Sadly, today the castle is much diminished. Although it still stands, and people still visit, most of the actual building is now off-limits to guests, after the discovery in 2020 of concrete cancer in the structure.

Yes, concrete cancer. Did you know that was a thing? Apparently that's a thing. Concrete can actually get cancer. You thought a castle on the Sunshine Coast was weird? Try concrete cancer on for size.

The concrete cancer means the castle is beyond saving. Efforts have been made to find a new location to rebuild it on, but the outlook is currently bleak. You are therefore encouraged to go see it while you still can, as any day now the part of the castle that remains open to the public will have to close down forever.

So please do get up to Bli Bli. Wander the courtyard. Admire the swords and shields. Do the treasure hunt. And, most of all, visit the dolls. For they remain there, in their glass cabinets, looking out with tranquil beauty on the world that has cruelly passed them by. They still stand in their finery, they still dance on their mechanical stage, they still gaze upon us with a calm acceptance of whatever fate they should come to.

Hopefully the dolls will be blessed with a dignified retirement. And hopefully one day Sunshine Castle will rise again, on a new site, with a less carcinogenic framework. For although a medieval castle is to some extent the least Australian thing imaginable, in another way the idea of building one thousands of miles away from anywhere that an authentic castle has ever stood, filling it with dolls and charging people to have a gander is the most Australian thing ever.

The Girl in the Cupboard

Fourteen-year-old Natasha Ryan was dropped at her Rockhampton school by her mother on 31 August 1998, and never came home. Her name was not marked off the roll. Nobody had seen where she went.

Her panicked parents reported her as missing, and a huge search commenced. Police and the State Emergency Service scoured the area for weeks without luck, but the community eventually began to succumb to despair as they lost hope of the schoolgirl turning up alive. 'I don't believe Natasha would have let me go through all the pain if she was out there,' said her mother, Jenny, to which someone privy to all the facts might have replied, 'LOL!'

The first inkling that there might be more to the case than met the eye should perhaps have entered investigators' minds when Natasha's parents revealed that she had a habit of running away from home. However, this time felt different, they told police. And they were right: this time was different, as this time she hadn't come back.

None of her friends could provide a clue as to Natasha's whereabouts. Her boyfriend, Scott Black, said he had no idea where she'd gone. Also, Scott Black was twenty-two years old, a fact that the cops presumably decided to come to grips with later on, because for the time being they seemed pretty okay with it.

Natasha's best friend, Maioha Tokotaua, was the first to fall under suspicion, as he had been the last person to see her alive. However, with no evidence to show Tokotaua had done anything to his friend,

261

the police were at a dead end, until an extraordinary piece of good luck fell in their laps.

Serial killer Leonard Fraser, aka the Rockhampton Rapist, a nickname which ironically gave him a little too much credit, had been apprehended and charged with the murder of four women. He confessed to killing a fifth: Natasha Ryan. Everyone believed his confession, because as he was a serial killer, people presumed he knew what he was talking about.

Fraser's confession put an end to any hopes that Natasha Ryan might be alive. A memorial service was held for her on her 17th birthday in 2001, and her family and friends did their best to move on after the unimaginable tragedy. Until there came what reality TV producers call the Twist That Will Change The Game Forever: on 11 April 2003, it was announced that Leonard Fraser was pleading not guilty to the murder of Natasha Ryan.

There was shock at the announcement, but even bigger shock when the reason for it was revealed: the night before, police had found Natasha Ryan, alive and well, in a bedroom cupboard in the North Rockhampton home of Scott Black. She had been living with Black for nearly five years, since the day she disappeared. Black's house was just a few kilometres from her family's.

After appearing at her own murder trial to testify that she had never met Leonard Fraser, clearing him of all blame (apart from all the other murders and rapes that he had done), Natasha Ryan faced charges of her own. She was convicted and fined for causing a false police investigation, while Scott Black pleaded guilty to lying to police and got a year in jail for perjury.

The case of the Girl in the Cupboard has a happy ending: after being found, Natasha Ryan signed up with celebrity agent Max Markson and scored a $200,000 deal for interviews with *Woman's Day* and *60 Minutes*.

Actually, on reflection, that's not a happy ending, is it? That's actually really horrible. Oh, well. How about this ...

The case of the Girl in the Cupboard has a happy ending: in 2008 Scott Black and Natasha Ryan got married and were paid $200,000 by

Woman's Day for the exclusive rights to their wedding photos.

That's horrible too, isn't it? Um ... Natasha Ryan and Scott Black had three children together and nobody knows what they're doing now. Is that a happy ending? I hope so.

The Bush Roars

It would be easy to think, looking at news reports over the decades, that Australia is positively swarming with big cats. It's only when you get out into the countryside and don't see any of them that you realise this is actually a depressingly megafeline-free land. Nevertheless, each story of an exotic beast stalking the outback is a thread in a rich tapestry of zoological quasi-plausibility that none of us would want to be without.

All of which is to say: let's talk lions.

Of course, there were lions roaming Australia in prehistoric times, but these were just marsupial lions – 'marsupial' here being used in the sense of 'not'. They had pouches, something that today's lions do not, and they have long been extinct, which, at time of writing, the modern lion is not.

But something that *is* true of the modern lion – or might be, anyway – is that one or more of them once terrorised the area around Jerrabomberra, near Canberra.

As *The Queanbeyan Age** of Tuesday, 5 August 1913 reported, the Jerrabomberra lion was witnessed the previous Friday by Mr W Brook, 'a gentleman to whom no one can fairly impute a state of nerves predisposing one to "seeing snakes" or other monstrosities the creation of a disordered brain – a gentleman, in fact, whose word may at all times be relied on for plain veracity'. Don't you wish newspapers still wrote like that?

Anyway, Mr Brook was up in the Jerrabomberra hills with his 'pea-rifle', a weapon that I assume was something other than a rifle that fired

---

*   50–34 million BC.

peas, because otherwise I do not see the point. He was looking to shoot some small animals and so satisfy the healthy bloodlust that dwells in the hearts of all men, when he came across a 'huge tawny animal'.

The Queanbeyan Age describes the scene: 'The Thing, scenting danger,* rose to a "rampant" position, and gazed at the intruding biped. This was quite enough for its disturber; for, recognising the beast to be a veritable lioness, Mr Brook ... beat a retreat at double-quick.'

This is a shame, really, for had Mr Brook been slightly less scared of being eaten, he might have gained a better look at the lioness and even been able to secure some solid evidence. Instead, he hurried off to the nearest police station and made a report, but the police informed him there was little they could do as it was not against the law to be a lion.

The story electrified Jerrabomberra, which had hitherto mainly invested its terror in legends of the 'hairy man' and so was quite pleased to have a bit of variety. For a while, anyone who disappeared without explanation or failed to show up at an appointed time was said to have been devoured by the Jerrabomberra lion, and local wisdom would have it that the lion was regularly gorging itself on human flesh. This seems unlikely; at least some of the missing people were surely taken by a wandering panther or tiger or bunyip or rhinoceros.

But what are we to make of the Jerrabomberra lion? We have the word of *The Queanbeyan Age* that Mr W Brook was a sober man of clear mind and not given to nutty raving, and he swore that he saw a lion. Unless he was completely round the bend, what else could it have been? Kangaroos are tawny-coloured, but their shape is not particularly liony. A quoll is a bit more catlike, but Brook would have to have had a severe problem with his perception of scale if he mistook one for a lion. Was it, perhaps, an especially fearsome golden retriever?

Perhaps we should follow the dictates of Occam's razor and simply accept that if a man says he saw a lion, the most likely explanation is that he saw a lion. It was the olden days, when travelling menageries and

---

* Presumably it did not realise Brook had only a pea-rifle.

circuses used to get about the country in colourful rickety wagons, so it's entirely possible a lioness could've escaped from one of these stereotypes and met Mr W Brook in the Jerrabomberra hills.

Sadly, both Brook and the hypothetical lion are long dead now, so we can't question either of them, or return them to their owners. Missed opportunities forever plague us.

This Effing Lady

Coral Browne was the kind of lady you'd love to be friends with, although you probably couldn't have been, because she would've hated you because you're nowhere near as awesome as Coral Browne.

Browne was born in Melbourne in 1913, and after beginning her career in the Melbourne theatre, understandably left to become a darling of the British stage and screen long before Australian actors became fashionable overseas. Indeed, back in the 1930s most British people would have been shocked to discover that Australia had electricity, let alone theatre.

Young Coral quickly established herself not just as a fine actress but as a woman who combined grace and wit with the priceless quality of not giving a fuck. She was bisexual, which in the prevailing showbusiness climate was considered perfectly fine as long as you never said it out loud. In another nod to showbiz convention, in 1950 she married actor Philip Pearman, in a ceremony that *The Argus* reported was attended by 'playwright Emlyn Williams and his wife, Jack Buchanan and Michael Redgrave'.

Philip Pearman, although married to Coral, was gay, and when the Royal Shakespeare Company told Coral that there was no role for him to perform alongside her in *King Lear*, she flipped through the script and said, 'There you are, the perfect part: A small camp near Dover.' With such impish humour and bitchy insults towards her own family did Coral Browne create her legend. On another occasion, according to Alan Bennett, 'When I said to Coral that I'd thought Cecil Beaton was gay, she remarked, "Not when he was with me, darling. Like a rat up a drainpipe."'

It was Alan Bennett who wrote *An Englishman Abroad*, a telemovie about Browne's encounter with the Cambridge spy Guy Burgess. It was one of the rare movies in which one of the leads got to play herself: Coral Browne delivering a scintillating performance as Coral Browne. Many said it was the role she was born to play, and felt very clever about themselves after saying it. Later on, *An Englishman Abroad* transferred to the stage and Browne saw other women playing her, to far less impressive effect.

She had met Burgess in Moscow, after he defected to the Soviet Union. While she was touring with the Shakespeare Memorial Theatre,* he pushed his way into her dressing room during the interval and put his communist moves on her. It happened in 1958, but she played the part in the movie in 1983, so nobody could say the woman wasn't well preserved.

Speaking of well preserved, after her first husband died, Coral later married the star of *The House of Wax*, Vincent Price.** According to her, she did so 'chiefly because, even if Vincent can be a bit moody and frightening at times, loneliness is even more frightful'. Which is bloody depressing, if also another delightful example of how mean she was to her husbands.

Coral was an actress, a raconteur, a charming dinner party guest and, it can be assumed, an absolute firecracker in the sack. She was also a skilled and enthusiastic swearer, as attested by the title of Rose Collis's biography of her, *This Effing Lady*. After Coral converted to Catholicism – which was a pretty weird move for a foul-mouthed, bisexual shag-rat such as herself – an acquaintance began telling her a juicy bit of gossip when she cut the story short, saying, 'I don't want to hear this filth. Not with me standing here in a state of fucking grace.'

It may be that 'weird' doesn't quite do justice to Coral Browne. But her eccentric vivacity, not to mention her talent and the fact she conquered the world long before far less interesting people like Cate Blanchett and Hugh Jackman came along, merits far more attention from her native

---

*   There doesn't seem much chance of anyone forgetting him, to be honest.

**   What a segue!

land, which seems to have forgotten her somewhat. In the words of Barry Humphries at Browne's memorial service:

> She left behind an emptiness
> A gap, a void, a trough;
> The world is quite a good deal less
> Since Coral Browne fucked off.

The Bloody Bridge

Few places on Earth are more beautiful and more possessed of horrific history than Norfolk Island. Caught up in the race between Australian colonies to see who could treat convicts the worst, Norfolk has a strong claim to be the winner. If they weren't being starved, they were being flogged, and if they weren't being flogged, they were being hanged en masse. Prisoners on Norfolk would make pacts wherein one man agreed to murder his friend, and consequently be executed himself, to spare both a moment's more life on the island. When disobedient convicts were rounded up and execution orders handed out, those men who were not to be hanged wept at their terrible luck.

The Bloody Bridge is one reminder of those days, set amid the stunning natural beauty of Norfolk. You will find it at the eastern end of Quality Row, the street that once housed the officer class of the island. It spans Music Creek, which sounds absolutely lovely, and is, as long as you don't think too much about how the bridge got its name. A task which I am, of course, making much more difficult for you.

The Bloody Bridge got its name due to the bolshie attitude of the convicts who built it. Getting ideas above their station, they grew weary of the abuse of their brutish overseer, who used to apply the whip more liberally than a Devo video. Deciding it was time that they took collective action to make management aware of their grievances and move towards a resolution satisfactory to all parties, they did so. And the action they judged most likely to achieve their aims was burying a pickaxe in the overseer's head. That this was effective is hard to deny. Although you could question the convicts' commitment to the mediation process, you had to admit that the overseer whipped them a lot less after receiving the pickaxe than he had before.

Unfortunately, the convicts had not entirely thought through the medium- to long-term ramifications of their plan. The pick had barely scythed through the overseer's temporal lobe when they realised that if they thought they'd copped some punishment before, that was as nothing compared to what was coming when the murder was discovered. They were, in a very pressing sense, for the high jump.

Luckily, this was a resourceful bunch – as you could guess from their elegant solution to the overseer issue – and they rapidly saw that the answer to their conundrum was right in front of them. They were building a bridge. They had a pile of stones they were supposed to put into the bridge. They had a corpse they needed to hide. Everything coalesced nicely. In the twinkling of a figurative eye, they'd slipped the corpse into the structure of the bridge and bricked it up inside.

When questioned, they swore blind that they had no idea where their beloved foreman had got to, and it seemed that all was well. Well, apart from the fact that they were still convicts, and probably the new overseer was a prick as well, but one dead bastard is better than nothing, as they say.

It was the perfect murder, the decisiveness of the strike matched by the elegance of the disposal and the excellence of the motive. Applause for the cheeky killers was in order, until – alas! Things went sideways.

It turns out that though possessed of infinite resource and sagacity, the convicts were not brilliant at attention to detail; perhaps this was why they ended up as convicts in the first place. For in walling up the tyrant's body, they had, appropriately enough, used mortar to stick the stones together. And mortar, when first applied, is wet. Another thing that is wet is blood. And when you've got a body oozing blood coming into contact with fresh mortar, what you get is bloody mortar.

When the new overseer saw the blood seeping out of the bridge, he was surprised, not to mention quick-witted enough to realise something was up. It had been such a good plan, but the game was up, and once more the lads were for the high jump.

A grisly tale indeed, and one in which nobody got a happy ending. Except us, for these days the Bloody Bridge is a gorgeous place to visit, and well in keeping with that famous Norfolk Island slogan: 'Come for the scenery, stay for the blood-drenched ghosts.'

The Occasional Crimes of Long Harry

Between Port Fairy and Portland, on the Princes Highway on the south-west coast of Victoria, you will find the tiny town of Codrington, home of the Codrington Wind Farm, the Yambuk Wind Farm and just about enough people to fill a phone booth. Besides its much-admired ability to grow wind, Codrington boasts an achievement that no other town can: it is the only one in Australia to be named after a bushranger.

Which seems weird, right? I mean, we love our bushrangers. You'd think somewhere there'd be the City of Ned, a hamlet called Mad Dan or East Thunderbolt. But no. Even the suburb of Kellyville was named after someone called Hugh Kelly, who never so much as shot a policeman.

Codrington, though: now there's a township with true respect for this nation's history.

Our story begins in Leicestershire in 1818, when an adorable baby was born by the name of Henry Rouse. He grew up to be a tall, thin young man whose career as a cooper awkwardly intersected with his career as a thief, the latter resulting in his transportation to Australia for ten years.

Somehow surviving the depredations of convict life in the hellholes of Norfolk Island and Van Diemen's Land until his release, Rouse then made the mistake generations before and since have made: moving to Victoria.

Henry's soul yearned for a more exciting and violent life, and so in 1850 he entered the most noble trade of all: bushranging. Dispensing with his birth name as too prosaic, he assumed the alias 'Codrington Revingstone', planning to lull his victims into a false sense of security by making them think he was an English stately home.

Codrington Revingstone began his illustrious career on Portland Bay, bailing up the Portland to Port Fairy mail coach three times in 1850. The area where he would descend upon the coach became known as Codrington's Forest, and the post office tentatively inquired whether the people of Port Fairy really *needed* their mail.

Henry's ambitions went beyond mail, however. Having changed his name to Henry Garrett, he settled in Ballarat, where he was known as 'Long Harry' due to being, you know, long. Well, not really 'settled' – he was just using it as a base for his continued naughtiness. In 1854 he gathered three pals who, like him, enjoyed money, and they robbed the Bank of Victoria.

The respectable folk of Victoria were outraged at Rouse's escapades. Governor Charles La Trobe offered a £30 reward for his capture, to which the bushranger responded with a newspaper notice offering £100 to 'any man or old woman* who will deliver into my hands Charles Joseph La Trobe, and my word if I get hold of him I'll work the shine out of his carcass!'

Sadly, the predicted carcass-deshining never happened. Instead, Harry took his loot and hopped on a ship to England, where he discovered just how poorly he had chosen his accomplices: one of them had dobbed him in. Long Harry was arrested and taken back to Melbourne, where he was sentenced to another ten-year stretch on a prison hulk.** As he had withstood his first term of imprisonment, he endured this too, and on his release in 1861 set off for New Zealand, where he'd heard people were pretty lax about their possessions.

He'd heard right: in New Zealand he robbed a gunsmith and fifteen gold diggers and took off back to Australia with a pile of cash, whereupon he was arrested in Sydney because he had once again allied himself with a dirty snitch. This time the authorities, sick of Harry's recidivism, cracked

---

* New women he would not accept anything from.
** An enormous ship used as a prison to keep social misfits in a state of continual immiseration. Like P&O.

down seriously hard and sent him to Dunedin for eight years to think about what he'd done.

In Dunedin he found God, despite the incredible unlikelihood that He'd be there. Harry was released in 1868 and went back to Victoria. Victoria didn't want him and sent him back to Dunedin. Deciding that maybe what he'd found wasn't God after all, Long Harry decided to stick to what he knew and robbed a chemist. In a reminder that he wasn't actually that good at it, he was arrested, tried and sentenced to yet another ten years. In 1882 he was released, stole some wine, was arrested and got another seven years. It is at this point a pattern begins to reveal itself.

The seven-year term was one of hard labour, but Henry Rouse was now in his sixties and in no state for such work. Sick and tired, he was admitted to hospital and died of bronchitis at the age of sixty-seven in 1885.

It was a sad end, but to die in your sixties of an ordinary illness was a pretty good outcome for a bushranger – as a profession, it doesn't lend itself to old age or peaceful demises on clean sheets. And although as an outlaw he had the fatal flaw of constantly getting caught, he had also the virtues of persistence, courage and flair. And even if we do not remember him the way we do more celebrated bushrangers, at least we know there's a little hamlet on Portland Bay that testifies to the one-time reign of terror of Henry Rouse, aka Long Harry, aka Codrington Revingstone.

Under the Odds

Greg Chappell was fed up. As captain of the Australian cricket team, he had been through the wringer. In the last couple of years the international cricketing schedule had gone into overdrive, the calendar filling up with more and more matches as the TV rights-holders who now called the tune of the newly commercialised game sought to squeeze every drop of revenue from what had, a few years earlier, been a sport but was now irrevocably a product.

The result of all of this, as far as Chappell was concerned, was sheer bloody exhaustion. Now, on 1 February 1981, things had reached crisis point, at least in the skipper's fatigue-addled brain. The best-of-five one-day international finals series against New Zealand was poised at 1–1. If Australia could win this third game, and then the fourth, he could finally have a day off.

Chappell had hit ninety in Australia's innings, before bowling ten overs and taking three wickets in New Zealand's. He had already told wicketkeeper Rod Marsh that he was stuffed and wanted to leave the field, but Marsh told him he had to stay on, which wasn't the kindest thing to do. Victory had seemed well within Australia's grasp, but the Kiwis were simply refusing to go away, and as the last over of the innings loomed, a superb century from Bruce Edgar had brought them to the brink of what would have been a mighty – though, from Greg Chappell's perspective, intolerable – victory.

New Zealand needed fifteen off the last over. With his best bowler,

Dennis Lillee,* having exhausted his allowable overs, Greg Chappell entrusted the bowling to his brother Trevor, an unimposing slow-medium pacer who nevertheless was an effective operator in one-day cricket, his humble dibbly-dobblers often difficult to smite.

With Edgar at the non-striker's end, helpless to affect proceedings, Trevor trotted in and bowled to the great Kiwi all-rounder Richard Hadlee. Hadlee wound up and smashed the ball back past the bowler to the fence. Four runs. Eleven more needed.

Hadlee swiped hugely at the next ball, but missed and was hit on the pad. Trevor Chappell leapt in the air and beseeched the umpire for a decision. The umpire, not noticing that the ball had pitched considerably outside leg stump,** raised his finger. Out – Hadlee had to go.

New Zealand wicketkeeper Ian Smith was next in. He swatted his first ball off his legs into the deep and sprinted two. To the next he heaved with all his might, squirting it off the inside edge and again, though just barely, getting back for a second.

Seven runs to win. Two balls left. Chappell trundled in. The ball scuttled low, Smith played a clumsy mow over the top of it and the stumps were scattered.

All hopes of a New Zealand victory were now gone. But they could secure a tie if they hit a six off the last ball. As Greg Chappell watched the New Zealand number ten batter, the burly fast bowler and sometime rugby international Brian McKechnie, walk in, he closed his eyes and saw all his nightmares coming true. If McKechnie could clear the fence, the tally would remain at 1–1, which meant an extra game in the series. The captain could not stand the thought of it, and as his overheated brain contemplated the possibility, he made a decision that would change cricket history, and his own life, forever.

----

* And I think nobody will have failed to notice that this book has three examples of Australian cricketers embarrassing themselves, all of which happened between 1979 and 1981, involving teams captained by Greg Chappell and including Dennis Lillee. Take that however you like.

** If you don't understand the terminology, don't worry. It's just cricket stuff.

Greg strolled over to Trevor. 'How are your underarms?' he asked his little brother.

Trevor, nonplussed, replied, 'All right.'

Greg nodded. 'Right, bowl one,' he said.

The tactic was, in and of itself, a cunning one. An underarm delivery would run along the ground and be impossible to hit in the air, thus removing any possibility of a six and ensuring Australia went ahead in the series. The problem was that, though underarm bowling remained legal, nobody had actually made a habit of it since the 19th century – and to introduce it for one ball just to make sure a tailender couldn't hit a six was dirty, dirty pool.

Trevor Chappell informed the umpire that the ball would be an underarm. Rod Marsh shook his head, calling, 'No, mate,' knowing this was no way to play the game. The umpire told the batsman. McKechnie stared in disbelief.

Trevor stood at the crease, bent like an old lady on the green and rolled the ball gently down the pitch. The furious New Zealander blocked the ball derisively, then threw his bat away before storming off.

And all hell broke loose.

The crowd roared boos. New Zealand skipper Geoff Howarth ran on to protest to the umpires, but there was nothing they could do: the underarm was a legal delivery. Off the field, the television commentators – including the eldest Chappell brother, Ian – looked on aghast. Back in New Zealand, Prime Minister Robert Muldoon began preparing a strongly worded statement. He declared it 'the most disgusting incident I can recall in the history of cricket ... I consider it appropriate that the Australian team were wearing yellow.' His Australian counterpart Malcolm Fraser agreed that it was 'contrary to all the traditions of the game'.

Closing the match broadcast soon after, veteran commentator Richie Benaud delivered a calmly scathing analysis, calling it 'one of the worst things I have ever seen done on a cricket field'. Pretty much everyone agreed. Later, Greg Chappell would express his regret, saying the decision had been the result of exhaustion and stress and that he had at that moment been mentally unfit to captain Australia. It became a byword for Australia–New Zealand hostility, and for poor sportsmanship and underhanded tactics.

And yet, in the end, it would be a shame if the underarm incident had never happened. For sport is the richer for such bizarre occurrences, and the story of cricket in both Australia and New Zealand is a tad more colourful thanks to that memorable summer day when the Aussie skipper went out of his mind.

Acknowledgements

My appreciation is unbounded for those whose assistance and support I've relied on in making this book. To wit: Kevin O'Brien, Dana Anderson and all at Affirm Press, who've been backing me for years. Shoutout to Les and Helen Pobjie, Emily Maguire, Rebecca Davis, Alice Pobjie and Freda Stozki for moral support and spiritual succour. Thanks to Colette Harrison for general saviourhood. Huge props to Caitlan Cooper-Trent for making my life so much easier. Infinite love to J, K and L. Most of all, thank you to Australia itself, for being, from the very start and for all time, as relentlessly weird as you are.